SOUVENIRS

OF

TRAVEL.

BY

MADAME OCTAVIA WALTON LE VERT.

VOL II.

MOBILE:
S. H. GOETZEL AND COMPANY, No. 33 Dauphin Street.
New York: No. 117 Fulton Street.
1857.

JOHN F. TROW,
Book and Job Brinter,
379 B'dway, N. Y.

CONTENTS.

SOUVENIRS OF TRAVEL.

CHAPTER XXXVII.

After leaving Seville, we drove over a great plain to *Alcalá*, the "City of Springs," and likewise the "City of Bakers;" for all the bread used by the *Sevillanos* is made there, (and admirable light, white bread it is.) Then, too, aqueducts take thence the pure water of the hills to them. There are fine Moorish walls, and a castle in excellent preservation. Beyond Alcalá there are plains covered with olive trees, and now and then a grove of orange trees. But the olive is here the great wealth of the land. The trees are usually planted in rows, and are about the size of a willow tree. The gray tinge about the leaves imparts a sad and mournful aspect to them. Their flowers are very small, but with a pleasant perfume. In the autumn the fruit is gathered, and pressed by machinery until it yields up all the oil. Those for the table are thrown into salt and water. They are much richer and larger than the olives of France or Italy.

Next we came to *Mairena*, where the great horse-fairs are held, and where the gipsies and majos are always assembled in vast numbers. Then to Carmona, a city founded by Cæsar, and strongly fortified by the Moors. We dined there, and journeyed on slowly, although we had ten mules in the diligence. There was a *mayoral* (the driver) and *zargalis* (postillions) running alongside the carriage, and beating the mules, which all had names. The mayoral talked to them constantly as though they were "sensible brutes," urging them on, and comparing the strength and power of one with the other, to excite emulation. He would exclaim, "Ah! Petronilla, will you let Catalina outwork you!" Then came similar admonitions to Juanita and Josefa, and supplications to Perilla and Mariquita to sustain their high reputation. The poor, meek creatures pricked up their ears as though they heard, but did not quicken their pace.

We had most pleasant companions in the "Interior"—three Spaniards, gay, witty, and agreeable. One was an Andalucian, a noble specimen of manly comeliness, attired in his handsome and picturesque national costume. They all wore immense cloaks, thrown around them in a graceful fashion, very like the drapery of the Roman toga. Journeying along, they related to us many incidents of historic interest, and many wild Moorish legends of the valleys, towns, and plains through which we passed. We were delighted with their courteous bearing, and their unaffected civility to us as strangers. They even gave up their adored cigars, when they discovered by our averted faces that the smoke was disagreeable to us. As all Spaniards smoke every where, this abnegation of a luxury may well be deemed a chivalric regard for woman's comfort. Tobacco is universally used in Spain, in cigars and in snuff, but it is never *chewed*. This disgusting use of the weed is a peculiarity of the Americans.

Near *Ecija* we crossed a bridge, famed as the lurking-place of a bold band of robbers, called "The Boys of Ecija." Their daring exploits furnish material for many of the ballads of the country. It was bright moonlight as we passed this dangerous spot, and near by we saw men with long carbines. When they spoke to us we found they were the *Guardia Civil*, and away vanished "into thin air" our visions of a night-attack on the wide vega of Andalucia.

Ecija has many associations of the past. The Romans, the Goths, and the Moors, all embellished it. As we drew up at the *Posada* (inn), where we were to sup, the mayoral drew me aside, saying, "Señora, let me show you the very house where St. Paul lived while in Ecija." Following him around the corner of a narrow, dark street, he showed me an old, decaying mansion, which assuredly looked as though two thousand years had passed since its erection.

After a good supper at the inn, we continued our journey through the night. Our charming travellers left us there, so we were alone in the "Interior," and endeavored to sleep. But not succeeding, I spent the time looking out over the great white plains, seeming in the moonlight as though covered with a sprinkling of snow. In the glorious days of the Moors these plains were perfect gardens, filled with groves of the olive, citron, and orange; watered by canals and shaded by the royal palms of Africa. Now it is a sterile waste. At intervals a few olive trees appeared, rising up like pale spectres of long gone years. The profound silence was only broken by the cries and entreaties of the mayoral to his wearied mules. Every few hours we stopped to change them; then, although it was deep night, around the diligence would gather a throng of miserable beggars, holding up their meagre hands for charity. By dawn we were travelling along the bank of the Guadalquivir. There was not a tree in sight, and not even grass. The only vegetation was a beautiful blue lily, resembling very much our hyacinth. They were so numerous upon the barren plain that they seemed like a delicate purple mist hovering over it.

Just at sunrise, from the summit of the "Hill of the Thorn" we espied Cordova, the birthplace of Gonvalve de Cordova, whose adventures, written by Florian, had been one of the joys of my youth. The great dome and the minarets of the *Mezquita* (the cathedral) were distinctly visible; so, urging the mules onward, we soon came to the gates of the stupendous fortifications, and drove through them rapidly, and along the winding streets, to the hotel, where we breakfasted.

"And this mouldering and crumbling city is Cordova!" we exclaimed, as we looked upon its desolation and its beggars—"Cordova the Learned and Wise"—Cordova, so prosperous under the Carthaginians, and famous under the Romans—the native city of the philosopher Seneca and the poet Lucan—the city which gave to Rome her bravest soldiers, and which clung the longest to the fortunes of Pompey. For this fidelity Cæsar murdered twenty thousand of its gallant soldiers at one time, and almost destroyed its temples and splendid edifices. After the Romans came the Gothic rule, and then the Moorish dominion, when Cordova was spread out over the plains, and one million was the number of its inhabitants. During the reign of Abderahman it became the rival of Bagdad and Damascus.

No wild dream of the enthusiast can equal the strange and wondrous history of this Abderahman. Born in Damascus, and closely allied to the royal fa ily, he was driven by them into exile, and passed long years amid the Bedouins, and the Zenetas tribes in Northern Africa. Flying from place to place, and incessantly pursued by those sent to take his life, he became a wanderer in the dreary desert, and amid the Mountains of the Moon, hiding himself by day in dark caves, and creeping warily along by night. At length, a noble sheik received the fugitive with kindness, and having learned his history and royal descent, vowed to espouse his cause. "After the darkness came the morning;" and soon envoys from the moslems of Spain found him out, and offered him the sovereignty of their native land. He accepted the trust, and went with them; landing with only one thousand men, he soon made himself master of the rebels, and fixed the capital of his kingdom in Cordova, which he embellished and beautified. Then began the golden age of Cordova; while nearly all the rest of Europe was engaged in frightful wars, literature, the sciences, and the fine arts, "flourished like the rose," in this favored city.

Abderahman built the mosque, which is even now a marvel of architecture. Though mutilated and stripped of many of its precious adornments by the *Berbers*, (savage barbarians from Africa, who devastated the fair plains of Andalucia,) it was the intention of this noble man that the vast and grand structure should only be second in holiness to the *Kaaba* of Mecca. And thus it was, that pilgrims came from Barbary and moslem Spain, and kneeling, made their devotions as at the "Holy of Holies." The exterior is not imposing, but within is a forest of hundreds and hundreds of pillars and columns, of marble, of jasper, of porphyry, brought, many of them, from the ruins of Carthage, from Asia Minor, and from Rome even. There is a perfect labyrinth of these pillars, while far above is the delicate tracery of the roof, almost like the foliage of trees.

Abderahman had a long and prosperous reign, and after him came two other monarchs of the same name, who constantly increased the grandeur of the kingdom. It was during the time of the last Abderahman that the gardens and palace of *Jehra* were constructed, a few miles from the city. They were of fabulous magnificence—the halls of audience paved with silver, and the fountains encircled by trees of gold, thronged with birds made of precious jewels, which, moved by some secret machinery, gave forth exquisite notes of melody. His officers and household numbered thousands of men, and his *seraglio* contained the rarest beauties of the world. He was the patron of the arts and of letters. Nearly one hundred great cities were subject to him, and along the banks of the Guadalquivir were twelve thousand villages. There is a story that after his death, in a closet was found a writing by him, in which he recorded, "With all the riches, the honors, the triumphs of the world, I have only been happy *fourteen days of my life.*" What a pity he had not revealed to us in what consisted the happiness of those "fourteen days." In 1808 Cordova was taken by the French General Dupont, and multitudes of its inhabitants were killed; the venerable Mezquita plundered, and immense treasure seized by the victors.

Near the great walls, whose foundation was laid by Cæsar, we saw the tower called *Mala Muerta*, built in 1406 by Enrique the Third, and not far from it an ancient convent, noted for its "Court of Palm Trees." The first palm tree ever planted in Cordova was brought from the East, by the order of Abderahman, who placed it in the earth with his own hands, and when it became a tall and graceful tree, delighted at evening to gaze upon it. There is a pretty little poem, said to have been written by him, which was repeated to me by our handsome young Andalucian:

"Ah! my beautiful and graceful palm tree,
Thou art here a stranger! The west wind woos thee
Gently, sweetly, with its tender voice of love,
Softly caressing thy rich luxuriance; fertile earth
Thy roots are gladly nourishing, and high thy head
To heaven thou raisest. Ah! noble tree,
Hast thou no grief for thy deserted home?
Must I alone endure the pain,
And weep the tears of deep regret, in vain,
For thy companions! thy sister trees,
So freshly growing, crowned with feathery diadems
Along the flowery banks of Forat's stream."

The most dreary and sad emotions oppressed us while we tarried in Cordova. There was about it the gloom and desolation of a deserted grave-yard, and little effort of imagination did it require to convert the pale and spectral creatures around us, holding up their skeleton-like hands for charity, into ghosts of the departed. Walking along the streets, we found the grass growing, as though months had passed since a foot touched it; and from the tops of houses hung down long vines, waving mournfully in the breeze. And this was once the "Beautiful City," so famed for its ten hundred thousand private houses—for its palaces, its gardens, and baths—its literature—its chivalry—its noble mosque, with the most gorgeous mosaic of the world, and its arches of marble, carved so delicately, they resembled the richest lace woven in the looms of Brussels. Silence, gloom, and starvation, are now the peculiar attributes of Cordova, and we gladly welcomed the approach of the diligence which should take us away from the tomb-like city. Our companions in the "Interior" were this time quite different from the merry, courteous Andalucians of our first day's travel. There was an aged man, frightfully ill, accompanied by a young and buxom wife, and his father confessor, a learned monk from a convent near Granada. The wife of the aged invalid was his niece. The custom is very general in Cuba, as well as Spain, for uncles to marry their nieces, (first obtaining a dispensation from the Pope). They told us, it resulted from the desire to keep all the wealth in the family; and thus youth and loveliness were often mated with age and ugliness. The poor old man was going to Madrid for medical aid, saying, "A few weeks will quite restore me." Never was the shadow of death more visible upon any face. His lustrous-eyed young wife was tenderly watchful of him, as though he were her father.

While we had been wandering about, M. D. had remained in the diligence. A grand assemblage of beggars had gathered around him, and he, wearied of shaking his head in refusal of their entreaties, at last affected to be *deaf*. So, when we returned to continue our journey, they all rushed to me, exclaiming, "Ah! Señora, we have unfortunately fallen upon a deaf gentleman; can you not assist us in our efforts to make him hear?" Ere they could receive a reply the mayoral slashed his long whip among them, and we drove out of Cordova. Crossing the Guadalquivir upon a splendid bridge of dark-colored marble, we came to the village of *Alcolea*, which was once celebrated for the Cordevese horses bred there. Our road passed through fields of corn and groves of olive trees, with the Sierra Morena mountains rising like a great bulwark to the north. The women no longer wore the poetic mantillas, but had a covering for the head of some coarse green cloth, called a *saya*.

At *Adujar* we dined in a very nice posada, and then, recrossing the Guadalquivir, parted with it, "perchance for ever." Soon we reached the hills, advanced guards of the frowning mountains, and came to the plain of *Baylen*, where the battle was fought between the Spaniards and the

French, in which the former were victorious; thus causing the flight of Joseph Bonaparte from Madrid, and a temporary freedom of Spain from the oppressions of the French soldiers. Very short, however, was the respite; for the great Napoléon was only preparing a terrible revenge, which soon burst upon them with appalling power. The Spaniards, fancying from the decisive victory of the battle of Baylen that their army of recruits was invincible, rushed down from their mountain retreats, and abandoning the guerilla warfare, which was their "tower of strength," they unwisely fought upon the plains, where they were constantly defeated, until advised by the Duke of Wellington to return to the "wild foray" mode of battle.

Baylen is a miserable town, through which we quickly passed. The road now turned northward. and was among the hills. The monk pointed out to us many places famous as the battle-ground of Christians and Moors, and described the wonderful victory achieved upon the plain over which we were passing, by one hundred and ten thousand Crusaders who came from England and France at the call of Pope Innocent the Third, when he proclaimed in 1212 a crusade against the moslem of Spain. When this gallant army of Crusaders reached the mountain passes of the Sierra Morena, they found them all guarded by the Moors, and a pass-way quite impossible. In this dilemma, a shepherd, poor and scantily clad, came to them, and proposed to show them a secret path by which they could reach their enemy. Most gladly they accepted his offer, and falling suddenly upon the Moors, killed them by thousands and thousands, and destroyed their armies. This poor shepherd proved to be *St. Isidro*, and his act of faithfulness is immortalized by one of the greatest artists of the land. At Madrid, the monk told me the picture might be seen.

At *La Carolina* we found a gay little town, with green

trees and neat houses. The people looked like the Swiss peasants, and upon inquiry we learned that during the past century these plains had been peopled by Swiss and Germans, brought there on a speculation. Many pined and died from the *mal de pays*, while others prospered and gave their own nationality to the plains and villages.

Driving slowly "upward ever," we ascended the mountain-chain of the Sierra Morena. The scenery is very grand and striking, from its deep abysses and abrupt precipices. The name of "Brown Mountains" must arise from the dark brown hue of the rocks near the summit. We crossed over by the pass of "Despeña Perros," (Throw over the Dogs.) This singular appellation comes from the fierce battle fought in the narrow gorge, with unfathomable depths on every side, by the Christians and Moors. In that terrible struggle the war-cry of the Christians was "Despeña Perros!" which they carried out by throwing over the precipices the moslem soldiers, whom they termed "Infidel Dogs"—thus destroying hundreds by a cruel death. This pass is really a fearful spot, shut in by sharp, dark crags, and on the verge of an abyss, so gloomy and dim, it seems like a great cavern. With only a slight fortification, it might be made as strong and inaccessible as the famed Thermopylæ of ancient days. During the war with France, the Spaniards often contemplated doing so, but never accomplished their proposed work.

After we crossed the "Despeña Perros," we entered the country of Don Quixote, *La Mancha*, over which his adventures have thrown an interest very necessary to aid one in enduring the barren monotony of the great plains, quite unbroken by tree or shrub. There are a few towns, intolerably wretched and poverty-stricken in appearance, and the inhabitants miserable and poor, dressed, or rather wrapped up, in brown cloaks, with sandals of hemp upon their feet, and a high ugly cap upon their heads. These *manchegos* (peasants) are noted throughout Spain for their honesty and truth; and although so starved and poor, they are passionately fond of their national dance, the *seguidillo*. Several times, when we stopped at the inns, we heard their guitars, and saw them dancing on the ground-floor of their hovels. Since the desolation occasioned by the march through La Mancha of Soult and Dupont, the manchegos have rarely re built their hamlets, but live in the ruins.

Just as in Don Quixote's time remains La Mancha—no improvement, no progress, in man, beast, or earth. Now and then we saw a mule, almost entirely hidden by the pig-skins, filled with wine, which he carried along to market. They were very like indeed to those attacked by the valiant old knight. Constantly in view were great wind-mills, almost as numerous as when Don Quixote and his faithful squire, Sancho Panza, rode forth to fight them.

We stopped at the town of *Val de Peñas*, and supped at a capital inn, where we were waited upon by two handsome peasant girls. Finding myself alone with one of them, of a wild and oriental type of beauty, I inquired from what part of Spain she came. With a sweetly expressed gratitude for the interest I manifested in her, she told me her singular history. She was a zingali (gipsy), who about fifteen years ago had been abandoned by her mother and the tribe to which she belonged, and left in a dying state upon the ground. A little lad, son of the inn-keeper, roving about the deserted encampment, heard a feeble moan; and seeking out its origin, discovered a child about two years old, senseless, and apparently dying. He caught up the poor sufferer, and carried it to the stables of the inn, where he wrapped it in straw, and brought it food; not daring to allow any one to know of his act of charity, for violent was the hatred towards the race of the gipsies. At last his mother, seeing him always carrying food to the stables, watched him, and found a child instead of a pet dog, as she first imagined. Touched by the tenderness of the boy towards the deserted child, she gave him permission to bring it into the house, where it was reared, and given the name of Maria, as it was rescued from death on the birthday of the holy Virgin. Often in after years, when she became useful, the zingali mother strove to take her away; but so dearly did she love the friends the "Virgin" had given her, she would never leave them, but labored assiduously for them. "And where is the boy who saved you from death?" I asked. "Ah, Señora! he is a soldier, and far away," she replied, while her glorious eyes filled with tears; then reading a warm sympathy in my face, she continued, "but when he comes back, he has promised I shall be his wife. He is not too proud to love the poor zingali girl." Just then came a loud call, "Maria!" and she started to obey the summons. Seizing her hand, I said, "Stop; tell me—do you love the boy?" She gazed at me in mute amazement, as though she did not hear aright; then looking up to heaven, exclaimed, "No, no; I do not love him, I adore him next to God." Then kissing a little crucifix around her neck, his parting gift, she ran off. "Truth is strange, stranger than fiction," involuntarily burst from my lips, as I thought over the little romance of the zingali girl and her boy-lover.

Around Val de Peñas are vineyards of a grape brought from Burgundy, and planted on the sterile plains, which have proved so congenial to them; they produce an incredible amount of fruit, from which "the rich blood" is pressed, and made into a wine, certainly the most delicious and luscious in the world, called "Vino Val de Peña." It cannot bear transportation, and is therefore drunk near where it is made. In place of water upon the table, there were large earthen vessels filled with this rich and fruity wine, worthy of a place at the banquet of an emperor.

We remained at the posada until the moon arose, and then continued our journey over the barren wastes. All the occupants of the diligence were soon asleep save the old monk, who kept me company in the lonely hours of the night. He was a learned old man, in whose veins flowed the Moorish blood, of which he seemed quite proud. Kind old monk! how pleasantly passed away the time, listening to the stories of the grandeur of the moslems of Spain, and the magnificence of the Alhambra in its days of glory. When he found I was from America, he burst forth into glowing expressions of admiration of Washington Irving, whom he had known while he lived in Granada, saying, "He is as noble as he is eloquent, as truthful as he is learned, and to the Moors he has been just; therefore we honor him!" Washington Irving's eloquence and excellence was a charming theme to me, for in my heart of hearts is cherished the memory of his genial and cordial kindness to me, long, long years ago.

When daylight came, we were passing over a still more miserable country than that of yesterday. The wretched peasants were clustering round their mud-houses, seemingly in a state of actual starvation. We passed an inn, styled the "Venta de Quesada," where Don Quixote was knighted, according to Cervantes, and soon we saw large ponds, called the "Eyes of Guadiana," said by Don Quixote to be filled with the tears of Belerma and her seven daughters at the loss of Durandante. In the distance was pointed out *El Toboso*, and the house wherein lived the fair *Dulcinea*. Then we passed the mountains of Tolédo, whose gentle slopes are covered with olive trees, and whose valleys are fresh with wheat-fields. There are no country houses, or even hamlets. In consequence of the unsettled and war-afflicted state of the country, people gather in villages for mutual protection, going thence at morning to work in the fields. Thus we drove through multitudes of towns, until we came to a miserable one, where there is the prison in which Cervantes wrote "Don Quixote." It is called *Argama del Alba.* At *Villarta* we entered *New Castile*, as barren as La Mancha, and drove on rapidly, passing many a fac-simile of Sancho Panza riding on a lean mule, until we stopped at *Temblaque*, a desolate spot, sacked by the French in 1809. There we left the diligence to take the railway. As the train had departed ere we arrived, we were compelled to wait until evening. There was no inn, only a great barrack-room, where we all assembled, and soon after our clever courier, Luigi, after making a foray in a neighboring village, brought us a very acceptable and respectable dinner. This over, and farther inquiries made, we had the comfortable assurance of leaving at six o'clock. Five long hours were then to be disposed of. So while the others scolded and quarrelled at the delay, I found consolation in my journal, upon whose pages I recorded the events of our three days' journey from "Proud Seville" to cold Temblaque. In all times of weariness and anxiety, I have sought forgetfulness in the journal, as to a good and true friend, pouring out all my thoughts and my impressions. Railways are not "cosas de España," and hence they are not prompt and swift as ours. It was a long time ere the friends of progress (*prograsistas*) could induce the people to allow them to pass through their country. They fancied they were inventions of the devil, and therefore to be shunned.

Luigi has just entered, with the pleasing tidings that the train is approaching; so adieu to Temblaque.

The diligence was soon placed upon the railway, and attached to the long train of cars. Then we began slowly to move onward, stopping now and then as though the engine were wearied. In a short time fierce blasts of wind came down from the Guadarama mountains, so powerful as almost to blow the cars from the track. At length we came to a decided halt. The cold wind was roaring around us, and at intervals a spasmodic shriek or consumptive whistle of an engine was heard; then all was silence and darkness. We endeavored to open the doors of the diligence, but they were locked on the outside. Our calls to the guard, or conductor, were unanswered, and in patience we were forced to "bide our time." After an hour or two we moved on again, and by twelve at night reached Madrid. Taking a carriage, we drove through the gate into the city, and found ourselves in the midst of gay groups of people. The houses were all lighted up, and the cafés thronged with men smoking and talking. Upon the balconies were well-dressed women, laughing, with their attendant cavaliers, and splendid equipages dashing along. It was like a radiant vision uprisen by the wave of an enchanter's wand, and in strong contrast with the darkness and chilling blasts of the preceding hours.

We drove to the *Calle de Carretas*, where our good friend N. had obtained lodgings for us, in a *casa de huespedes*, (boarding-house.) The servants were awaiting our arrival, and soon brought in a most appetizing supper. Our rooms were magnificent, almost equalling the "St. Nicholas;" and undressing for the first time in four days, we soon were enjoying the luxury of an excellent bed, and thinking with Sancho Panza, "Blessed be the first inventor of sleep."

CHAPTER XXXVIII.

MADRID, *March 16th*, 1855.

IT was mid-day ere we awakened, for the rich brocade curtains hanging from the windows quite shut out the morning light. Quickly making our toilette, and partaking of a delicious breakfast, we started forth to view the city. "It must be a fête-day," we all exclaimed, as we entered the gay and joyous throng of the crowded streets. Soon we came to the *Puerta del Sol*, (Gate of the Sun,) which is about the centre of Madrid. All the streets diverge from it, like the rays of a star. It seemed an exchange or bourse *al fresco*, for there were evidently discussions upon trade and money, as well as politics and the last intelligence from the Crimea. Like the orientals and ancient Athenians, the Spaniards delight in sunlight, and are eager for news. The Puerta del Sol is therefore the great focus where concentrate all the animation and life of the capital.

A fine, stalwart, and noble-looking people are the Madrileños, with their large cloaks faced with crimson velvet, so gracefully thrown around them. By the fountain in the small Plaza we tarried awhile to remark the variety of national costumes assembled there. Every province in Spain has its own; many very quaint and fanciful, but none so handsome as the picturesque dress of sunny Andalucia. Numerous vendors of the journals were around us, nearly all *blind men*, and well-formed and comely women, with long black veils covering their heads, and muffs to keep the hands warm; for although it is spring, the cold blasts from the Guadarama mountains render it quite necessary to be *bien abrigado* (well sheltered), as they say in Madrid. There were a few bonnets visible, and we were told they were coming in vogue, and that soon the poetic mantilla would give place to these inventions of the Paris milliner. Multitudes of people were crying out the different prizes of the lotteries, and imploring the assemblage to buy the tickets. All manner of things were raffled for, from a splendid painting to a small pig.

Leaving this busy and tumultuous *reunion*, we walked slowly along the *Calle de Alcalá*—a broad and magnificent street, where there are palace-like houses, occupied by the nobility of Madrid. This noble street ends in the *Prado* (the Meadow), the Hyde Park and Champs Elysées of the capital. This Prado in the time of Philip the Fourth was a great barren waste, noted for the murders perpetrated there; but Charles the Third, who came after him, commanded it should be planted with trees, embellished with flowers, and adorned with statues and fountains. Now it is deemed one of the most pleasant paseos in Europe. Although not yet in its full beauty (as the trees were just putting forth leaves), we could well imagine its charming picturesqueness in the summer-time. Then, evening is the fashionable hour of the promenade and the drive, but in the cold season, at three o'clock the élite of the gay world appear in splendid equipages with dashing outriders. Gallant-looking men, on the most superb Andalucian steeds, were riding rapidly along the avenues, and multitudes of handsome, dark-eyed Marileñas, with fluttering fans (the fan is quite as necessary to a Spanish woman as her dress). Upon the grass, which runs like a green band along the gravelled avenues, were throngs of lovely children attended by their nurses in quaint, queer costumes of the different provinces from whence they came. The day was exquisite, the sky of a deep turquoise blue, and the scene around us really charming. By the fountain of *Cybele* we stopped to see the water-carriers fill their barrels. They were a curious, wild-looking class of people. Then, crossing over, we saw the monument called *Dos de Mayo* (second of May), erected to the memory of the victims of Murat, who were shot upon that spot by his orders in 1808, because they refused to yield up their cannon to the French. It is only within the last ten years this tribute to their loyalty has been raised by the Spanish Cortes.

So many praises had we heard of the collection of pictures in the *Museo*, that we left the gay and brilliant spectacle without, and eagerly hastened to that vast edifice, with a clumsy portico, whence we entered a grand vestibule, and then, ascending a wide stairway, found ourselves in the *Tribuna*, wherein are gathered the most glorious gems of the old masters. The room is oval, with an opening in the centre, encircled by a balustrade, over which we looked down upon a fine sculpture-gallery. But the walls of that Tribuna—they were absolutely glowing, radiant with the most precious and eloquent pictures of the greatest artists of the world. First, ever first to my heart and my memory, was the divine "Assumption of the Virgin," by Murillo. It filled my very soul with joy, while it thrilled with bitter anguish. In that face of perfect beauty I beheld the exact resemblance of my angel-child, now rejoicing near the throne of the Almighty. Long, with tears dimming my eyes, I gazed upon it. To me it seemed like a message from the spirit-world, that thus in heavenly peace she was hovering over me. Blessed picture! again and again I returned to look upon it! Hours passed away while thus employed, and a pure and holy light from those soft eyes shone sweetly upon the tumultuous tide, which often sweeps over my soul, and soon all was peace and resignation—the rebellious murmurs stilled, and the heart ready to say, "Thy will, not mine, be done." This picture of Murillo is surely one of the greatest creations of his genius. It seems to breathe upon the canvas. The tender expression reveals the perfection of joy, as though no trace of sorrow could ever rest upon that angelic face, so fresh and radiant with undying youth and immortal beauty.

Farther on was the famous "Perla" of Raphael, and the "Venus and Adonis" of Titian; both wonderful and exquisite paintings. Then came the "Santiago" of Guido, the "Magdalena" of Correggio, and "Christ at the Column" of Michael Angelo. The painting by Raphael—of Christ falling beneath the weight of his cross—is remarkable, and most touching. Each figure is a study. There is the divine expression of the Saviour's face—the anguish of the mother—the bitter grief of her attending women, and the stern faces of the Roman soldiers,—all are types of character, and bear with them the history of that awful and sacred scene.

Advancing farther on, we came to the great picture of Velasquez, styled "The Lances." It is a representation of the surrender of Breda, and is admirable for color, attitude, and the bright atmosphere, so distinctly defined, it seems as though the figures moved in it. All the varieties of national characteristics are most faithfully preserved in the faces of the Flemings, the Italians, and the Spaniards.

The conqueror, General Spinola, (who captured Breda in 1625,) is portrayed by the side of his vanquished enemy, with a glow of generous feeling in his dark face, as though uttering words of consolation.

It is only in Madrid, and in this Museo, that Velasquez lives in glowing pictures. He was a native of Seville, but lived the brightest days of his life in Madrid, and dying here, was buried in a church which the French destroyed, thus scattering the dust of his body to the "four winds of heaven." It is a singular coincidence that the remains of Murillo shared the same fate from the hands of the French soldiers. Velasquez was emphatically a *painter of men*, (just such noble specimens of men as one sees now in Spain.) But the faces of his women lack the entrancing beauty and spirituality of Murillo. The bold and chivalric nature of the Spaniard he admirably represents in all his pictures of kings, dukes, and peasants. His holy subjects did not strike me as possessing the impassioned zeal and soft tenderness of the paintings of Raphael and Titian.

Many of the noblest pictures of Salvator Rosa, of Leonardo da Vinci, of Carracci, of Claude Lorraine, of Rembrandt, of Rubens, of Vandyke, are in this Tribuna, which contains the richest treasure, assuredly, of any other apartment in Europe, to those who, like me, regard pictures as a glorious wealth.

The Museo was built by Charles the Third, to contain the national paintings of his kingdom; but his intention was never fully completed. When the French entered Madrid, they turned the Museo into a barrack for the soldiers. Upon the return of Ferdinand to his capital, he ordered the building to be repaired, and the great rooms and corridors to be converted into picture-galleries. When Spain was almost mistress of the world, in the renowned days of

Charles the Fifth and his son Philip the Second, hither thronged, by royal invitation, the finest artists of Italy and Holland; and here they painted their noblest pictures, inspired and encouraged by the appreciation of the monarchs themselves, who delighted to receive with friendship and social courtesy, Rubens, Titian, and Velasquez. Charles and his son Philip were the patrons of the arts of that period, so fitly styled *Renaissance*, (the awakening,)—truly the awaking of the *love of the beautiful* from its long slumber, when, like a fresh flower of the spring-time, it came radiantly forth, enchanting the eyes of kings as well as those of their subjects.

While Murillo, Velasquez, and Ribiera, artists of the three schools of Seville, Madrid, and Valencia, were painting great pictures, the viceroys in Italy and the low countries were collecting the most valuable and costly works of foreign artists to send to the mother-country. Generals, officers, and even soldiers, home-returning after victorious battles, often brought with them precious pictures, which they placed as offerings upon the altars of their patron saints. In this manner almost every church and convent could boast of some painting of inestimable value. When the sequestration of the monasteries and religious houses became a law, their property reverted to the Crown, and by a royal command, the pictures were all removed to the Museo. Thus has been gathered the most beautiful, rare, and choice collection of the works of the great and famous artists whose names are glorious in the annals of painting.

The saloons are divided into a vast number of galleries, appropriated to the Dutch, Italian, French, and Spanish schools of art.

We made several visits to the Museo, and passed entirely through it. Murillo, however, always attracted me more than any other artist. His pictures are so dramatic that they take instant possession of the interest, and impress the heart far more than the creations of any other painter. The complexion of his women really seems the reality of the warm, rich, Andalucian skin—there is such vitality and clearness in the tints mingling and melting into each other like those of nature. There is a blending of the noble and the beautiful, the graceful and the gentle, which is strangely fascinating to me.

Madrid is a city of three hundred thousand inhabitants, built upon "more than seven hills," near the *Manzanares*, a small stream which is dignified by the name of river. It is enclosed by low walls, and has many fine public buildings. Except the Calle de Alcalá, the streets are narrow, and the houses five or six stories high, with delicate balconies to the windows. Madrid has no environs, like all other cities we have visited, and as it does not cover much space of ground, we were quite at a loss to know how the people were accommodated, until we heard that twenty or thirty families often live in one house, which, like those of Paris, have a common stairway, and are let out by floors for the rich, and single apartments for the poor; thus one roof often covers magnificent luxury and wretched poverty. The houses are not built like those of Seville and Cadiz, around a pleasant court with trees and fountains in it; but are great masses of stone, with walls of immense thickness.

We are delightfully lodged in the gayest portion of the city, and from our balcony we look down upon an animated throng, warm and glowing with life and energy. Multitudes of soldiers mingle with the crowd, and, in their gorgeous uniform, seem like tulips in a parterre of flowers—they are so bright and gaudy with their red and yellow trimmings, and their helmets shining like silver in the sunlight. Frequently whole regiments march by, with bands of music and streaming banners. There is an unceasing bustle and activity on all sides; a quick and busy air about the people, which speaks of eagerness in the battle of existence.

The shops along the Puerta del Sol are filled with gay and brilliant merchandise, resembling much the Boulevards of Paris. But nothing is of Spanish manufacture. The shop-keepers always told us " every thing needed in Spain is made in France." The streets are clean and nicely paved, and at every corner is a vendor of water with his little stand decked out with gilt balls, so fanciful, we never failed to stop and look at them.

Our Minister, Mr. Soulé, had just left, but we called upon the Secretary of Legation, Mr. Perry, who has recently married a Spanish poetess.

Mr. Perry informed us that intelligence had come that morning of the death of Don Carlos, uncle to Queen Isabel the Second. He died at Trieste, on the 10th of March; and although a fierce enmity existed between them, and for seven years he had waged a relentless war against her, the royal etiquette demanded the Queen should assume deep mourning, and that all the gaiety of the court should be suspended. Her Majesty had left the city for the retirement of one of the country palaces. Thus we were disappointed in seeing her. Since the death of Don Carlos there are many apprehensions of a revolution, for the Count de Monte Molin (his son) is still of the "seed of Banquo," and has many warm partisans in Spain.

At our casa de huespedes, where we lodge, we dined today at eight o'clock. Upon entering the saloon, we found a large assemblage of the members of *Las Cortes* (the Congress), now in session. They were a distinguished body, and elegant in appearance, dressed with great taste, and of evident refinement of manner. They all bowed with the courteous grace so peculiar to Spaniards, and we commenced our dinner. The conversation interrupted by our entrance was then resumed with great animation. Its theme was the debate in that morning's *Cortes* on the subject of forming a new constitution. One of the members, to whom all listened in wrapt attention, gave his views on the subject, and his peroration was uttered with the enthusiasm of a *devotée*, and in perfect unconsciousness that we were Americans. "In truth," he exclaimed, in a rich, sonorous voice, "there is upon the earth but one model government—but one we should strive to imitate—for it alone is worthy of man in his true majesty! It is the government of the United States!"

Pride and exultation thrilled my very soul, and sent the warm blood glowing to my cheek. My eyes must have told my delight; for, meeting their glance, the speaker said instantly, "The Señora must be American!" Then came many inquiries concerning my dear country, and appreciative praise of its onward progress. Oh! it is a glorious thing to be an American! There is a spell about the name which awakens interest, while it commands respect, from the high as well as the lowly.

During our sojourn in Madrid, we made the acquaintance of many of the members of Las Cortes. We found them charming in conversation, intellectual, and exceedingly well informed. They gave us much information concerning Spain, and freely discussed her present position. Many of the people are eager for a republic, and all are anxious for some improvement in the government. The Cortes is now occupied with a new constitution, which they are striving to make acceptable to all parties.

The eloquent eulogist of our country we soon discovered was the Marquis de Alviarde, leader of the "Prograsistas," the party who are strong advocates for progress. He is a man of noble talent and chivalric impulses—enthusiastic in debate, and feared by his enemies. Only a few years ago all his possessions were confiscated, but have since been restored to him. He seemed just the man to be the idol of the people, warm, frank, and sympathetic. It was really a delight to listen to his impassioned words, when he spoke of his country, of its past grandeur, and its present agitated and reckless existence.

It is nearly thirty years since the civil war began, soon after the death of Ferdinand the Seventh, and during that long period fearful and frightful has been the desolation of homes and hearts. Kindred blood shed by kindred hands has deluged the land. Parties and fierce factions have risen up, each contending for power, while the wretched country was tossed from one to the other, as though it were a football. Yet with all this demoralizing strife, and its attendant evils of poverty, rapine, and murder, the loyalty and chivalry of the Spanish character have never been extinguished. It still possesses the noble bearing, the love of independence, and generous ardor of those ancient days when Spain was first among the nations of Europe; and though dimmed by its surroundings of discord and internal warfare, its elements of greatness and true dignity still live in many and many a heart. Spain is really a wonderful country; for none other could have so long sustained itself under such trials and difficulties. Often is my admiration called forth by the firm faith with which its people look forward to the future, always picturing it as bright and prosperous, and saying, "After the storm comes the sunshine;" and though constantly disappointed, they are ever hopeful. Never has any country been more calumniated by the false impressions which have gone abroad of its inhabitants. Before we came to Spain, persons were frequently warning us of the rough and terrible roads; of the dangers of the mountain-passes, where wild and fearless banditti held supreme control; of the miserable inns and lawless peasants. All of these stories have proved utterly false, and absolutely a myth. The roads are good, the inns excellent, the mountain-passes well protected by the Guardia Civil, and the people most instinctively polite and cordial to strangers. Spain is the land of romance and of beautiful legends. Then it is truly rich in the memories of the past. In all our wanderings we have never heard an uncivil word, or seen a rude action. Amid all classes of persons, from the nobility to the poor peasant, we have received the kindest and most genial attentions.

We passed a morning in the royal armory, which is kept in a large building erected during the reign of Philip the Second, by Gaspar de Vega. It contains a curious and rare collection of the trophies won in battle, and memorials of the ancient grandeur of the nation, when the Spanish flag of *red* and *yellow* (emblematic of blood and gold) waved over the New World, and the Islands of spices, and the Gold Coast of Africa. We entered a gallery of immense length, along which were arranged knights in armor near the wall, and equestrian statues along the centre. Above them hung the banners taken in war. There were coats-of-mail of the Spanish soldiers, from the time of the Cid to the latest days in which they were used. The armor of Columbus was of black and white, with silver plaitings. Several worn by Charles the Fifth were exquisitely chased, and all with the image of his tutelar saint (the Virgin) engraved upon them. Then there was the armor of the Cid, of Pelayo, of Philip the Second, of Isabella of Castile, of Ferdinand her husband, of Garcilarco de Vega, of Fernando Cortez, and Don John of Austria; besides multitudes of others of the heroic Spanish captains. There were helmets and shields, and standards brought from Lepanto, and swords of wondrous antiquity and variety of forms. The sword has always been the favorite instrument of Spain, and its keen *toledos* have a world-wide fame. First there was the scimitar of Bernardo del Carpio, and that of Orlando, or Roldan; the sword of brave old Bernal Diaz of Castille, who, following the fortunes of Cortez, wrote a history of their victories in Mexico. Next came the swords of Pizarro and of Cortez, of the "Great Captain," of Charles the Fifth, and of the Prince of Condé. Thousands of other relics of the chivalric days of Spain met our eyes at every turn.

From the armory we drove to the *Museo Naval*, founded in 1853 by Isabel the Second, and adorned with a full-length picture of her Majesty. The figure is full and well formed, and the face decidedly Austrian, or rather of the Bourbon stamp. In this Museo are gathered many precious memorials of Columbus. Of course these souvenirs had for us an especial interest. There was an admirable picture of him—the model of his caravel—the original chart he carried with him to America, and the marks made upon it by his own hand, indicating the new discoveries. Several paintings represented his first landing in the New World! Then came portraits of Pizarro, of Cortez, of Balboa, and of Fernando de Soto. His burial in the Mississippi formed the subject of a large and most touching picture. The scene is night upon the river, illumined by the lurid glare of the torches held by the soldiers. The priest in his robes is reading the service for the dead, while the comrades of the brave De Soto, holding the emaciated body of their commander in their arms, are about to cast it into the dark and turbid waters. There are numerous models of ships, and arms, and trophies taken of late years from the pirates of the Philippine Archipelago.

In the *Sala de la Reina*, (which contains his portrait,) is a picture of the Battle of Lepanto, given to the Museo by the Marquis de Molins, to whom the Museo is indebted for many improvements and additions. This noble Spaniard, a man of talent, courage, and energy, is now an exile from his country. He was one of the ministers at the period of the revolution, when Calderon de la Barca was driven from Spain. It was a source of deep regret not to have met again Señor de la Barca, and his gifted and charming wife. In America we had known each other, and had hoped to meet in Spain. But when we reached Madrid, we found them also wanderers, and their elegant palace silent and desolate.

We were quite captivated by a modern picture, portraying the incidents of the visit of his Holiness Pius the Ninth, to the flag-ship of Admiral Bustillos, while the Spanish fleet lay at *Mola di Gaëta*, in Italy, where they had been sent by the Government to aid the Pope if necessary. The scene is brilliant, and the waves of the Mediterranean, sparkling in the sunlight as they break against the great ships, have a look of singular reality.

The national *Biblioteca* library is exceedingly interesting. There are vast treasures of the lore of olden time in musty manuscripts, (which I would gladly have explored,) and then two hundred thousand volumes of rare and excellent works in many languages. The coins and medals are very curious. They are Gothic, Moorish, and Spanish. "Hard money" was not known to the Iberians until it was introduced by the Carthaginians. During the dominion of the Romans, however, there were great numbers of mints, and hence the profusion of coins now found in the museums. Upon those of Moorish origin were Arabic words, and on others strange arrow-headed cuneiform letters, said to be words from the Punic.

Returning from the Biblioteca, we passed through the *Plaza del Oriente*, which is a fine square, with a *glorietta*, or flower-garden, in the centre. This is raised from the surface, enclosed by a fanciful railing, and planted with trees and parterres of delicious flowers. Around the Plaza are numbers of statues of the kings of Spain; beginning with the Gothic line of Astolfo, and thus on to Pelayo, (of the Asturian race,) to Isabel and Ferdinand, and other representatives of the monarchs of the land. From the midst of the trees rises a tall "Monument to the Arts," erected by Isabel the Second. Four great lions are placed at the base, and near them fountains are pouring forth streams of water. The glorietta also contains the equestrian statue of Philip the Fourth, deemed by many the most admirable in Europe. It was carved in wood first by Montañes, and was then cast in bronze at Florence, by Tacca. It was for years in the *Retiro* gardens, but recently has been removed to the Plaza del Oriente, where it attracts the attention of all beholders—there is such bold spirit in the form of the horse, and in the figure of the kingly rider, whose cloak seems floating out upon the air. The finish and perfection of the workmanship are remarkable. The Palace of the Queen fronts upon this square. It is of enormous dimensions, with an entrance and courts like those of the Tuileries. It is built upon the spot where the Moors first erected their Alcazar, which was burned in 1734. Philip the Fifth then resolved to raise up a structure which should rival the Palace of Versailles. It is of white stone from Colmenar, and by the moonlight seems a huge "palace of marble." The interior is gorgeously adorned with frescoes, carving, gilding, tapestry, and a few paintings. The chief saloon of reception, or the throne-room, has beautiful furniture of crimson and gold; chandeliers of vast size, and immense mirrors cast at the manufactory of *San Illdefonso.*

The afternoon was delightful; so we extended our walk to the *Buen Retiro.* These are beautiful gardens, walks, and avenues, first designed by the gallant Duke of Oliravez as a "retreat" for the sovereign Philip the Fourth, when the cares of state pressed tóo heavily upon his mind. For his amusement saloons were built, and adorned with regal magnificence, where masques and gay balls gladdened the night, and fêtes amid the groves of the gardens made joyous the hours of the day. There was, too, a theatre, where the plays of Lope de Vega were enacted in the presence of the sovereign, while the author of them, with Murillo, Velasquez, and Calderon, were among the honored guests. All these remembrances crowded upon my mind as we wandered through the flowery labyrinths, or seated ourselves in bowers of jessamine.

The Retiro was long in the occupancy of the French, who quite destroyed the trees, cutting them down for fire-wood. Upon the return of Ferdinand the Seventh to Madrid, he devoted immense sums of money to the restoration of the gardens. The medallion-like parterres, planted with violets, heliotropes, and hyacinths, are really beautiful, and the atmosphere is filled with their sweet perfume. Numbers of people, in various costume, were wandering through the grounds or seated beneath the trees. Around the little lake were groups of merry children, feeding the flocks of white ducks upon it

We passed several private palaces, of noble and imposing architecture. That of the Dukes of Medina-Cæli is of vast size, and has great numbers of balconies along the prado. In the *Plaza de las Cortes* we saw the statue of Cervantes, modelled by Antonio Sola, of Barcelona. The figure is represented in the old Spanish costume, and the cloak falling around it conceals the mutilated arm, which was wounded at Lepanto. Cervantes deemed that poor maimed arm quite the pride of his life, and loved to display it. On the pedestal are *relievos*, picturing the adventures of Don Quixote. These were ordered and paid for by a religious society. Thus again was Cervantes indebted to the monks, for the "Brothers of Mercy" ransomed him when he was a prisoner in Algiers. During life Cervantes was often starving. All his entreaties to the Government for aid and succor being treated with a contemptuous silence, now that he is dead, a great monument rises to his memory, and the entire nation proudly claim him as compatriot.

In this Plaza is the *Descalzas Reales*, a church founded by Juana, the daughter of Charles the Fifth; also a great nunnery, or convent, where the daughters of Cervantes and of Lope de Vega took the veil. It was designed by Queen Barbara, wife of Ferdinand the Sixth; and endowed most richly by her. The high altar is wonderful for its pillars of serpentine marble from Granada, very rare and precious. Coming so recently from the splendid cathedral of Seville, we were not anxious to visit all the churches of Madrid, as they are not remarkable in architecture or adornments.

There are multitudes of hospitals and houses of charity founded by persons of wealth, or belonging to different churches. These are conducted by priests or nuns, and are most excellent institutions.

In spite of the many asylums for the poor, we often met beggars, whose pitiable and pathetic words were very touching. Yesterday a little girl, about nine years old, caught my dress in her hands, and appealing to me with her large, tender eyes, at last said, "Ah! Señorita, a little charity—God will repay you!" Giving her some money, and asking her of her situation, she told me she was lame, and had two brothers and a sister younger than herself, and that they had never had either father or mother. Theirs was certainly a peculiar state. Like Topsy, in "Uncle Tom's Cabin," they must "have growed."

Often were we warned, during our stay in Madrid, of the danger of *pulmonia*, a deadly malady, induced by sudden exposure to the cold air which comes down from the Guadarama mountains. This wind is so subtle and insidious that there is constant necessity of care to guard against it. Hence the people wrap themselves in wide cloaks ere they leave a room. An old adage describes it thus:

> "Too slight to blow out a candle,
> Yet strong enough to kill a man."

Madrid derives its name from *Magerit*, an Arabic word signifying a "current of air." Its position on the summit of rude and bare mountains, renders it particularly under the "dominion of the winds," and therefore rather unfavorable to health. The summers are fiercely hot, and the winters intensely cold,—so said the Madrileños; but we could scarcely imagine it to be so, for the houses have very few chimneys. In the centre of our elegant drawing-room was a large gilt bowl, (very like a giant punch-bowl.) This was a *brasero*, into which was placed burning charcoal to warm the room. Although the men were so carefully sheltered from the cold winds, the women wore only lace mantillas over their heads, on the prado, in the streets, and at the opera.

We accompanied Navarro, the evening after our arrival, to the *Teatro del Oriente*, in the Plaza del Oriente. The house is magnificent, with six tiers of boxes, and a splendid parquette. The hangings are rich crimson velvet, with gold fringe. The façade of the boxes is white, gilded and enamelled, and the ceiling exquisitely frescoed. The opera of

"Lucia di Lammermuir" was admirably rendered by Spezzia, Malvezzi, and Guicciardi. The orchestra of eighty musicians was delightful, and the scenery excellent. As it was a benefit night, the theatre was well filled with the high people of Madrid; and never have I seen a more noble and distinguished-looking audience. The women were all in black, (as the Court was in mourning,) though amid their "sable drapery" were glittering diamonds and precious jewels. The Queen's box was superb, with gorgeous curtains and great mirrors. It was not occupied, as grief for Don Carlos keeps her Majesty away from all amusements. In a private box near the stage was seated the Duchess of Alva, sister to the Empress of France. She is a lovely, graceful creature, with dark hair and eyes. The Duke of Alva, (whose name has so often appeared in our journals in connection with Mr. Soulé and his duels,) was with her. He is quite young, of mild and gentle aspect. Not far from us was an elegant and dignified old man, with the most genial expression of countenance. It was Martinez de la Rosa, often Minister of State, and several times Ambassador abroad. Although a statesman and a politician, he is a poet and author. Just now his party is out of power, but he is "biding his time."

Las Cortes, the building where the deputies, or members of the national congress assemble, is built upon the spot where once stood the convent of *Santa Catalina*, pulled down by the French. It is a large edifice, with columns and statues in front. Stormy sessions are held within its walls, and ministries made and destroyed therein. The Spaniards are extremely free in their expressions of opinion concerning the Queen and her Government, and appear to have no fear of the *surveillance* of the police.

CHAPTER XXXIX.

THE ESCORIAL, *March 17th*, 1855.

AT dawn we left Madrid, passing through the deserted Puerta del Sol, by the great Palace of the Queen, and on to the avenue called *La Florida*. The trees are planted near the Manzanares, and their vigorous life is in strong contrast to the sterility beyond them. The plains are parched, and the hills gray, and entirely without verdure. At intervals we saw the peasants working amid the rocks, for there did not seem to be a vestige of soil upon them. The snow-capped peaks of the Guadarama mountains soon met our eyes, gleaming brightly in the morning sunlight, as we journeyed pleasantly along the *camino real*, (the royal road,) which leads from the capital to the *Escorial*, a distance of twenty-five miles. The road is really magnificent, with a parapet raised up on each side, and grand bridges spanning deep chasms, where far below trickle slowly on diminutive streamlets, dignified with the name of river.

Many leagues away we caught sight of the Escōrial, rising in gloomy yet majestic grandeur, near the highest point of the mountain region of the Guadarama. It is built of granite, and absolutely seems a part and portion of the "everlasting hills." It is a glorious old palace, monastery, and mausoleum, erected in 1563 by Philip the Second, (son of the famous Charles the Fifth,) in compliance with a vow made to St. Lorenzo (so says tradition) during the battle of St. Quentin. The Saint granting the monarch's prayer for victory, this colossal and sacred edifice was dedicated to his honor, and constructed in the form of a *parrilla* (gridiron), as San Lorenzo suffered martyrdom by being broiled upon one. Hence it presents the most singular appearance. Four enormous towers indicate the feet of the gridiron, while the interior is divided into cloisters like its bars. The handle contains the palace. In the centre of the building is the immense dome, and beneath it the church. We drove through a poor little village near the palace, and stopping at the posada, obtained a guide, and went immediately to the Escorial. Its proportions are gigantic, and it seems intended for eternity,—with its arched corridors, its spacious porticoes and wide courts, its lofty galleries and noble saloons. There are eleven thousand windows, in holy remembrance of the "Virgins of Cologne," slain by the Huns, and fourteen thousand doors. Twenty-two years were occupied in its construction, and its cost was six millions of crowns.

We spent all the day following our guide, Cornelio, through the windings of the building, almost as intricate as those of the Cretan labyrinth. Cornelio was entirely blind, and had been so for *forty-eight years*. Still, in his "mind's eye," he sees all the glories of the Escorial. It was so strange to hear the sightless old man exclaim, "Now, Señora, remark the effect of the sunlight upon that picture!" and then he would stop as though looking upon it, and point out all its beauty. "See the deep shadows cast by those columns; they have the form of a king upon his throne!" again would he say, as we passed along with him up the great granite stairways, and through vaulted cloisters, to the royal apartments, where

Isabel the Second spends her summers. These are fitted up with luxurious elegance, but not by far so exquisite as that portion of the palace embellished and adorned by Charles the Third. It is quite unique in style. The floors and walls are composed of a mosaic of different-colored wood, and the furniture inlaid with ivory and pearl-shell, and glittering with stones and gems.

The view from the balcony of these rooms is admirably picturesque, looking down upon the *lonja* (terrace), planted with box, cut into fanciful shapes. Beyond this terrace are the hanging gardens, and the little lakes and fountains; then great groves of elm and oak trees, all brought from England. Enclosing the lovely picture, as though with a dark frame, were the gray summits of the Guadarama chain. Gazing over the wide expanse, it appeared to me the realization of the wild dream of an enthusiast. The creation of such a paradise, beneath the shadow of the snow-topped mountains, upon whose highest peak is the grand Escorial, justly styled by the Castilians *La octava maravilla del mundo*, (the eighth wonder of the world.) Philip the Second was a man of most indomitable will and religious zeal. Thus, inspired by a holy purpose, and aided by the great magician of earth, mighty gold, he accomplished almost a miracle. Possessing infinite taste in the fine arts, and a love of the beautiful, he adorned the vast halls, galleries, and libraries, with the works of distinguished artists and authors.

When we came to the door of the great library, blind Cornelio gave me to the charge of an aged monk, who became the cicerone of our wanderings through it. There are thirty-five thousand volumes resting upon the shelves, and multitudes of manuscripts in Arabic; then noble portraits of Philip the Second, in his early youth and in his manhood. There is a superb picture of Charles the Fifth, taken in the glorious days of his life, when he ruled nearly one-half of Europe. We also saw the portraits of Herrera, architect of the Escorial, and of Montano, the first librarian. The ceiling, which is extremely lofty, is painted by Carducho, and is now as fresh and bright as when painted, some three hundred years ago.

The old monk was learned, kind, and courteous. He gave us most interesting and valuable information concerning the former occupants of this wonderful place. He showed us the small room in which Philip died, in 1598, at the age of 72. His last illness was of frightful duration, and he commanded his people to remove him to a spot whence his eyes could look constantly upon the great altar of the church. We also saw the seat where he was wont to place himself among the monks in the coro, and listen to the music swelling out from the giant organ. In his old age he was rigid in the observance of his religious duties, casting aside all the regal splendor of the monarch. Just in the rear of the coro is the statue of Christ upon the cross, carved by Benvenuto Cellini, and given to Philip by the King of Sardinia. It is of exquisite workmanship, but painful to look upon. So precious was it deemed, that it was brought all the distance from Barcelona on the shoulders of men, for fear the shaking of a carriage might injure it.

Although many of the paintings have been removed to the Museo of Madrid, multitudes still remain, of rare excellence. There are many of Raphael, of Tintoretto, of Murillo, of Titian, and Velasquez. The monk often paused before pictures by Navarrete el Mudo (Navarrete the Dumb), and commended them to my especial attention. They all portrayed the sufferings of our Saviour, and were indescribably affecting. This Navarrete was a poor deaf and dumb boy, who was permitted to wander unheeded through the long cloisters and amid the picture-galleries of the Escorial. At last his genius and his talent found utterance through the pencil and brush. The eloquence of the soul seems infused into them. "The Temptation of Christ upon the Mount" is a perfect history of the fierce struggle and trial of the passions. "Christ bound to the Column" touched me even unto tears. The divine face of our Lord, although bitterness and humiliation are expressed in it, has also a holy calm in the beautiful eyes irresistibly impressive. There were other paintings of Navarrete the Dumb besides these, which were remarkable for the coloring and admirable life-like attitudes. From the saints and martyrs his subjects were all taken.

In the private chapel was the grand painting of Titian, representing San Lorenzo bound to the gridiron, and the fire just kindled beneath it. A most gloomy and sad picture it was, with the stern and fierce faces of the persons clustering around to gaze upon the agonies and martyrdom of the saint.

We passed through a long subterranean passage, under a portion of the edifice, and came out just near our inn. A crowd of beggars was watching for us, and we were quickly assailed by plaintive entreaties for charity. Miserable beings! how wasted and worn they look. It needed no words to tell the sad story of their starvation; it was written in their staring eyes and trembling limbs.

Our posada is extremely neat, with a floor of great blocks of granite, and walls hung with pictures of the saints. The wind is roaring wildly around us, bringing with it the icy coldness from the Guadarama. Not far from our window rises up a grand mountain-peak, covered with snow, and seeming in the dim twilight like an immense white palace with towers and turrets.

M. D. and Octavia, wearied with our busy day, have retired to rest; but the thronging memories of the olden time so press upon my mind, I cannot sleep. Thus, seating myself by the small fire in the wide hearth, I yield myself to the influences and associations of the spot, recalling the brilliant days of the Escorial, when gorgeous pageants and splendid festivities filled the hours; and then the gloomy period when Philip, discarding the gentler charms of life, gave himself to nights of penance, and long hours of severe mortification of the flesh. Wandering amid these remembrances, I was startled by the deep tone of the monastery bell striking the hour of one. And now, away with the past; it is the present which commands me.

March 18th.—The pealing bells awakened us, and as it was Sunday, we quickly dispatched our breakfast, and hastened to the Escorial to hear mass. The church is under the dome, and is of grand proportions and majestic elegance. The great altar is superb, with a crucifix of blood-red jasper, upon white marble, and pillars of porphyry and gilded bronze. The height of the cupola from the pavement is nearly four hundred feet. The coro (choir) is of carved oak, and the missals of music are all of parchment, exquisitely illuminated. Far above us, in the dome, were the frescoes of Lucca Giordano, so varied, bright, and beautiful in color, they seemed freshly strewn with flowers. There were statues of Charles the Fifth and of his wife Isabel, of Philip the Second, and of the San Lorenzo. As we stood looking upon the pictures, the mass began. How glorious was the sound of the organ, pealing through the perfect forest of marble columns, and growing louder and louder as it swelled beneath the vaulted dome. Deep and holy emotions possessed my soul, and never before did I so fully realize the sublime grandeur of the Catholic worship.

When the religious services were ended, one of the priests accompanied us to *Pantéon*, the burial-vault of the kings of

Spain. We descended a long stairway of black marble, the walls on each side lined with green and yellow jasper, until we reached an octagon room of great height. It seemed all of dark-hued marble, and of bronze gilt, not in harmony with the solemn gloom of the place. There were niches containing urns, in which were placed the mortal remains of the royal dead, with their names inscribed upon them. When Philip the Second built the Escorial, he designed this Pantéon as a mausoleum for his father, Charles the Fifth; but his intention was not fulfilled, and upon his death his son, Philip the Third, completed it, and placed within it the bodies of his grandfather and of his father. Since that period the home of the dead has been well filled. The last placed here was the infant child of Isabel the Second. The old monk held aloft his lamp, and pointed out all the peculiarities of this sanctuary, dwelling with particular delight upon the crucifix by Pedro Tacca. Oh! how cold and gloomy were the feelings which stole over me as we looked upon these dark urns. Within them were all that remained of the men who once swayed millions. A small vase of marble and a few Latin words are the only record—they lived and died.

We gladly left the chill atmosphere of the Pantéon, and ascended to the cloisters, passing the tomb of Don Carlos, the son of Philip the Second, whose romantic story has been the theme of poets. Schiller and Alfieri have both invested his sad fate with a touching interest. Hated by his father, he was loved and cherished by his young and beautiful stepmother, whom, when he reached the years of manhood, he adored with a wild and frenzied passion. Then, reckless of the strict conventionalities of court etiquette, he often gave expression to his admiration. This reaching his stern father, caused an increase of the detestation with which he had before regarded him; and forthwith the wretched son was imprisoned, and died shortly after, "a natural death," said the historian of the times. But there are many legends of the love of the fair Queen and the hapless Carlos, and of his murder by hired assassins.

Our guide showed us next the *Anti-Sacristia*, with fine arabesque ceilings painted by Granello and Fabricio. At one end of this room is the *Retablo de la Santa forma*, in which is kept the holy wafer. It was said to have bled at the battle of Gorcum, when trampled upon by the heretics. When the French took the Escorial, in 1808, and destroyed many precious pictures and statues, this wafer was miraculously preserved. When Ferdinand the Seventh regained his kingdom, he returned it with great pomp to its sanctuary. Twice each year it is *manifestada* (that is, exhibited for adoration). A noble painting by Coello, an admirable Spanish artist, represents the apotheosis of the wafer. The good old priest permitted me to see the vase containing it, (although none but Catholics are permitted to look upon it.) He did not inquire concerning my religion. No doubt he was satisfied with the devotion expressed in my face, when gazing upon the heavenly picture of our blessed Saviour painted by the divine Raphael, and needed no other evidence.

In the *Sala de Batallas* (the Battle-Chamber) are curious paintings, in fresco, of the fierce encounters between the Moors and Spaniards. The costumes are singular. These pictures are copied, it is said, from an old painting found in the Alcazar of Segovia, of vast antiquity. On one side is the Battle of St. Quentin in Flanders, and the Sea-Fight of Lepanto, when Don John of Austria, (the brother of Philip,) achieved so grand a victory. Then came multitudes of minor battles, by land and sea.

The Escorial, we were told in Madrid, was in a state of decay; but we perceived no signs of "defacing time." It seems to defy even that conqueror. In the days of its glory there were three hundred monks in the monastery; now, since the sequestration of the convents, only twenty-five are allowed to remain there. They take care of the building, and devote themselves to good works of charity, and instruction of the poor peasants. We conversed with several of these excellent men, and found them well informed, intellectual, and actuated by a holy zeal for their religion in all their efforts and purposes of life.

Old Cornelio insisted that we should ascend to the summit of the cupola, whence we obtained a most extensive view, for many miles, of the mountain region. Every peak was glittering in the sunlight, for upon them lay the pure white snow which had fallen during the past night. Around the dome there is a gallery in the wall, quite wide enough for three persons to walk abreast. Well may it be said, "the Escorial was built for eternity." The thickness of the walls is more than seventeen feet through. In the "Court of Kings" there are gigantic figures of scriptural kings, each carved from one block of granite, with gilded crowns around their brows.

We spent two days within the gray walls of the Escorial, exploring the arched corridors and lofty cloisters. One evening we walked in the "Plantation of Oaks," as it is styled. It contains a small *casita*, a kind of toy palace built for Charles the Fourth.

In the afternoon of Sunday we left the Escorial, and entering the diligence, drove rapidly through the little village. The sunshine fell lovingly upon the vast edifice, and long shadows of the turrets streamed over the parterres of flowers, like clouds in the bright atmosphere. "A palace for God," exclaimed Philip the Second, when he stood upon the mountain-pass which divides the possessions of the monks from those of the State; "a palace for God and a hut for myself is all I require."

The mayoral and his zargales (driver and postillions) were very eloquent in their entreaties to the mules to quicken their pace. "Ah! Coronella, will you let Generala outdo you? See, now, Pia is worth five of you." And thus with caressing words they urged them on; but as the poor wretches heeded them not, blows from great poles were resorted to. The miserable mules constantly awakened my sympathy, they are so patient and so ill-treated. Then the donkeys, brave, industrious little animals! how would the peasants exist without their aid? They seem as necessary to them as the reindeer to the Laplander. There is about them such an appealing look of suffering! Often we would meet long strings of them, when, without a word from their driver, they turned out of our way. The peasants were all in their holiday dresses, bidding us good day as we passed.

Along the rocky glens we drove until we came to the cross marking the boundary of the monkish dominion. Then ceased the oaks and elms, and all was a barren waste. Four leagues away we caught sight of Madrid, rising up with its spires, its domes, and cupolas. The picture was a fine one, enhanced by the surroundings of gray hills. It really seemed a city in a great desert. Approaching the Manzanares, we encountered throngs of people from the city. They were well dressed, and apparently happy and contented. There were several parties with guitars, playing and singing most gaily. We saw, too, the peculiar type of the Madrileños called the *manolo* and *manola*. These are bold, daring, reckless men and women, remarkable for their wit, their repartee, and wild *abandon* of character. They have a picturesque costume, a graceful walk, and strikingly handsome *physique*. The men wear a jacket covered with a profusion of little silver buttons, a red sash, wide pantaloons, embroidered shirt, and a broad-brimmed hat. The women have short petticoats, exquisite stockings, delicate slippers, and a mantilla falling over thick braids of hair. They told us these peculiarities of dress and manner were fast passing away, and it was only upon a day of *fiesta* they were now ever seen.

Beyond the river we saw the hermitage of *San Isidro*, the Patron Saint of Madrid, whose praises were so sweetly written by Lope de Vega. It was this saint who was supposed to have revealed the secret pass of the mountains to the Christian army of Alonzo the Eighth, by which means he fell upon the Moors and destroyed them by thousands. During the month of May a festival, called *La Romeria*, is held in honor of San Isidro. Then along the banks of the Manzanares assemble happy crowds, who with songs and dances, castanets and guitars, pass the merry hours in joyous pleasure.

As we drove through the city we met so many soldiers in the streets, that we at first imagined a revolution had broken out, (having heard many prophecies of one;) but found they had only been without the walls to celebrate a fête-day. They were a fine-looking set of men.

We tarried for the night at a hôtel on the noble street of Alcalá; and at early morning, March 19th, left Madrid, passing along the Prado, and by the lovely Retiro, through the northern gateway. From an eminence beyond the walls we took our last look of the city, gloriously bright in the sun's early rays.

For miles our road was through a dreary country, but

little cultivated. At *Alcalá de Heneres* we breakfasted. This old town was the birthplace of Cervantes and of Antonio de Solis. It was here, too, that the first Polyglot Bible was published, in 1514, by Zimenes. On to *Guadalajara*, the route was still through cold and sterile wastes. In this ancient town desolation and despair seem to hold their court, for misery is every where visible. We saw the ruins of the palace from whose gorgeously decorated balcony Francis the First beheld the tournament given to him by the Duke of Infantado. The Palace of the Mendozas, and various half-ruined churches, are objects of interest. Guadalajara was conquered from the Moors by Alvar, the friend of the Cid, whose exploits are still sung in all the ballads of the country.

The Cid (Ruy Diaz) was born in 1026, and became at an early age the hero of Spain. Like our own Washington, he is even now considered the property of the nation. His deeds of arms still shine forth through the dim mists of the past. Upon his shield were blazoned his two good swords, which he named Tizona and Colada. His daughters became queens, one of Navarre and the other of Aragon. Although often in peril, he appeared protected by some spell of enchantment. While thousands of his followers fell around him, he passed on unharmed amid countless hosts of his Moorish enemies. "Soy el Cid, honra de españa," we heard a cracked voice singing, as we passed along the deserted streets.

Just at night we reached Alhama, a wretched town, but once renowned in the ballad of

"Woe is me, Alhama!"

We were now in Aragon, and journeyed along the banks of the Jalon to Calatayud, where we breakfasted. The appearance of this old Moorish city, with its noble castle, is very striking. It was here that Martial was born, the famous poet of the Emperor Domitian. After an absence in Rome of thirty-five years, the poet returned to his native city, heart-sick from the neglect of Trajan. Being his countryman, he had expected great favors at his hands; and when disappointed, he sought again the rude home of his youth, whence he wrote those eloquent letters to Juvenal, so well known to Latin scholars.

All the day we journeyed along the Jalon, passing Lupiana, where the first convent was established in 1330, and Torija, famous for its Moorish tower, still in a fine state of preservation. There were numbers of vineyards and groves of olive trees. A most delicious wine is made here, called *cariñena.* On the white and treeless mountain of *La Muela* we perceived afar the towers of *Zaragoza*, and beyond them, like a dark cloud along the horizon, were the Pyrennees.

On the road we have constantly met clumsy, huge wagons, with singular-looking people driving them. Upon inquiring of one of our travelling companions, he told me they were *Maragatos*, a type of people peculiar to Spain, and supposed to be Moorish Goths. They are entirely different in appearance from all the other Spaniards. They are tall, robust men, with a vacant, expressionless face; slow of speech, and totally unlike the demonstrative inhabitants of these regions. They are the *arrieros*, or carriers, of Spain, and more than one half of the rich merchandise of the country passes through their hands. So wonderful is their honesty and truth, that vast treasures are often entrusted to them to be conveyed from the sea-coast to the great inland cities. Even the robbers respect them, or rather fear their long carbines.

The women and children cultivate small fields in the

depths of the mountains, but the men deem agriculture a disgrace to them. There were many characteristics about them very like our Indians. They have a language of their own, as harsh as that of the tribes along the Northern Ocean. In religion they are supposed to be Mohammedans. They never intermarry with the Spaniards, or hold with them any social intercourse. Like the zingali race (gipsies), their origin is a mystery; although it is said they are the descendants of the Goths, who embraced the cause of the Moors, and thus retain the most inveterate hatred for the Christians.

CHAPTER XL.

Zaragoza.—Zaragoza was the Salduba of the Celts, and, under the Roman Emperor Augustus, was decorated with splendid temples and noble palaces. The Moors and Spaniards destroyed them all, using the fine and rare marbles in the construction of their dwelling-houses. There is only one bridge remaining upon the foundation laid by the architects of Rome. This is across the Ebro, upon which the city is built. Although it is said to be in a state of *décadence*, there are still sixty-five thousand inhabitants, and the street through which we drove, the *Coso*, had lofty houses on each side, strong and substantial as castles. It was well paved and brilliantly lighted, and throngs of people were sauntering along, seemingly prosperous looking, and very vivacious. We stopped at the *Leon de Oro*, an immense hotel, with a superb saloon, where we supped. The ceiling was richly frescoed, and long lines of marble columns sustained the vaulted roof.

Zaragoza had always possessed a charm for me, since reading in my youth the thrilling description of the "Maid of Zaragoza," rushing forth to avenge her lover's death. Byron has almost made her name immortal. A bright young officer was my *vis-à-vis* at supper, and during our conversation we touched upon the exploits of the fair maiden, to whom Southey, in his interesting history of the Peninsular War, has devoted a whole chapter. Augustina was her name, and she was celebrated throughout Aragon for her pure and delicate beauty, for her soft and gentle manner. Poets had sung the praises of her fairy-like grace, of the sweet enchantment of her words, and the tenderness of her nature. Many gallant hearts adored her, but all her love was given to a brave young soldier, whose wife she was soon to be, when "war's alarms" summoned him to his post upon the walls of the city. Augustina, in spite of his entreaties, followed him to the ramparts, resolved to perish with him. Standing by his side, she saw his comrades fall one by one. At length a bullet pierced his bosom, and exclaiming wildly, "Augustina, revenge my death," he fell dead at her feet, his life-blood bathing them with its rich, warm current. Springing to his gun, she seemed endowed with the power of an avenger, and with unerring aim she killed multitudes of the French soldiers.

"Her lover sinks—she sheds no ill-timed tear;
Her chief is slain—she fills his fatal post;
Her fellows flee—she checks their base career;
The foe retires—she heads the sallying host:
Who can appease like her a lover's ghost?
Who can avenge so well a leader's fall?
What maid retrieve, when man's flushed hope is lost?
Who hang so fiercely on the flying Gaul,
Foiled by a woman's hand before a battered wall?"

Thus wrote the poet of her heroic deeds. The Junta of Madrid awarded her medals and orders.

The officer, after giving me many other incidents of her history, told me there were now in Zaragoza many fair and beauteous women, capable of a similar devotion to their lovers. With a beaming eye he said, "Ah! Señora, love with us is the impassioned adoration of the soul, capable of all sacrifices, faithful and enduring, and not like the cold sentiment of your northern land, which is but the shadow of feeling." Knowing full well his heart was filled just then with a devotion he described, I turned to watch its influence upon a lovely little Spanish girl seated near me, and caught the electric glance passing between them, and quickly divined she was *his* Maid of Zaragoza. How often in my wanderings have scenes of uncommon interest sprung up before me like sweet flowers! and that night was revealed to me, in a singular manner, the heart-history of two young beings chance had cast in my way. The officer had been stationed in the town where the pretty Inez lived, had seen and loved her, but was refused by her parents. They, to cheer the sadness of their child, resolved to send her to Barcelona, and gave her in charge of a relative who was passing through their village. The good fairy who watches over lovers brought the officer to the same hotel the same night, and they met at supper. Looking upon them, I read their story in their expressive eyes. A younger sister, who accompanied Inez, soon told me all the particulars of the affair, and of their mutual resolution to die for each other. Just then a summons came to them that their diligence was ready, and the young lover had the joy of travelling all the night with his beloved—her protector being quite ignorant they had ever met before. The little sister whispered to me, as we parted, "Oh! is it not charming! I shan't tell Señor —— who it is." And thus they left me quite alone; for M. D. and Octavia, taking no interest in our conversation, had retired before me. Often since have my thoughts gone back to that handsome young couple, so bright and loving.

Zaragoza is the capital of Aragon. It was the first city

of Spain which abandoned the worship of the gods, and became famous for the piety of its Christians. It has been for many centuries a kind of Mecca, or Jerusalem, to which pilgrims came from long distances. There is a church within its walls, called *El Pilar*, containing an image of the Virgin, said to have descended from heaven, sliding down a great marble pillar or column in the centre of the edifice. Upon the anniversary of that day, they told me, fifty thousand people often came and knelt before the shrine, placing offerings there and invoking the aid of the Virgin with humble and devout adoration.

Zaragoza has withstood many fierce sieges. In the eighth century it was captured by the Moors. They held it until the twelfth century, when it was taken by Alonzo the Conqueror, after a siege of five years. During that period vast numbers of the inhabitants died of starvation. In 1809 the French found the same determined resistance, and it was only after sixty-two days of severe fighting, and terrible bloodshed, the city capitulated. Lannes and Junot, with all their forces, aided in the attack.

The Aragonese are said to be the most obstinate and determined people of the Peninsula; great lovers of liberty, bold, athletic, and courageous; fond of the dance; of which the *Jota Aragonesa* is the favorite. This gay and exciting measure often drives them half frantic when far away from their native province. Like the Swiss, they adore their own country.

At dawn we left Zaragoza, passing by the wall where Augustina so nobly filled her lover's post; and crossing a noble bridge over the Ebro, we travelled all the day through the "Desert of Aragon," a wild, barren waste. At *Velilla* we stopped for two hours, and saw the immense bell cast by the Goths. Into the burning metal was thrown, so says tradition, one of the thirty pieces of silver paid to Judas Iscariot for the betrayal of our Saviour; and it also tells that when any calamity is about to befall Spain, the bell rings of itself. Thus it tolled a mournful peal in 1516, when Ferdinand the Catholic expired, and upon other occasions also.

At evening we crossed the *Cinca*, a rapid river dividing Aragon from Cataluna. From the verge of the water rose up a steep mountain, upon whose summit was ruined *Fraga*. Never have we beheld such desolation as there prevailed. Every house was in a state of decay, and the miserable inhabitants, wandering along the river-bank, were the illustrations of the damned spirits waiting by the terrible Styx.

At twilight we reached Lerida, an old Celtic town upon the Sagre. It was strongly fortified by the Romans, and even now has fine castles and long lines of battlements. It was captured by the French under Suchet, after a fearful loss of life among the occupants of the city.

After supping at Lerida, we continued our journey. It was bright starlight—the atmosphere soft and balmy; so, yielding up my thoughts to the associations of this chivalric land, I passed the night without fatigue. There is a charm of romance thrown around every village, every mountain, tower, and city, awakening enthusiasm and delighting the imagination.

When the morning came, a most perilous and dangerous road was revealed, passing along the side of huge mountains, on a narrow shelf, as it were, cut in them. The sure-footed mules appeared to shrink from the edge of the precipice, and almost clung to the rocky base of the cliff, often rising perpendicularly three or four hundred feet. There were no parapets to protect us, as across the pass of the Sierra Morena mountains, and it was absolutely terrific to look from the window of the diligence down into the frightful abyss below.

These Monserrate mountains are wild and grand in scenery. For many leagues along their summit extends a singular rampart. It has the appearance of being carved out of granite, in colossal figures, which have the resemblance of castles, of towers, of turrets, of steeples, of the battlements of fortresses. Then comes a portion precisely like a procession of monks, with cowls drawn over their heads; and enormous statues, and lofty pinnacles, hundreds and hundreds of feet in height. The legends of the peasants tell that this mountain-ridge was thus rent into fantastic forms at the moment of the crucifixion of Christ. From the top of this curious rampart the view was of wondrous extent, embracing the far-away town of Manresa and the Pyrennees. Apparently just beneath our feet were several green valleys, with vineyards and groves of olive trees. Amid the most desolate portions of the mountains we saw the ruins of the hermitages once occupied by holy men, but burnt and destroyed by the French.

Near the mid-day we descended the Monserrate mountains, dashing along at a terrific pace. At the town of *Igualada* we breakfasted. The posada was dark and gloomy, and was really the only inn where we have not been well and plenteously served since we came to Spain. After our *slight repast*, we went down a long stairway to continue our journey. At the door stood "four and twenty beggars, all in a row," imploring charity. When we entered the posada a similar assemblage had attended us, to whom we had given every cent in our purses, so we were copperless. To escape their entreaties, we opened the door of the diligence and jumped out, concluding to await there the coming of the other passengers, who were not ready to depart. But the beggars followed us, and still we heard their plaintive cries. Quite in despair that I had no means to relieve them, my eyes happily fell upon a large box of choice crackers, which a kind friend had insisted we should bring with us, to use in "time of need." My hands seemed endowed with a strength I am sure they never possessed before, and I broke open the box, and dealt out the crackers by dozens on one side, while Octavia gave them on the other. The miserable creatures clustered around, with famine most legibly written on their wretched and withered faces. O heavens! how fearful it was to see their gaunt hands, so thin and fleshless, they appeared like talons of birds of prey, clutching with frantic haste the bread we gave, while others afar off cried, "For the love of God, do not forget me!"

Quickly the news was carried to the by-streets and dim alleys, as speedily as though by telegraph, and hurrying along came crowds, calling out, "There is a kind woman giving bread to the hungry." There were men, women, and children; the crippled, the blind, the aged, and the young. Their furious efforts to reach the diligence were appalling. Seeing this assemblage of beggars, all the idlers of the town collected around, and the street was entirely blocked up. We kept on giving out the crackers until the supply was exhausted, but the people still coming. Just then the mayoral (driver), finding they would not give way for him, jumped on his seat, and slashing his long whip to the right and left, and urging the mules forward by wild cries, dashed through the crowd. We waved our hands in adieu to them. Then from the throng of beggars arose loud shouts, "Go with God! Go, beloved of the Virgin! Joy will come to the good heart! Peace will never leave you! God will bless you! The saints will repay you!" Looking back we saw the maimed hands raised to heaven, and the sightless eyes turned upward, all invoking blessings upon us. All sympathetic hearts can imagine the emotions that rolled over my soul, and the gratitude I felt to these poor wretches. Leaning back in the *berlina*, I wept many, many tears, that for such a trifle blessings like these had been called down from the good God upon me; and long did the remembrance of that scene linger around me, as a sweet strain of music. How fervently did we exclaim, "Thank God! We can never behold misery like this in our own happy country." Ah! in that favored land it is impossible to imagine the sufferings of our race, from hunger, cold, and destitution. And yet Spain should be a land of plenty. There are vast fields of wheat, and vineyards, and "sheep upon a thousand hills." Still there are legions of beggars, with starvation looking out from their glaring eyes, and sadly visible in their emaciated forms. At last we succeeded in steeling our hearts towards the young beggars; but when the white-haired old man, or the tottering old woman, held out their aged hands, and said, "Charity for the poor old beggar," I could not refuse.

Not many miles from Igualada is the small town in which Ignacio Loyola was born, in 1491. He was a soldier in his youth, and being wounded in battle, lay for many months in a horrible state of suffering. While near unto death he vowed, should life be permitted to him, he would become the follower of our blessed Lord. He recovered, and then sought a wild cave in the Monserrate mountains, where he endured severe penance for one long year. At its expiration he gathered a few disciples and went to Rome, to ask permission to found the Order of the Jesuits. It was granted him, and he ruled over it for fifteen years. He died in 1556, and was canonized by Gregory the Fifteenth.

During the reign of Charles the Third, the property of the Jesuits was reckoned by millions and millions, and they became so powerful in their influence, they were exiled from the country—driven out with cruel persecution.

During the afternoon we passed through a country resembling Switzerland. There were little valleys well cultivated, vineyards on the slopes of the mountains, orchards of fruit-trees, and groves of the olive. There were no farmhouses; all the people live in the towns and villages, from fear of the lawless bands of revolutionists, who place whole districts under contribution. However, since the establishment of the Guardia Civil, there was no longer the same danger as in former years. We met these men on all the roads from the Atlantic to the Mediterranean sea. They were armed with carbines, robust, and courageous-looking, and very obliging in escorting us over the wild passes of the mountains where robbers were supposed to be lurking. We often saw their stone cabins, far up on the highest peaks, whence they could overlook the road for miles.

A deep sadness has rested upon my soul all this day. It is the anniversary of the first great sorrow of my life—the death of my noble brother, who died six years ago, in the glorious prime of his manhood. That was my first entrance into the realm of suffering. Alas! how often since has "my heart travelled the dark track." Ah! in the loneliness and silence of the mountain-world, my spirit went forth to my precious mother, desolate in our home, thinking, I knew so well, of her dead and living children, and the thought of her anguish at this day's return thrilled my heart with fierce pangs of agony, and all was forgotten but her. At length the mayoral called out, "Look, Señora," and a long line of light gave indication of a large city in the distance. We soon felt the soft breeze from the sea, which wooingly came to me, and called me back from the memories of that dread past, which, "ever and anon, with fresh bitterness imbued," seizes upon me.

CHAPTER XLI.

March 23*d*, 1855.—We have delightful apartments at an excellent hotel upon the *Rambla*, a wide and handsome street, very like the Boulevards of Paris. It takes its name from an Arabic word, signifying "rocky river," as it once was the bed of a rapid stream, whose waters were turned into another channel when the town became a city, and more space was needed. There are splendid houses along it, and rows of trees in the centre, which form a pleasant and shaded walk.

Barcelona is a busy, bustling place, reminding one vastly of New York, from the strong vitality and activity of its inhabitants. Every one seems occupied, and no longer do we see the smiling faces and *dolce far niente* attitudes of charming Andalucia. Here, too, as in the great cities of Northern Europe, "commerce is king," and hundreds of ships from distant lands fill the harbor. The people of Cataluña, from their energy and industry, from their money-making and money-keeping peculiarities, are called the "Yankees of Spain"—an appellation of which they appear exceedingly proud.

Barcelona is a very ancient city, since it claims to have been built by Hercules. However, it certainly was founded by Amilcar Barca, the father of Hannibal. The inhabitants are the descendants of the Goths, and are in strong contrast with the other Spaniards, being of fair complexion, with light hair and blue eyes. They speak a *patois* styled *Catalan*, a harsh, disagreeable language. Not a sound of the noble and flowing Castilian can be traced in it.

There are several fine churches in the city, and the cathedral is large and massive, with lofty towers, and a great bell cast in the tenth century. Beneath the grand altar is the tomb of Santa Eulalia, the Patron Saint of Barcelona. In the "Street of Paradise" our guide pointed out some Roman columns, now forming a portion of the walls of houses.

The *Muralla del Mar* is an enchanting promenade, upon a parapet built up just on the verge of the sea. The view thence of the Mediterranean is extremely fine. In the harbor of Barcelona was made the first trial of steam as a motive power. It was the invention of *Blasco de Garay*, who in 1543, in the presence of the great Charles the Fifth, gave a successful evidence of its usefulness. In consequence of the enmity to him of the King's minister, he was refused money and encouragement to carry out his project, and to succeeding generations was left the priceless advantages of this wonderful "annihilator of time and space."

The fortress of *Monjuich* is perched upon a lofty eminence, called by the Romans *Mons Jovis*. It entirely commands the city, and controls it in times of revolution, which often occur, as the people are impatient of imposition, and, like the Americans, strong advocates for their own rights.

As in all Spanish towns, we saw many handsome paseos and alamedas; then also the *Plaza de Toros*, where during the summer season there are "glorious and splendid bull-fights," to use the words of a Catalan who was regretting to me that I was not here at the proper period to see them in all their magnificence.

There are numerous manufactories, and every where we remarked the women weaving lace and fringe. The beautiful mantillas of the Spanish women are all made here.

At night we went to the *Teatro del Liceo*, to witness the representation of the last week of our Saviour's life. Every detail of those last days was given with a painful minuteness. All the interviews with his disciples—the parting with his mother—his trial before Pontius Pilate—the betrayal of Judas—the denial of Peter—the scourging at the pillar—and the crucifixion. Ere that act arrived we made our escape, the preceding ones being most fearful to behold. The words of the tragedy were in Catalan, and the *mise en scène* taken from the ancient pictures. The actor who personated Christ was wondrously like Raphael's great picture of our Saviour, and the touching tones of his voice, and the eloquence of his gesture, were deeply affecting. The audience often wept aloud; and being very sympathetic in my nature, I wept also. Judas, after receiving the money, hangs himself to a tree; whereupon the devil, dressed in an armor of red and gold, comes in, cuts him down, and bears him off to the regions below, where multitudes of fiends receive him, and, making a bonfire, burn him up, much to the delight of the people, who cheered them bravely in their work. The "last supper" was a *tableau* from the world-renowned picture of Leonardo da Vinci, and was admirable.

We were told this tragedy was played throughout the country during the last week of Lent, to prepare the minds of the people for the solemnities of Easter.

The next night we heard the "Barbière di Sevilla," most charmingly rendered by the artists of the Italian Opera. The *prima donna*, although excellent, could not compare with our poor Sontag. Ah! how memory fled back to that evening when she filled the *rôle* of Rosina! when, bright and captivating, she enchanted us by her exquisite melody and wondrous grace! Never again shall we hear that voice of matchless sweetness.

After waiting two days at Barcelona for the Spanish steamer, in which we intended going to Marseilles, we were compelled to proceed by land, as the severe *mistrale* then prevailing prevented the coming of the "Vifredo." Glad were we afterwards that this adverse wind detained her, for our journey along the shores of the Mediterranean was really delightful. On the 25th of March, at dawn, we left Barcelona, and proceeded by railway to Mataró, a flourishing town sixteen leagues to the northward. The road is built by the margin of the sea; so near, the waves almost touch the rails. The scene was beautiful; on one side the Mediterranean, bright and calm as a silver mirror, save near the shore, where its waters, rolling lazily in, broke into creamy foam upon the sands, with a faint, low murmur; on the other side were the hills, or rather mountains, covered to their summit with groves of the orange, the lemon, the olive, and the citron. Then came vineyards, and where the hills receded, fields of wheat, and pretty little villages. Prosperity and plenty were every where visible. We breakfasted at Mataró, and then continued on in the diligence, still journeying by the Mediterranean. How precious are the remembrances of that radiant day, realizing in truth the poet's description—

> "A day so calm, so clear, so bright,
> It seemed the bridal of the earth and sky."

At Gerona we passed the night. This is an ancient town, with a noble castle and grand cathedral. In the olden time it was (so says tradition) the resting-place, for the night, of

St. Paul and St. James, when they travelled through Spain to convert the people from their worship of false gods. During the next day we passed along the banks of the Fluvia to Figueras, a wild, vagrant-looking place, where crowds of soldiers were assembled. The town is upon a plain, quite encircled by mountains. Near it are rice-fields and *esparto*, a kind of reed deemed valuable here. There is a strong citadel, fortifications, and arsenals. In all the towns along the route, we still saw evidences of the desolating power of the French army. One by one they had been besieged and taken by the conquering foe.

Soon after leaving Junquera we began the ascent of the Pyrennees, by the pass called the *Col de Pertus*. The road was admirable, upon a ledge cut along the mountain-side, and defended towards the precipice by a high parapet. The scenery was not wild and startling like that of the lovely passes of the Sierra Morena and the Monserrate, but lovely, calm, and peaceful. There were myriads of cork trees, even to the summit of the highest peaks. These valuable trees are very like our live-oak. The bark is taken off once in three years, and Nature, kind dame, then restores it, to be again appropriated. Thousands of people are engaged during the season in stripping the bark and sending it to the sea-shore.

Perched upon the loftiest point of the mountain, we saw the Castle of Bellegarde, erected by Louis the Fourteenth, to guard his new possessions. How the workmen ever got up to build it is a mystery, unless they were carried up in balloons. Along this mountain-pass Pompey marched after he had conquered Spain, and, stopping on the highest eminence, erected a monument, upon which he inscribed his glory. When Cæsar had vanquished him, he placed another monument by its side to record *his* victory. This is probably a legend of the past, as no trace of either remains. On the summit of the Pyrennees we lingered for a time to enjoy the view, extending over France and Spain. The mountain-tops were still covered with snow, although the valleys were green, and the fruit trees in full blossom. From that elevated point I looked my last upon Spain, with regret in my heart. There is a warm and genial kindness about its people, extremely captivating—a noble and romantic chivalry of character, unique and agreeable. Happy days have been mine there, and "pleasant to the soul" is their remembrance.

A rapid descent brought us to "El Balon," where the custom-house officers took possession of us for a time, making the most minute examination of the baggage, and inquiring particularly if the mantilla purchased in Barcelona was truly for my own use; whereupon I affirmed most energetically that it was intended as a covering for my own head. Having said this, the officer rose up from his kneeling position, and with a dignified wave of the hand and theatrical voice, exclaimed, "Proceed onward immediately." With infinite pleasure we availed ourselves of the permission to enter the "great empire," and soon reached Perpignon, a fine, strongly-walled city of twenty-five thousand inhabitants, and a multitude of soldiers, as it was a frontier town. We remained there one day, and during the afternoon had a pleasant walk in a charming paseo just without the walls. There are avenues of trees of immense height, and a stream of water rushing through it, fringed along the banks by flowering shrubs. Around it are numerous gardens of rare and beautiful flowers.

From Perpignon we travelled all night along the shores of the Gulf of Lyons, and the chill wind came roaring over its turbulent waters. We passed several large towns, and stopped at Cardona to breakfast, where we were offered oysters as large as those of Mobile.

About mid-day we reached Montpellier, a handsome city, renowned for its healthful situation, and a great place of resort for invalids during the winter-months. The streets are wide, and the public buildings numerous. In the *peyroun* (promenade) is an equestrian statue of Louis the Fourteenth.

Taking the railway at Montpellier, we passed rapidly through a luxuriant country. There were often five or six large cities in view at one time. The prosperity and fine cultivation were very like that of England. At Nismes we were detained an hour, thus giving us a glance at the Roman amphitheatre, still in a remarkable state of preservation. By half-past ten o'clock we were at Marseilles, and soon reached the *Hotel Beauvau*, where we found comfortable rooms awaiting us.

Marseilles, March 29th.—We were awakened this morning by the sound of drums and bugles, then the tramp of soldiers, and the loud cheers of the people. Springing up in alarm, we almost fancied we were in the midst of a revolution, when our nice little *bonne* came in, and informed us it was only regiments marching down to the quai to embark for the Crimea. Raising the window, she begged we would look at them. They were all young men, fresh and rosy with health; laughing merrily, as though going to a *fête*. Poor fellows! how few will ever return!

We spent the morning driving around the city and in the *Prado;* then made a charming visit to a family of American descent, whom we found graceful, agreeable, and intelligent. At night we went to the *Alhambra*, a coffee-house, fitted up in the Moorish style. The room is octagon, and the walls composed entirely of mirrors, except where they are broken by delicate arches of white and gilt. Next we visited the

Café Turque, arranged in true oriental magnificence. The coffee was clear as amber, and delicious, but most effectually "murdered sleep" for the whole night. There must have been in it some of those wondrous preparations like the *haschish* described in "Monte Christo;" for the most strange and singular sensations possessed me after drinking it. In a dream I seemed floating in the air, and wandering amid gorgeous scenes of wild fascination. The morning light only summoned me from this realm of imagination back to the realities of the present.

March 30th.—We are now on board the "Corrière Siciliano," steaming out of the harbor of Marseilles, and passing the *Chateau d'If.* The day is lovely, and in our cabin on the deck we are cozily seated, enjoying the view of the coast with its white villages, and the clear and sparkling sea.

Genoa, March 31st.—Again we are in "Genoa the Superb." Eighteen months ago we parted from it, as I thought, for ever, but here we are once more, and right welcome is the sight of the noble city. We have magnificent apartments in the *Hotel d'Italia*, overlooking the harbor. As M. D. had never been in Genoa, we became his guides through the palaces and churches, and with delight revisiting the picture-galleries with which they are enriched.

Among the pilgrims who are going with us to the "Eternal City," I have been charmed with a young Spanish priest. He looks as pure and holy as a saint. In a long conversation with him this evening, he told me the story of his life. His father was rich, and one of the grandees of Spain. He designed his son should inherit his wealth and titles; but the youth, even in his tenderest years, was devoted to the church; and, when his father bade him leave the convent where he was educated, declared to him his purpose of becoming a priest. Terrible was the rage of the parents, and every effort was made to change his purpose. Calmly and resolutely he told them, to the service of God he should devote his life, and implored them to give all their riches to his younger brother. After months of entreaty, they yielded to his wishes, and he entered the priesthood. His learning and piety had reached the ears of his Holiness the Pope, and a summons from the "Propaganda Fide" was taking him to Rome, when doubtless great honors awaited him. With simple and innocent frankness, he related the trials and struggles of his heart to give up the affection of his parents. As for their wealth, it was but as a feather in the balance. His father and younger brother (now heir to the titles of the noble family) accompanied him. As though he were a child, they sought to shield him from all troubles and inconveniences of travel. Often the old father would turn to me and exclaim, "Ah! Señora, what a sacrifice it was to give up my eldest-born; but now that I see him so happy in his beautiful faith, I am content."

After writing several letters, I seated myself by the window, and drank in the wondrous beauty of the scene. It was a glorious night, cloudless, and lighted by the full moon. One by one the sounds of the city died away, and intense silence, like that of the Guadarama mountains, prevailed. How often in my childhood had a vision of this tideless sea floated over my imagination; and now it was before me, more radiant than even that rosy dream of youth, glittering and gleaming in the moonlight.

April 1st.—At dawn our courier, Luigi, awakened us, and soon we were *en route* for the villa of Pallavicini, ten miles from Genoa. We drove along the embankment by the sea until we passed the great walls which encompass the city, and then came to the palace-crowned heights beyond. The gardens of these noble edifices were filled with orange trees laden with fruit and flowers.

Arriving at the villa, we halted at the porter's lodge, and sent in our permission from the Count, and were admitted at once. Walking up the broad avenue, hedged on either side by trellises of roses, we entered the palace, a large building with a splendid terrace in front, and a marble stairway leading from the orange grove below. The view thence of the Mediterranean was superb. We did not linger long within the palace, as the gardens and grounds were the objects of our greatest interest; therefore, passing through the richly frescoed and gilded saloons, we proceeded up the gravelled walk to a marble temple, adorned with exquisite statues by Canova—a *basso relievo* of the "Feast of Bacchus." A flight of steps conducted us to a darling little room, frescoed in the Pompeian style, and decorated with Etruscan vases. Leaving this, we passed beneath a marble arch, elaborately sculptured, and with a touching religious inscription. Next we entered a rustic cottage, where we tarried for a time, and then began our "winding way" through the mountain-paths, shut in by tall trees and flowering shrubs. We wandered for hours amid scenes of enchantment, so unique and beautiful, no description can picture them. Yet only twelve years ago these wonderful grounds were wild mountains, covered with pines or vineyards. The mighty power of gold has converted them into a paradise, where it seems I could linger for ever. Constantly ascending, we often came to repose-inviting bowers, entirely shaded by rose-vines, and surrounded by banks of violets. Then a sudden turn of the pathway would bring us to a cataract of water, rushing down the rocks, and disappearing in the deep glen below.

On the highest peak of the mountain there was a castle, built in imitation of those of ancient days; and toiling up to its summit, near one hundred feet, we were rewarded by a glorious prospect of Genoa, its fortresses, and encircling villages. The deep blue sea lay apparently at our feet, and afar off the snow-crested Apennines. Over the keep of the castle is an octagon room, with four windows of stained glass, looking through which the landscape is revealed in different aspects. The *blue* gives it the appearance of being covered with snow; the *yellow* shows it glittering in the sunlight; the *red* presents it glowing in a fiery hue, like the volcanic light of Vesuvius; while the *green* clothes it in the verdant garb of spring. The ceiling of this almost magic room was blue and gold, and the floor of mosaic. Around the castle were placed portions of ancient ruins, arranged so artistically, they seemed the work of "defacing time." Then in a grove of yew trees was a monument to the supposed general who defended it, with some spirited words of eulogium, and a resemblance of him in *basso relievo.* In one of the rooms there were many curious arms and suits of armor. Our guide, however, would not permit us to remain long within the castle-walls; he urged us to leave, saying, "Hasten on! there are many more wonders to see."

So, leaving the tower, we walked on through a densely shaded path, until we came to the mouth of a great cave in the mountain-side. We entered it, and soon were in perfect darkness. The guide seized my hand, and led me on to a grotto, where from openings above, fringed with creeping plants, shone in the daylight, discovering to us the vaulted roof hanging with stalactites, dazzling and bright as the "Mine of the Gnome King." Various galleries diverged from this central chamber, through which we passed. In the deepest recesses of the cave we reached a clear lake, in which were mirrored the quaint forms of the crystallizations above. We stopped to admire them, when, lo! from the shadow of a jutting rock out darted a small boat, with a picturesque-looking boatman. He invited us to step in. We did so, and he rowed us beneath the rocky arches for a while, and then passed out into a fairy-like lake. In it was an island, containing a marble temple, in which was standing a statue of Diana, of exquisite proportions. Perfect trees of the *Camellia Japonica* grew upon it. They were all in full blossom, and of every variety of color. The mimic beach was thickly strewn with the petals of the flowers, and even upon the tiny waves created by our boat they floated like "foam upon the billows." Ah! a vision of beauty like this dwelt in the heart of Moore, when he wrote,

> "Oft in my fancy's wanderings
> I've wished yon little Isle had wings,
> And we, within its fairy bowers,
> Were wafted off to seas unknown,
> Where not a pulse should beat but ours,
> Far from the cruel and the cold."

So enrapturing was the "Isle of Beauty," that we could not withdraw our eyes from it until our boatman called us repeatedly to look seaward. Through an arch of green the Mediterranean seemed to unite with the calm lake. So perfect was the illusion, that although the sea was half a mile away, we could have sworn its waves were flowing in to meet the waters upon which our little boat was floating. A slight strip of greensward appeared alone to divide them. Down the mountain, in front of us, rushed a bold waterfall. A deep abyss received it, and within the spray arising thence was a rainbow, like a beautiful bridge across the chasm. Turkish kiosks and Egyptian obelisks crowned the summits around.

When we had made the entire voyage of the lake, our

boatman landed us upon a marble quai, where two most lovely statues of Spring and Summer stood as sentinels on the shore, to guard, as it were, this domain sacred to Flora. It was entirely shut in by giant orange, lemon, and citron trees, so smoothly trimmed, they seemed a deep green wall, to protect this paradise from the outward world. In a marble temple was a statue of Flora, and beyond it a pavillion, or saloon, richly adorned with frescoes and paintings. Encircling this were vases, containing rare and gorgeous flowers, forming a colonnade around it. Their perfume filled the air with the most delicious fragrance. Never have I beheld a spot more sweet, more tranquil, more enchanting. It seemed the fit abode of joy, where even love might fold his wings, and never wish to rove again. Many entreaties from our party were needed, ere they could withdraw me from this "valley of delight," to climb a steep mountain, near whose topmost peak was a shrine, with a fine painting of the Blessed Virgin, by Isola. The scenery was wild and rude, and a strong wind, coming directly from the Apennines, brought with it fleecy particles of snow. Not finding these very genial, we quickly descended to a vast garden, and crossing a Chinese bridge, thrown over a clear stream, we entered a rustic bower, crimson with myriads of roses. We seated ourselves to repose awhile, when suddenly a gently falling mist enveloped us; then jets of water darted between the rose-vines and through the doorway. Starting up, we ran out, when all around us were springing tiny fountains, filling the atmosphere with delicate spray, picturesque certainly to the eyes, but rather uncomfortable to the feelings. After the guide had enjoyed our surprise, and laughed at our efforts to escape the falling waters, he explained that multitudes of small pipes were placed just under the surface of the earth, and along the pillars which sustained the bowers and arbors. These conducted the water to the plants and flowers, thus refreshing them every day. By touching a spring, the fountains began playing, adding a new feature of interest and amazement to this wondrous place.

Leaving the radiant flowers, we went down into a gloomy vale, darkly shaded by cypress and weeping-willow trees. In it was a monument to the memory of *Chiabiera*, a poet of Savona, who lived two centuries ago. Passing a dense forest, we saw magnolia trees, (pointed out by the guide as the greatest treasure of the grounds,) camphor and cork trees; in fact, there appeared a gathering of all the trees of the universe, from the cedar of Lebanon to the North Carolina pine. Hundreds of birds were fluttering and singing amid them. Our path was along an arch cut out with Gothic regularity through the woods, and our feet absolutely pressed upon banks of violets and daisies. On every side we heard the music of the waterfalls, and almost with regret emerged from the soft "twilight of the forest shades," into the clear daylight.

Again we were upon the marble terrace, after having wandered many miles through verdant labyrinths, and grottoes whose arches were like congealed cataracts; then over the lake, with its island gem; from the quiet glen to the bold cliff upon the mountain-top; across the graceful bridges, spanning the partings of the huge rocks unto the vale of sweet delight, sacred to Flora. All the enchantments and marvels of the villa we have seen. Like precious pictures I will hang them in memory, and, often recurring to their beauty, summon up the joy which thrilled my heart when first I looked upon them.

From Pegli, the village near the villa, we drove rapidly back to Genoa, and hastened on board the steamer. The sky was overshadowed by dark clouds, and a fierce wind came down from the Apennines, sighing mournfully through the rigging of the ships around us as we rowed off. With infinite difficulty we climbed the ladder, and sought the shelter of our little state-room. Soon a message came from the captain that he feared to venture out, as the *tramontana* was blowing. We resigned ourselves to the disappointment, and were preparing to pass the night on board, when we received an imperative command to leave the vessel, and return to the shore. It was almost dark, and the wind from the mountains "roared like caged lions." The sailors told me it was really dangerous to stay there, for if the storm increased we might be dashed against some of the larger ships, and utterly crushed. Again we were forced to "tempt the raging blast." It was really a frightful effort to enter the boat. We were compelled to wait until a great wave raised it to a level with the steamer, and then, being seized in the stout arms of one of the sailors, were thrown to the persons in the boat, who adroitly caught us as we fell. Our courier had obtained a large tarpaulin, in which he wrapped Octavia and myself; thus we made the voyage back to the quai, trembling with fear and cold, but perfectly protected from the dashing waves. Again we sought our rooms in the Hotel d'Italia (once the Grimaldi Palace); and to console myself for the detention, I have written the description of the villa of Pallavicini. The storm is wild without, and beyond the mole the great waves of the Mediterranean are rolling in, breaking with a deep booming sound upon the protecting bulwarks.

The excitements of the day so crowd upon my mind, they drive away all thoughts of sleep, and I have been walking to and fro in the vast drawing-room of our apartments, looking upon the pictures, and conjuring up the gay scenes of revelry once enacted within these walls. It is long past midnight, and I must seek repose. With blessings upon the dear ones in our far-away home, I bid the world good night.

Harbor of Genoa, April 2d.—Several hours ago we came on board the "Siciliano," but there are no signs of departure, and the anchor quietly rests beneath the waters. Three great carriages have been brought off in enormous boats, and numerous people are hoisting them on deck. Our courier tells us they belong to a royal personage, and slyly whispers our captain delayed a day purposely to have his "distinguished excellency" on board, laying all the blame of the detention upon the *tramontana.*

The view is beautiful. The city has precisely the form of one half of the amphitheatre of Verona, while the streets rise up one above the other like the ranges of seats in that well-preserved monument of Roman antiquity. Just beyond them are the mountains, with great castles and frowning battlements along their loftiest heights. The snowy peaks of the Apennines are clearly visible, while near the shore the vegetation is richly luxuriant, and the orange and lemon trees are as large as the oaks of our forests. The day is delightful in its balmy loveliness, and the scene gay and spirited. Numerous ships are ranged along the quais, with the flags of different nations floating at their mast-heads. Dozens of boats are bringing off Sardinian soldiers, about departing for the Crimea. Three or four ships and steamers are near us, quite filled with them. They are a noble, handsome-looking people, but seem very sad and mournful as they part with friends, who in little skiffs are lingering around the ships, not being permitted to accompany them on board. Poor fellows! we hear they go with heavy reluctance. Their hearts are not in this terrible war. They have no enthusiasm or love of country to urge them on in this encounter with the Russians. Alas! how few will ever return to tell the story of their sufferings.

A large barge, manned by Sardinian sailors, and filled with officers, is now approaching the steamer. With great *empressement* the captain rushes to the gangway, and ushers on board Prince Adalbert of Bavaria. His Highness is a tall, stalwart man, very fair, and not at all handsome. He questions the captain particularly concerning the dangers of the voyage, and quickly retires to his state-room on deck, being, as he expressed it, " a martyr to sea-sickness." With an important air, the captain orders the anchor to be raised, and a wild tumult of cries and imprecations from the sailors attend its elevation on deck. At last we are off, passing between the moles which form the harbor of Genoa, and are now upon the Mediterranean, the sea of historic memories! It is smooth and calm as an ice-bound lake. Like a great mirror, it reflects the mountains rising abruptly from its shores. These are dotted here and there with villages and small fields of grain. The fishermen are returning homeward in their little boats; for it is sunset upon the sea, and glorious tints of rose-hue, of amber, and purple, are flaming up the western sky. We are so near the land that we pass under the shadow of a grand jutting point projecting far out. Upon it are the ruins of an ancient castle, with a tall tower still standing. The sunlight, streaming through the broken windows, gives the old structure the appearance of being illuminated.

Now it is quite dark; so I will throw away my pen, and go out on the deck for a promenade with the young Spanish priest, whose conversation is truly quite delightful to me.

Leghorn, April 3d.—About daylight we anchored in the harbor of Leghorn, and soon after landed, and passed through the usual examination of the passports, although we only intended to remain one day in the city. As soon as these important documents were *viséd*, we were permitted to enter. Just by the quai we stopped to look at a curious statue, supported by four kneeling figures, whose arms were bound with chains. A cicerone quickly appeared, and informed us this monument was erected to commemorate the capture of four noted pirates who lived on the island of Samona, and for long years had been quite the terror of land and sea. At last they were taken prisoners by Ferdinand the First, and executed. The statues are admirably sculptured, and the different expressions of the faces are very striking, portraying anguish, despair, humiliation, and hatred.

Leghorn is a fine modern city. The streets are wide, and the houses spacious and elegant. In the great square, or piazza, there is a noble statue of the Duke of Tuscany, who gave the inhabitants the blessing of fresh water from the distant mountains. An aqueduct brings it fourteen miles from the interior, and it is received into a reservoir covering a vast space. The roof is lofty, and sustained by graceful rows of arches; these, reflected in the clear waters, make a charming picture. A balcony runs entirely around the area, and forms a delightful walk.

As we passed across the prado (promenade), we encountered an immense crowd who had gathered around a vendor of elixirs, a veritable Dulcamara. He was standing in a chariot, attired in a superb costume, and eloquently recommending a powder he held up, as a cure for "all the ills of life." Two heralds accompanied him, who through long trumpets proclaimed their master "the wonder of the nineteenth century." Multitudes were pressing forward to buy his nostrums.

After a fine breakfast at the restaurant, we drove to the Jewish synagogue, said to be the richest in Europe. We entered it during the morning service. All the men wore white scarfs, striped with blue. The girls and the youths were absolutely beautiful, but the old men and women were decided specimens of ugliness. Two of the rabbis had long beards reaching to their girdles. Upon the altar were splendid vessels of gold and silver.

From thence we went to the Greek church, where the priests were officiating, very much after the fashion of the Catholics. When the mass was over, they showed us some excellent paintings, and vases encrusted with precious gems, presented by the Emperor of Russia.

Without the walls of the city, we visited the English cemetery, and saw the tomb of Smollett, who is buried there. Until a few years ago, all Protestants dying in Italy were brought here for entombment. Hence the grave-yard is filled with monuments. Near by it there is an Episcopal church, where services are held each Sabbath.

At the "Royal Oak" Hotel we found Com. Stringham and his family, and met our dear friend Captain Morris. He told us the Cumberland U. S. frigate was in the offing, and invited us to go on board with him. Our row of five miles across the sparkling Mediterranean was enchanting. Ah! how freshly to my memory came up

"The days that are no more,"

when over the glittering waters of as fair a bay, we two had often glided in the

"May of the year, and in the May of life."

We spent some charming hours on board the frigate, happy to be once more beneath the stars and stripes of our own noble flag. The Cumberland is a splendid ship, in admirable order. Captain Morris detained us until the afternoon, and then sent us in his own gig back to the "Siciliano." The oarsmen were all Americans, bold, independent in manner, healthy, and happy looking. When they had seen us safely on board, and had pushed off from the steamer, they all sprang up in the boat, and gave "three cheers for America!"

In Leghorn the number of our passengers was greatly augmented by the pilgrims, hurrying on to Rome for the ceremonies of the Holy Week. They seemed to be of all the nations of the earth, from the polyglot conversations heard on every side. There was a tall, gaunt monk of La Trappe, who spoke Latin to Gaspar (the Spanish priest). It was delightful to hear this rich and sonorous language, and I often drew near them to listen. Amid other oddities were the perfect originals of Thackeray's "Dodd family"—fussy, vulgar, and pretentious people. It was a delicious evening, and we walked the deck until a late hour. We passed Corsica, the birthplace of the great Napoléon, and Elba, his island of exile after the Russian campaign. Like dark clouds they faded away in the distance as we proceeded southward.

April 4th.—At six this morning we anchored in the harbor of Civita Vecchia. It is a vast basin, constructed by the command of the Emperor Trajan, and defended from the waves of the sea by a strong wall. A splendid fortress is near the quai, and a great prison, always filled, we were told, with convicts. Gasparoni (the "Fra Diavolo" of Terracina) was long confined within it.

After various delays we were permitted to land, and walked up to an old barrack-like house, styled an inn, where we breakfasted. Then began the trials and troubles which always beset the pathway of the pilgrim to the "Sacred City." Many hundreds had arrived before us, all equally eager to go on to Rome. Happily for us, our courier was an Italian, and being quite *au fait* with the ways of the people, he soon obtained a carriage for us, and we gladly left the town. Of all places upon earth to try the patience and to exhaust the purse, commend me to Civita Vecchia. Permission is required to enter the place, and permission needed to leave it. There is *buono mano* in advance for the postillions—fees for the conductors—bribes for the owners of horses, and charity for a legion of beggars.

Soon after leaving the city we entered the *Campagna*, a green undulating plain between the Mediterranean and the mountains. There were no houses upon it, except the rude stone huts where the post-horses were kept. Shepherds guarding their flocks were the only inhabitants we perceived. Now and then we passed lofty watch-towers, used by the Pretorian Guard in former days. On a point of land jutting out into the sea was a wild and picturesque ruin of an ancient castle, said to have been once the stronghold of the Tyrrhenian pirates. Our road was quite near the Mediterranean, and the silence of the vast Campagna was only broken by the sound of the waves, as they wildly dashed upon the shore. Looking over the barren waste, I thought of the cheerful villages, the fair cities, the noble villas, and gorgeous palaces, which adorned it, in those glorious days when Rome was indeed "mistress of the world." Then came the remembrance of the great armies returning from triumphant wars, led on by conquering generals to the capital, where the laurel crown of victory awaited them; and of the barbarian hordes desolating and destroying, ere, like a mighty avalanche, they overwhelmed the city. As these visions of the past were floating through my mind, we were suddenly startled by a loud cry from the postillion, "Roma! Roma!" Eagerly we looked out, and afar off, rising up as though it were a mountain between us and the gray sky, was the dome of St. Peter's. Grander and more majestic it became as we approached the walls. At the *Porta Cavallegieri* we were only detained a short time.

"At last in Rome!" was the joyous exclamation bursting from my lips, while a new and tumultuous delight filled my soul. Ah! the recollection of that moment will be to me "a joy for ever." It was rapture to repeat again and again, "I am in Rome!" and so deep was my gratitude, I would gladly have knelt and kissed the sacred earth. We drove slowly around, and through the dim twilight saw the statue-crowned colonnade and fountains of St. Peter. Crossing the Tiber, we passed ruined arches and massive columns. The "Eternal City" was around me, and thoughts of her departed glory came rushing over my mind, and on a flood of giant memories swept away the drifting present. Ah! I could have quarrelled with our travelling companions, who were constantly asking me, "Where will you find lodgings?" A matter of stern importance I soon discovered it was, for hotel after hotel was tried, and always the same answer, "No rooms vacant." A violent rain-storm pattered against the windows of our carriage, and even my enthusiasm was almost chilled, when we drew up within the portico of the "Hotel of the British Isles," and fortunately found good apartments.

Wearied and exhausted with the thronging emotions of the day, we declined the supper offered to us, and quickly sought our chamber. Then soon, wrapped in the soft mantle of sleep, I was borne by the fairies of the dream-land over the great ocean to my own home, and to the fond caresses of the dear ones there.

CHAPTER XLII.

April 5th.—A ray of morning sunlight touching my eyes, awakened me. I sprang up, casting aside the dreams of night, while my heart thrilled with the enrapturing consciousness of being in Rome. I ran to the window, and, in place of towers and temples, a beautiful garden met my eyes. Myriads of flowers were glittering with dew-drops, and giving forth their precious perfumes. Sparkling fountains were falling into marble basins, pretty statues were half revealed, half hidden amid the clustering roses, and birds singing and fluttering beneath the jessamine bowers. It was a sweet, fresh morning-scene, and the deep quietude was unbroken by any murmur of city life. Soon there came a rap at the door, and an entreaty for us to hasten our toilettes, as the "Washing of Feet" was to take place at an early hour. We quickly dressed ourselves in black, throwing long lace mantillas over our heads. The carriage is ready, so now for St. Peter's!

From the vestibule of our hotel we drove out into the *Piazza del Popolo*, a large paved square, with a grand obelisk in the centre, brought from Egypt, and said to have adorned the Temple of the Sun during the time of Moses. Two churches precisely alike were before us. They had graceful porticoes, towers, and cupolas. On one side was the *Porta del Popolo*, (the People's Gate.) Through this once passed the Flaminian Way, leading from the walls of the city up to the capitol. We soon entered the *Corso*, the gay street and fashionable drive of Rome. It contains many splendid modern palaces and fine houses, and derives its name from the races of wild horses, which are let loose upon it during the last days of the Carnival.

Turning down a narrow street, we crossed the "yellow Tiber," upon a noble bridge, and soon were in the *Piazza di San Pietro*, (the Place of St. Peter.) A great concourse of people were hastening up the steps, and we joined the throng. Lifting the heavy curtain hanging before the door, we entered "the most glorious structure that has ever been applied to the uses of religion." With a bewildering joy my eyes wandered through the magnificent aisles, while my feet seemed transfixed to one spot, as though the sense of sight had absorbed all other powers of my being. It was only by repeated entreaties that Octavia could induce me to follow her to the chapel of St. Michael, where the ceremony of washing the feet of the apostles was to take place. The crowds I had often encountered at Washington, "long years ago," in the Senate-chamber, to hear the immortal Clay, or the majestic Webster, were but shadows to the substantial throngs in this chapel. Such rushing, crushing, fussing, and eagerness, defies all description. A crowd of women is always very troublesome, in consequence of their dresses, whose trimmings, laces, fringes, and hooks and eyes, are catching in every passing object, and thereby exciting the fierceness of the fair ones. Absolutely, the legends of the wild and frantic Amazonians appeared perfectly credible to me, as this feminine flood swept onward, almost crushing any poor creature who should attempt to stay its progress.

The English and Americans were exceedingly determined in the " go-a-head " principle, yielding not one inch to male or female, while the Italians, Spanish, and Germans, kindly made way, and even assisted us to obtain a good position to witness the ceremonies. There were long rows of benches, rising one above the other, covered with crimson cloth, called the *tribuna*, where the audience were seated. To this we had tickets, procured from one of the cardinals. When we had " fought and won the battle " of obtaining a pleasant seat, we looked around upon the immense multitude filling the aisles of the chapel. There were cardinals, bishops, priests, ambassadors, French soldiers, Swiss guards, and gorgeously attired chamberlains. It was all like a grand fancy ball by daylight.

Soon there came a deep lull in the storm of voices, and his Holiness the Pope walked slowly up, and ascended his glittering throne, whence he blessed the vast assemblage. His attitude was noble, and his face beaming with a pure and sweet benevolence. He was clad in a crimson velvet mantle, richly embroidered with gold, and sparkling with precious jewels.

On a high bench, just near us, were seated the " twelve apostles," dressed in white, with high white caps upon their heads. They are usually poor priests, chosen from one of the convents; and the ceremony is intended to preserve the memory of that night when our blessed Saviour washed the feet of the apostles. It is likewise an occasion when the Supreme Pontiff publicly manifests his admiration for the lesson of humility taught by the Redeemer of all men. We fancied the faces revealed the characters of the apostles, for that of Peter was kind and good, while Judas had a fiendish expression. The attendants of the Pope removed his velvet robe, and tied a white apron around him; whereupon he proceeded to wash the feet. A servant went before him, who removed the stocking with quick despatch, while another held a basin. From this the Pope took water and poured over the foot, wiping it carefully, and then kissing it. Thus he passed on from one to another, until the ceremony ended. To each one of the twelve, he gave a piece of money and a bouquet of flowers. Immediately after the *lavanda*, the apostles were conducted to the banquet-room, a long and handsome apartment, where they were all seated at a table raised on a platform. It was spread with dishes, and numerous bottles of wine, and decorated with enormous gilt vases filled with beautiful flowers, and statuettes of the different saints. The Pope first washed the hands of the apostles, then served them with various viands, and goblets of rich-looking wine. After placing before them the dessert, he bestowed his blessing, and calmly withdrew with his cardinals, bishops, and noble guard.

As in the chapel of St. Michael, the crowd was boisterous, furious, and overwhelming, becoming more tumultuous when his Holiness had departed. In the frantic rush, I found myself caught up in the strong arms of a grenadier-like Russian woman. My first emotion was of terror; but soon a kind, warm voice whispered to me in French, "Be quiet; I saw, poor little creature! that you would be crushed, so I lifted you up. That is an advantage my height gives me. Now look about you, and see all you can." Imagine my gratitude to the brave Russian, who, after holding me awhile, placed me in safety in the recess of a window; and then diving down amid the rolling waves of the human flood, she fished out Octavia, and held her aloof until she implored our kind protectress to place her by my side. From our retreat we looked down quietly upon the surging crowd, and saw the ending of the feast. Twelve large baskets were brought forth, into which were placed every article used by the apostles at dinner—knives, forks, spoons, wine, food, napkins, and even the bouquets from the vases. These, of course, being very heavy, required several assistants to bear them away. The apostles followed after, very merry, with flushed cheeks and sparkling eyes. Our Russian friend left us to enjoy the scene, until the throng had departed; then lifted us from our retreat, as though we had been infants, and gracefully receiving our thanks, bade us farewell, saying, "Don't forget me when you think of the apostles' banquet."

Next we went to the Paulina chapel, which was illuminated with six hundred candles, and thence returned to the grand aisle of St. Peter's, where we found M. D. in great terror concerning us, as he fancied we had lost our way in the myriad corridors of the immense edifice, or had been crushed by the throng, as several women had fainted from the heat. Happily for us, we had been bravely cared for, and even in that great world of strangers I had found good friends.

Driving rapidly to the hotel, we quickly dined, and returned to St. Peter's just at twilight. In the Choral chapel they were singing the *Miserere*. Seating ourselves by the open door, a perfect flood of melody swept over us, swelling and seeming to linger long beneath the mighty dome and around the lofty arches. When the music ceased, a procession of cardinals, bishops, and priests moved slowly up the aisle to the grand altar, which they washed with wine, chanting in a solemn manner during the time. The darkness was intense, (save where the monks held lamps in their hands.) The crosses were all wrapped in black, and the pictures veiled. At intervals a wild and plaintive cry would break the monotony of the chant, and increase the strange and awe-inspiring mystery of the scene.

When the altar had been washed, and wiped dry, by

numerous hands, we perceived, far above the statue of St. Veronica, a bright and glowing light. Soon upon a small gallery appeared a priest, holding in his hands the precious relics of the Basilica. These are enshrined in glass cases, encrusted with rich jewels, and guarded with ceaseless care. At certain periods they are exhibited for adoration. Numbers of persons fell upon their knees as they were held up. These relics consist of "a piece of the true cross;" "a part of the lance which pierced the side of Christ;" "the handkerchief which St. Veronica spread over his face, on his way to Calvary;" and some others of great value.

One by one the lamp-holders vanished, and the throng departed, leaving only a few kneeling figures before the great altar, who appeared earnestly and deeply absorbed in their devotions.

It is impossible to describe the holy calm which fell upon my soul as I sat within that dim and silent church. The very air seemed filled with beautiful spirits, who were weaving around me a spell of enchantment, and bearing me far away from the present into a glorious world of the future. I felt as though I had lost my own identity,—when hurried steps and voices approached me. "Where have you been? where have you hidden yourself?" were the eager words addressed me; and thus returning to the actualities of life, we left St. Peter's, and drove to the *Trinitá dei Pelligrini*, to see the noble Roman ladies wash the feet of the pilgrims, and wait upon them at table. These poor creatures are real beggars, who come from the neighboring towns, are half starved, wretched, and travel-worn. The hospital is divided into two departments. In one the male pilgrims are received, and waited upon by princes and noblemen; in the other the female pilgrims are cared for by princesses and women of the highest rank. They not only wash their feet, serve them with food at the table, but undress them with their own white and jewelled hands, and then put them carefully into comfortable beds, where they at least enjoyed the blessing of one night's luxurious repose. Although this strikes one as an ostentation of charity, and rather a paráde of the virtue for public admiration, still many miserable beings were made happy by it, and cheered for a few hours of their weary pilgrimage.

Once more we are seated in our quiet chamber. The varied scenes of the day melt and mingle in my memory like the combinations of the kaleidoscope; while afar off is open the "beautiful gate of dreams," through which I shall presently pass. Good night! good night!

Good Friday.—By eight this morning we were in St. Peter's, where we remained until eight at night. During many hours we tarried in the Sixtine chapel, listening to the mass, celebrated before the Pope, and looking upon the wonderful "Last Judgment" of Michael Angelo, which adorns one end of the chapel. It has a terrific grandeur, and many portions realized the fearful descriptions in Dante's "Purgatorio;" especially where the damned spirits are striving to cross the Styx, and are stricken down by the "grim ferryman Charon." Beyond this dark and horrid scene the blessed are rising up, welcomed by angels, and conducted to the Saviour, who sits enthroned with the Virgin by his side, encircled by saints, patriarchs, and martyrs. Besides the "Last Judgment," there are many other glorious frescoes, representing subjects from the creation to the deluge. In the "Fall and Expulsion from Paradise," the serpent is painted with a woman's head. It was always the custom of the old masters to present his snakeship thus adorned. The figure of Eve is exquisite, glowing rich and warm in color and outline. Not far from us, his Holiness was seated in his chair of state; and if there be truth in physiognomy, he is kind, just, good, and benevolent.

When the mass was over we wandered through the vast aisles of St. Peter's until two o'clock, when we returned to the Sixtine chapel. During the morning we had made acquaintance with several charming and noble Italian women, who invited us to accompany them back to the chapel, that they might give us good places to hear the *Miserere.* They told us the throng to listen to this famous chant quite equalled the fierce crowds of the preceding day. Hence we gladly profited by their kindness, and, seated with them, awaited the hour of four, when the Pope and his suite of cardinals entered. "See Naples, and die!" say its enthusiastic people; and all who have revelled in the enjoyment of that musical wonder, the *Miserere*, may in the same feeling listen, and then for ever close their ears. One by one the fifteen candles burning upon the triangle were extinguished, and a dim twilight filled the chapel, throughout which a deep silence prevailed. Suddenly from a dark recess stole forth a sweet and tender wailing cry, like the murmur of a breaking heart. An electric thrill seemed to strike to my very soul, as I sank upon my knees while the coro (chorus) chanted in touching strains, "Christ is gone! we are orphans—all orphans!" Again and again the atmosphere around us quivered with the long wild note of anguish and the answering voices of the coro; now swelling into a tempest of sighs and sobs, and then melting to the softest and faintest echo, like an Æolian harp. The hour, in its twilight gloom, and the strange and mournful melody, were fearfully sublime. Tears burst from my eyes, summoned from the deep heart by the spell of that plaintive voice leading the sacred chant, and appealing to tender memories, from its startling resemblance to the soul-entrancing voice of our loved and lost friend, James Drake.

This world-renowned *Miserere* was composed more than two centuries ago, by Gregorio Allegri, a priest, and singer in the Pope's chapel. Since that period it has been the wonder and the attraction of millions of enraptured listeners. But nowhere save in the Sixtine chapel, with its effective surroundings, can this chant produce the same bewildering and impressive charm. Indeed, a story exists that Leopold the First, Emperor of Austria, asked of the Pope a copy of this *Miserere*. It was given to him, and upon his return to Vienna he commanded all the finest musicians to sing it in the cathedral. So entirely different did it sound to him, that he instantly wrote back to Rome, saying he had been deceived, and dull, common-place music sent to him in place of the wonderful *Miserere*. Inquiries were made, and the chapel-master testified to the correctness of the copy forwarded to the Emperor. Thus it is evident, although a grand composition, it loses half of its dramatic power when heard elsewhere than in the Sixtine chapel. Allegri, no doubt, calculated on all these local accessories, and wrote up to them. The same results attend other musical works; for what would be the incantation scene of "Der Freyschutz," or that of the ruined abbey of "Robert the Devil," but for the wild and striking effects accompanying them?

When the last faint echo of the thrilling *Miserere* died away, the Pope and cardinals passed out in a grand procession to St. Peter's, where again the relics were exhibited, while hundreds fell prostrate on the pavement, as they were held up. When the Pope withdrew, the crowd departed; and we, following their example, drove speedily to our hotel.

April 7th.—At an early hour on Saturday morning we went to the church of *St. John of Laterano*, which is said to occupy the spot where the Emperor Constantine was baptized. In the piazza we saw the colossal obelisk of Thoutmosis, brought from Egypt by Constantine. It is of red granite, one hundred feet in height, and is covered with hieroglyphics. The Basilica is grand and majestic. The ceiling, by Borromini, is of wondrous beauty. In the centre of the principal nave is a singular Gothic tabernacle, containing, they told us, the heads of St. Peter and St. Paul. The altar of the holy sacrament is supported by four bronze pillars, made from the metal found in the ships captured at Actium by Augustus.

The great ceremonies of the day were the baptism of two Jews and one Turk. This over, we wandered for several hours through the long aisles, looking in upon the private chapels containing the tombs of noble families. That of the Corsini has a splendid porphyry sarcophagus of Clement the Twelfth. In the Torlonia chapel there is a superb "Descent from the Cross," by Tenerani. Magnificent pictures, elaborately sculptured columns, and precious statuary, adorn every portion of this grand old church.

Without its walls we saw the ancient cloisters, the baptistry built by Helena, and the immense vase of green basalt, called the "Baptismal Font." From the first days of Christian belief, it has been held most sacred. Constantine was baptized in it, and Rienzi was said to have plunged beneath its waters the night before he summoned the Pope to appear in his presence. Entire immersion must have been the rite of baptism, from the vast size of the vase.

Near the Basilica of St. John of Laterano, under the portico of Fontana, is the *Scala Santa* (the holy staircase). Church history tells us that these twenty-eight marble steps once formed the stairway to the house of Pontius Pilate. Our blessed Saviour descended them when he left the judgment-hall, and passed on to his crucifixion. They were brought to Rome after the destruction of Jerusalem. They are, of course, highly reverenced, and penitents ascend them only on their knees. Myriads of pilgrims flock to them, and they would soon have been worn away had not planks been placed over them. We stood for some time at the foot of the Scala Santa, to see the penitents ascend. It was a most singular sight. There were well-dressed men, neatly attired females (evidently gentlewomen), ragged beggars, squalid children, fresh-colored contadini (peasants), French soldiers, and Swiss guards. The men succeeded in getting up much faster than the women, whose petticoats clearly retarded their progress. Some of them stopped at every step to drop a bead, or stooped to kiss the plank covering the marble. Others hurried rapidly on, as though running for a wager. One wretched-looking creature all strove to avoid. She seemed to have just come from some hospital of disease. Her long hair was falling in wild confusion over her shoulders, while her skeleton-like arms were held up as though imploring assistance to reach the summit. The pale lips were muttering prayers, and the lustreless eyes dropping burning tears. At last she reached the platform above, where there is a figure of Christ, with wounds in the hands and feet. Before this the poor creature fell prostrate, seemingly insensible for a few moments; then rising up, she kissed the bleeding feet alone, with a humility so touchingly profound, tears of sympathy rushed to my eyes, and I turned away from the sad spectacle. When I looked again at her, all the wildness and anguish of expression had left her pallid face; a calm, holy, and beautiful light was beaming there. It was the light of divine faith irradiating her darkened soul, and revealing that glorious future, where sin, suffering, and sorrow shall be no more.

Just at the summit of the Scala Santa is a chapel, wherein is a portrait of the Saviour when he was twelve years of age.

They told us it was painted by St. Luke. After kneeling before the altar and telling their beads, the pilgrims and penitents descended by other stairways, of which there are two on either side of the holy one.

Driving along this almost uninhabited portion of the city, we saw many ruins and broken columns, half hidden by ivy and glowing spring-flowers. Before the Basilica of *Santa Maria Maggiore*, we stopped to look at the obelisk which was brought from Egypt by one of the Roman Emperors a few years after the birth of Christ. The church has a grand exterior, and stands upon the summit of the *Esquiline*, one of "the seven hills of Rome." There is a legend of its foundation, telling that a noble patrician saw, in a vision of the night, the form of a holy angel, who indicated to him the precise spot where the structure should rise. When the morning came, although it was midsummer, the ground pointed out was covered with snow. Forthwith this church was erected, and dedicated to the holy Virgin in the early days of the Christian faith. The interior is magnificent. There are many columns of white marble taken from the temple of Juno, and pillars of porphyry. The ceiling is gorgeously gilt, and the mosaics superb and rich in radiant colors.

When we reached the hotel, about sunset, we found quite a number of visitors awaiting our return; among them Señor Bañuelos, the Spanish Secretary of Legation (now the acting Minister), and his lovely American wife. Our good friend, Doctor Terrel, had given us letters to them, and they both came with the warmest cordiality to greet us. I had known Mme. Bañuelos in former years, when she was an admired belle of Newport, and was charmed to meet her again. She is a noble, elegant woman, with perfect grace of manner. Señor Bañuelos is a distinguished-looking man, intelligent and captivating in conversation. We were exceedingly indebted to him for many kind and pleasant attentions during our sojourn in Rome. He procured for us cards of admission to all places of interest, and entertained us delightfully at the palace of the Spanish Embassy, in the *Piazza di Spagna.*

The Conde of Peñalver, and his beautiful Condesa, were among our visitors. They were rejoiced to have such recent tidings from their Cuban home, to which they soon return by the Cadiz route.

Our American Minister, Mr. Cass, to whom we had many letters, we did not see. A terrible sorrow had just desolated his heart and home. His fair young wife had died a few weeks before we came, of some sudden and fearful malady. In the midst of her happiness and seeming health, death had snatched her away, ere she could speak one warning word of his approach. Every one mourned her, and even strangers to her told me of her sweet and gentle beauty, and spoke with warm sympathy of the grief of the mother and husband.

Our valued friend, Mr. Willis Hall, of New York, came also, and spent some hours with us. He was accompanied by his pretty little step-daughter, Louise, who has evinced great talent for painting, and is studying with one of the first artists of Rome. The Americans are very numerous here; there appear to be representatives from every State of our republic.

Easter Sunday, April 8th.—By seven o'clock this morning we were in St. Peter's. Early as it was, there were multitudes of women seated in the tribunes. These are temporary boxes, fitted up very handsomely, into which no one enters without a card of admission. When we had obtained a good position, we turned our attention to the scene around us. The great marble pillars were all hung with crimson cloth, striped with gold. The altar was covered by a drapery all sparkling with precious gems; while around the tomb of St. Peter a thousand lights in gorgeous candelabra were burning. The stairway to the vault below was wrapped around with white satin, heavy with rich embroidery. The noble-looking Swiss Guards, in their picturesque though gaudy dress, designed by Raphael, were drawn up in long lines, like a parterre of red and yellow tulips amid the black-robed priests, who flitted to and fro over the tesselated pavement, noiseless as shadows. Afar off in one of the chapels they were celebrating mass, and the wild, touching chant of the coro swelled above the tramp of restless feet and the rolling sound of the carriages without. A living stream poured constantly through the great doors, and flowed away into the isles and chapels. Here and there it was dotted by the white, lofty caps of the Sisters of Charity. Near the entrance were hundreds of French soldiers, with glittering bayonets.

At ten o'clock the trumpets sounded, and loud strains of martial music announced the approach of the Pope. He soon after entered. Quite a number of men supported upon their shoulders a platform. On this was an enormous chair, in which his Holiness was seated. Over his head was a white canopy, edged with gold fringe, held by his attendants. Two persons walked behind him with immense fans of white ostrich plumes, mingled with peacock feathers. Cardinals in scarlet robes and ermine tippets, and bishops in purple gowns with long trains, walked after him. Slowly they bore the Pope along, until they reached the throne, which he ascended, and the services began. The triple tiara was then placed upon his head, and all the dignitaries of the church in turn approached him and kissed his hand. After several other ceremonies, the Pope came forward to the grand altar, and commenced the mass. A profound silence fell upon that mighty crowd, while the sweet and clear tones of his voice resounded throughout the church. For two hours the services continued, and ended by the kiss of peace, given by his Holiness to the cardinals around him. Again he was borne down the aisle, in the same manner in which he entered. No one moved until the cortége had disappeared. Then came the impatient rush—the fierce eagerness to be the first out. A good Spanish priest, seeing us hurried so furiously along by the tumultuous crowd, kindly drew us from it, and conducted us by a side-door to the broad steps of the Basilica. What a wonderful spectacle met our eyes. The vast Piazza seemed paved with a mosaic of human heads. At least one hundred and fifty thousand people were there assembled, and carriages without number. Regiments of soldiers were standing like statues amid the surging crowd, while quite near us were the *Guardia Nobile*, the Pope's guard, consisting of young Romans, chosen from the noblest families of the land, all about the same age, and all of striking beauty of face and comeliness of form. Their uniform was splendid, with helmets like those worn by the ancient Greeks.

At twelve o'clock the Pope appeared on the balcony over the great door of St. Peter's. As he raised his hands to Heaven, one impulse of feeling seemed to touch the hearts of that multitude, for all sank upon their knees—princes, beggars, noble ladies, soldiers, peasants, and children. The silence was so profound, that the falling waters of the fountains could be distinctly heard. In a loud, clear, sonorous voice, his Holiness blessed the kneeling throng. What an impressive scene it was! Truly did I feel that even the strictest Protestant must cease, then at least, to protest, and feel upon his soul the influence of the benediction. When the blessing was over, the cannon sounded forth from the Castle of St. Angelo, and the military bands burst into triumphant strains of music. All sprang to their feet, and soon the vast concourse of people parted like streams and flowed away.

When we first went out from the church upon the Piazza, I had noticed a poor pilgrim laying on the step below us. He seemed overpowered by fatigue, and slept soundly amid all the confusion, his long staff lying by his side. When the Pope came out, my eyes again fell upon the sleeping man, and I stooped and awakened him. He raised himself up, and knelt in time to receive the benediction.

After the crowd had partially departed, we seated ourselves, to remark the strange contrasts around us. Gorgeous carriages of the cardinals and bishops, with various servants in splendid liveries, were driving up on one side, while on the other stood groups of beggars, with dark, scowling faces, hunger and despair looking out from their fierce eyes. Just then a hand grasped the folds of my dress. I turned quickly, and at my feet the poor old pilgrim was kneeling, and blessing me for the kind thought which prompted me to awaken him. Ah! what a trifle can sometimes give joy to a human being. Telling him I did not merit his gratitude, I asked him whence he came; and found that he had walked all night to be in time for the benediction. When he had seated himself on the steps to await the coming of his Holiness, he had fallen into a deep sleep, from excessive weariness, and nearly missed the blessing for which he had made a pilgrimage so long and toilsome. The day was of unusual loveliness, and the very earth and air appeared to rejoice; while the noble colonnades, glittering in the sunlight, were like two great arms stretched out to embrace the whole world.

It is only in Rome the majestic grandeur of the Catholic religion can be seen in its perfection. Constantly during the Holy Week have I been impressed with the solemnity of the ceremonies, and yet, even in the sanctuary, have we encountered persons who mockingly laughed at them. To me they were sacred, awakening only reverential awe.

After dinner we drove to Monte Pincio, the fashionable drive as well as promenade of the modern Romans. The carriage-way winds around it upon terraces cut into the hill. On the summit there is a beautiful garden, with statues, fountains, and delightful walks. Thence the view is magnificent. The entire city seemed spread out before us, while the matchless St. Peter's, "Earth's grandest Basilica," rose far above all else. Ah! what a wild delight came rushing like a bright stream over my heart, bringing with it the golden sands of classic and historic associations! Yielding myself to its resistless power, I was borne back to that glorious past, when Rome,

"She who was named Eternal, and arrayed
Her warriors but to conquer—she who veiled
Earth with her haughty shadow, and displayed
Until the o'er-canopied horizon failed,
Her rushing wings,—oh! she who was Almighty hailed!"

At sunset we drove in an open barouche to St. Peter's, and stopped just within the colonnades. An immense concourse of people, almost equal to the throng of the morning, was assembled in the Piazza. The carriages were drawn up in lines precisely as upon our race-courses in America. The mounted police, with drawn sabres, kept order over the movements of the crowd. A hoarse murmur, like the sound of a distant cataract, rose up from the dense mass of human beings. As twilight melted into darkness, along the front of the church, sprang up innumerable gleaming lights, until frieze, column, cornice, and pillar, were all traced out in fire. This was the "silver" illumination. We gazed upon this for some time, in wonder and admiration, when the great bell of St. Peter's tolled the hour of eight. At the first stroke a meteor, as though from the sky above, darted to the summit of the dome, and fixed itself upon the top of the cross; then as quick as thought, swift as electricity, thousands and thousands of blazing fires flashed over the noble structure, along the graceful colonnades, around the statues, and beneath the arches. The waters of the fountains, catching the vivid radiance, fell like drops of liquid gold into the marble basins. Glorious was the spectacle—a miracle of beauty! It seemed some vision of enchantment—a cathedral of flame, whose perfect architecture was all revealed in glittering light. A slight wind caused the fires to waver to and fro, as though they were stars which had fallen from their sphere above, and were now trembling and fluttering in their new abode.

For hours we continued gazing upon this last illumination, styled the "golden;" then slowly disentangling our carriage from the multitudes around it, we wended our way to the Pincian hill. The view thence was but another and more glowing revelation of its wondrous grandeur. All around was deep darkness, save the dome of fire, which absolutely appeared built in the heavens. Oh! it was a radiant mystery, wildly beautiful. Like a gorgeous dream, it seemed as though each moment it would vanish from our sight. Just above the luminous dome, the evening star was shining in the clear sky, almost eclipsed by the brilliant blaze below it.

Most reluctantly did we leave the Pincian hill, and look our last upon the grand cathedral. Long after the midnight, I stole gently from my chamber, and climbed a terrace above our hotel, whence I could still behold the "temple of fire." Not one light was extinguished, and thus it blazed and glowed until morning came.

The illumination of St. Peter's only occurs on Easter Sunday, and on the day of St. Peter. It requires six hundred men to accomplish it. A perilous task it is deemed, for they all confess and receive absolution before they ascend. Then over the whole building they spread themselves like a vast swarm of bees; upon a signal they light up the lamps for the "silver" illumination, and the fires for the "golden."

On the night after Easter Sunday came the *girandola* or fire-works. The place chosen for this marvellous display was the Pincian hill, which rises directly from the windows of our drawing-room. The position was, however, too near, so we hired seats in the Piazza del Popolo, just opposite the Monte Pincio. A dense mass of people were gathered within the square, while in their midst were many of the Pope's mounted dragoons, who with gleaming sabres enforced order. Along the summit of the hill, from time to time, flashes of light appeared; then the vast crowd would surge to and fro like great waves of the sea. At eight balloons, with lamps within them, ascended; as these sailed slowly away, flights of rockets rushed upward, and bursting, discharged beautiful flowers of red, blue, and yellow. Such was their profusion, that the sky above us seemed a garden, with flowers of flame and foliage of fire. These soon faded, even more quickly than the "flowers of earth," and night resumed its empire. Suddenly, as though by the touch of an enchanter's wand, up rose a magnificent Gothic cathedral, perfect in its graceful proportions, which were all expressed in fire, dazzling as the rays of the golden diamond. There were draperies to the great windows of crimson light, while the columns and noble façade were revealed in blue and white flame. Radiant and beautiful it glittered in the darkness, like some "glorified structure." As the cannon sounded forth, it vanished as swiftly as a gleam of lightning. The next moment raging flames darted from the summit of the Pincian; clouds of lurid smoke encircled it, and streams of burning lava flowed down the side of the hill. A fierce volcano in full eruption seemed before us, and the solid earth shook and trembled, as enormous blood-red stones rushed upward, then fell with crushing violence upon the ground. This seeming convulsion of nature soon ended, and again the Gothic cathedral appeared, disclosed to us in a soft light, like that of the moon. We were looking delightedly upon the sweet and gentle vision, when a fiery glare usurped the place of the moonlight. From every window, door, and column, sprang out serpents of fire, cataracts of red light, and showers of stars. The heavens were filled with blazing meteors, crossing and recrossing each other in such bewildering confusion, the eyes were absolutely blinded by their excessive radiance. One more terrific burst of flame, almost converting the air to fire, and the girandola was ended. Darkness came again, and Lent was over.

While in Paris, we had seen a grand display of fire-works on the fête-day of the Emperor, but they were as shadows compared to the wondrous beauty of the girandola. About them was something artificial and prosaic; but the gorgeous spectacle of the Pincian hill was perfectly unique in its grandeur and magnificence. It had the poetry of Italy, and its romance, kindling the imagination to wild delight.

CHAPTER XLIII.

NEARLY all the days of our first week's sojourn in Rome were spent in St. Peter's. It is indeed a glorious edifice.

> "What could be,
> Of earthly structures, in God's honor piled,
> Of a sublimer aspect? Majesty,
> Power, glory, strength, and beauty all are aisled
> In this eternal ark of worship undefiled."

At all hours it is grandly impressive; in the clear light of morning, and at mid-day, when the sunbeams, darting through the lofty windows, appeared like spears of fire, touching with radiant glow many a costly shrine and gorgeous mosaic; then at twilight, as music floated along the incense-ladened atmosphere, soft and sweet as the melody of "harps touched by angel-fingers;" and in the deep night, when its darkness was only broken by the lamps (likened by Shelley to "a swarm of golden bees") which burn unceasingly around the sacred sepulchre of St. Peter. An eloquent writer has said of this vast structure, "It is among buildings what Shakspeare is among poets; hence it cannot be defined by a single epithet." Infinite is its variety, and matchless its grandeur—a temple

> "Worthiest of God, the holy and the true."

Over the great marble plain, enclosed by massive walls, I wandered day after day, ere my mind could realize the gigantic magnificence of the consecrated building. The offerings of ages and the wealth of nations are gathered there. Painting and sculpture are the handmaidens who have aided in its wondrous adornments. Rich mosaics, rivalling the most exquisite efforts of the painter, and as imperishable as adamant, are scattered every where. Groups of statuary by Michael Angelo, Bernini, Canova, and Thorwaldsen, meet the eyes wherever they turn. In the grand nave there is a forest of columns, inlaid with beautiful marbles, which likewise decorate the tesselated pavement. Numerous chapels diverge from the centre aisle, and are shut in by sculptured pillars, and embellished with noble pictures and glittering vases. The lofty ceiling is shining with golden ornaments and elaborate carvings richly gilded.

So great are the dimensions of St. Peter's, that tens of thousands, nay even a hundred thousand people, appear in it but as a small crowd. Into the ocean many streams are swiftly flowing, which are quickly lost in its immensity; and thus it is with the human flood rushing through the portals of this Basilica. Once within it, like waves they glide away to dim recesses, and along the many-arched aisles, and are seen no more. Exalted emotions, and fervent admiration of the almost God-like genius of Michael Angelo, filled our hearts as we stood beneath the dome—

> "The vast and wondrous dome,
> To which Diana's marvel were a cell:
> Christ's mighty shrine, above his martyr's tomb."

Looking upward, upward, the gold-inlaid mosaics around it appeared as gleaming stars in a sky of the artist's own creation. The eye absolutely grew weary ere it reached the summit, four hundred and fifty feet from the pavement.

Just beneath the dome is the high altar. It is directly over the grave of St. Peter. A huge *baldachino*, or canopy of bronze, sustained by twisted columns ninety feet in height, rise above it. Not far from this altar is the statue of the saint, seated in an immense chair, with one foot extended. People were constantly kissing the great toe, and pressing their foreheads against it. After this act of devotion, they would humbly kneel before the figure in earnest prayer. Many antiquarians have contended that the statue of St. Peter, so devoutly kissed by millions and millions of Catholics, is but the figure of Jupiter. There is, however, only a shadow of probability in this supposition. The statue is stiff and formal, and lacks the graceful outline of the more classic period of the art. Besides, the head does not resemble any other representation of the majestic form of the mightiest of the heathen gods.

Ninety years after the birth of our Saviour, St. Anacletus built an oratory where now stands St. Peter's. He was the first Bishop of Rome, and was ordained by the hands of St. Peter himself. After the crucifixion of the holy man, his follower and friend buried the sacred body upon the very spot where many of the first Christians had suffered martyrdom, and raised over it an humble shrine. Two hundred years afterwards, Constantine, son of the pious Helena, erected a church upon its ruins, where for centuries faithful believers in Christ came flocking with votive offerings and with prayer. When near one thousand years had passed, and time had almost destroyed it, Nicholas the Fifth resolved to rebuild it. But this intention was abandoned, and then it was determined to raise up a structure equal to the temple at Jerusalem. Three hundred years elapsed ere it was completed, although but one hundred and eighty were required in the absolute work. It was dedicated in 1626 by Urban the Eighth. During the long centuries occupied in the building of St. Peter's, various plans of construction were adopted, and then abandoned. At length came the great artist, Michael Angelo, with his design of the Greek cross, and the glorious dome, "like the Pantheon hung in air." Happily, he almost completed this wonderful work, God having given him more days of life than often fall to the lot of man. He was seventy-two years old when he began the unequalled structure, and lived until he was eighty-nine. Della Porta was employed after his death, and religiously carried out the conception of Michael Angelo.

Nearly one hundred years after, Carlo Maderno was appointed by Pope Paul the Sixth to finish the Basilica. This architect changed the plan, and returned to the Latin cross of Raphael. In that form St. Peter's is built. At the extremity of the church is a group of four colossal bronze statues, representing the doctors of the Greek and Latin churches. They support a throne, upon which stands the patriarchal chair of Saint Peter. Angels, exquisitely wrought in snowy marble, encircle it, one holding the tiara and another the pontifical keys. Light falls upon the throne through the golden-tinted glass of an enormous window, upon which is traced the form of a dove. So radiant is the effect, that the dove, type of the Holy Spirit, seems surrounded by a halo of glory. In the transepts, or cross aisles, are confessionals in all living languages; not only Italian, Spanish, French, German, and English, but many of the dialects of remote lands. Before these, penitents may tell their sins in their own tongue, and receive absolution and consolation from priests who speak the language of their native country. Whatever our belief may be, we cannot refuse our admiration to the grand idea which thus brings a solace and a ray of joy to the soul of the wretched wanderer, who in the minister of

God finds a friend, and a memory of his far-away home, awakened by the accents of that language dear to his soul in the days of his youth.

Deeply as we were impressed with the stupendous magnificence of St. Peter's, as we lingered amid its wonders on the marble plain below, still more intense was our admiration, when, ascending by wide steps or *ramps*, we came out upon the roof of the church. There we found ourselves in a small town, about one hundred and fifty feet from the ground. Several broad acres of land, are roofed over by a marble covering, which, sustained by gigantic walls, seems indeed the work of Titans, and not the labor of man. In all directions are the houses of the workmen, who constantly live there to keep the roof in repair.

Next we mounted a stairway, and came out into a gallery around the dome, quite near the glorious mosaic inscription which encircles it, and which we could scarcely read from below. It is the blessed promise to the apostle: "Thou art Peter, and upon this rock will I build my church, and I will give unto you the keys of the kingdom of heaven." Each letter in these words, the guide told us, was six feet long. They appeared to us like masses of rough stone. Just near us were niches, with spiral columns, brought by the Emperor Titus from the temple of Jerusalem. From this gallery we looked down into the aisles, hundreds of feet below us. The men and women there seemed really like feathers wafted to and fro by the wind.

Passing upward still, we reached the staircase between the domes, (for there are an inner and an outer dome,) of solid stone, crowned by a lantern. There we had a fine view of the mosaic, wherein the Father is represented encircled by angels, and resting upon clouds. At the base of the ball, which is surmounted by the cross, we stopped, while some

Spanish friends ascended the slender iron ladder leading to it. A narrow gallery, quite invisible from below, runs around the ball. Out upon this we hastened, and beheld a scene of beauty to which earth has no parallel. Afar off was the Mediterranean, like a sea of lapis lazuli, sprinkled with silver; the Alban and the Sabine hills; the blue-tinted Apennines; Soracte, the lone sentinel of the vast Campagna, whose green and wave-like undulations were bridged over by long lines of aqueducts. Rome, the "Eternal!" Rome, the "City of the Soul!" was spread out at our feet—the forum and the coliseum, triumphal arches and temples, columns and ruined palaces. The first home of that wildly energetic Roman race, whose ever-widening circle of conquest spread over almost the entire civilized world, was before us. Immortal histories clustered about every object, and inconceivable grandeur of thought and memories of the undying past swept over my mind, as I looked upon these majestic ruins, ever entrancing to human interest, although

> "The Goth, the Christian, Time, War, Flood, and Fire,
> Have dealt upon the seven-hill'd city's pride."

Ah! what glorious hours we passed upon that narrow balcony, gazing from east to west, from north to south, and treasuring up soul-inspiring recollections. They absolutely appeared photographed upon the mind, with the same distinctness which attends the pictures traced indelibly by the rays of the sunlight.

All our party left me save Octavia. There we tarried, while our guide conducted several people into the ball, who all came down crying out upon the weariness of the ascent and the terrific heat within it. Finally, when the day was well-nigh ended, I consented to descend; a sharp pang thrilling my heart the while, for I knew that I could never again look upon a scene so sublime from association, and so perfect in its actual beauty.

Coming down quite rapidly, we passed numerous slabs of marble inserted into the walls, telling of the visits of crowned heads and important personages to *La Cupola Vaticana.* Reaching the church, we went out into the Piazza of St. Peter's, and walked around the famous colonnade of Bernini, which forms two semicircles of three hundred and sixty columns, crowned by colossal statues of saints. They are of travertine marble, and sweep around the Piazza with a curve of indescribable grace. In the centre of the oval space enclosed by these, is an obelisk of red granite, brought from Egypt by Caligula. There is an interesting story of this obelisk. When Pope Sixtus the Fifth resolved to place it in the Piazza, all efforts to raise it proved ineffectual. At last the architect Fontana consented to make the attempt once more, provided a command should be issued that no one should speak under pain of death, as the confusion of tongues had always retarded previous endeavors. Four gibbets were erected in sight of the people, and a proclamation told them the first who uttered a word should thereon be hung. Slowly and in profound silence the great Egyptian needle was raised, and when within one inch of the pedestal, the ropes, from the tension of the enormous weight, began to smoke. Then a workman cried out, "Aqua!" (Water.) The crowd rushed to the fountains and brought thence the pure water, which they dashed over the ropes. One more effort, and the obelisk was placed on its pedestal. Shouts of joy made the air quiver. But lo! the Pope, ordering silence again, called for the bold man who had dared to disobey his command and speak. The wretched workman came forward, pale and trembling, to meet his doom, when the assembled thousands fell upon their knees and cried out, "Mercy, mercy for him!

Mercy for the sake of the obelisk!" The Pontiff gave him his forfeited life, and any boon he should choose to claim. He asked that only he and his family should have the privilege to sell palm branches on Palm Sunday in the Place of St. Peter's. This was granted to him, and even to this day his descendants sell them there. Fontana, the architect, was made a Knight of the Golden Spur.

On each side of the obelisk are the fountains. A stream of water darts up about seventy feet into the air, and falling, is received into a basin of oriental granite; thence flowing over its edge, it falls in sheets of snowy foam into a larger one below. They surround the basins like a delicate drapery, and are beautiful in their restless play, and delightful from the music of their dashing waters.

Along the façade of the church are immense statues of Christ and his twelve apostles. Rising above these are seen the towers and cupolas, clustering around the peerless dome like a young flock beneath the wing of the parent bird. The spacious vestibule has two equestrian figures of Constantine and Charlemagne. Opening thence are five portals, near which stand the giant cherubs, holding vases of holy water.

Beneath St. Peter's there is a subterranean church, called *Grotte Vaticane*. It contains that portion of the ancient Basilica which was built over the graves of the first martyrs to our sacred faith. Long corridors and aisles stretch far away into dim obscurity, whose floor is paved with tablets of the "illustrious dead," and along the walls are sarcophagi of popes, kings, and emperors. The dauntless Otho has there his last resting-place, and Charles, James, and Henry, sons of the hapless Stuart; and Charlotte, queen of Jerusalem, Christina of Sweden, and Nicholas Breakspeare, the only English Pope who ever occupied the pontifical chair. (He died in 1158.) The ashes of St. Peter and St. Paul are mingled into one dust, reposing beneath the gorgeous splendors of the high altar. We went down into the crypt, or sacred grottoes, by a stairway in one of the great pillars, upon which rests the dome. The chapels within them possess many fine paintings and *bas reliefs*, columns from Hadrian's villa, and exquisite frescoes.

The good old priest who was our guide told me of a singular marriage which had just taken place in the sacristy. The parties were English people. The woman had been long wooed by a devoted lover, whom she determined at length to reward by the gift of her hand, (and I suppose her heart and fortune, as she had boundless wealth.) But she made several stipulations with him ere she consented. First, he was neither to speak, to see, nor to write to her for one year; secondly, he was to forsake his Protestant faith, and become a Catholic; thirdly, he was to meet her on the anniversary of the engagement, in the dark and gloomy crypt of St. Peter's, and there, near the tomb of the Saint, swearing he had fulfilled all these promises, (for he had gladly acceded to all her propositions,) he should receive her as his wife from the holy friar. The year passed by, and, true to her word, she came to the sacred grottoes, where the lover joined her, and they were married, before the very altar where we stood. I asked the priest, "What kind of woman was she?" "Ah! Signora," he answered, "she was a dark, cold, stern-looking woman, with a fierce look of command in her eyes. I pitied the young man. He had a soft, fair face and gentle voice, but he really trembled in her presence. The fiend of souls has surely no greater tempter than cursed gold." I would fain have asked more of these nuptials, but the old priest, kneeling before a Madonna and Child, by Giulio Romano, ended the conversation. After a stay of several hours in the subterranean church, we ascended again into St. Peter's, and went directly to the Vatican, which is joined to it by a long gallery.

The Vatican is an assemblage of palaces built at various periods, by different pontiffs, and occupies an incredible space of ground. There are galleries, halls, courts, gardens, and more than four thousand rooms. It was begun about the seventh century, and was the dwelling-place of Charlemagne. It was not the residence of the Popes until after their return from Avignon. Previous to the period of the removal of their capital to France, they had lived always in the *Lateran Palace.* When, however, it was resolved to make the Vatican the pontifical abode, the greatest architects were summoned to erect a palace which should rival the grandest of antiquity. Portions of the magnificent plans of different eras are thus mingled in its architecture.

We entered by the stairway of Bernini, with its Ionic columns, deemed the most splendid in the world, and passed along the *Galleria Lapidaria*, containing sepulchral monuments. Upon the walls are inscriptions in Greek and Latin. On one hand are the Pagan, and on the other the Christian, taken from the catacombs. The first are full of words of hopeless sorrow, while the latter are strikingly expressive of a joy and a life beyond the tomb.

Next we came to the *Museo Chiaramonti*, arranged by Canova. Walking through this, we seemed transported to the city of the Arabian Nights, where all the men and women were turned in one instant, by the cruel magician, to marble. The vast number of statues was perfectly bewildering—emperors and gods, generals and citizens, satyrs and fauns, children and tritons; Venus stepping from her bath; the sleeping Fisher-Boy; the Cupid of Praxiteles; and the figure of Hercules found in Hadrian's villa, and which Michael Angelo declared to have been his model in the most admirable developments of the human form. The highest point of art had certainly been attained by the Greek and Roman sculptors in those early days. Impossible were it for imagination to portray forms of more enrapturing grace, faces of more real loveliness, or an air of dignity more befitting the "land of lost gods and god-like men." The bust of the Emperor Augustus charmed me. It is that of a youth, with a sweet and dreamy beauty lingering around the brow, and resting on the exquisite mouth, which nature seemed to have intended should only breathe words of love. Its resemblance to the great Napoléon is often remarked. Not far from this is a statue of Demosthenes, one of the noblest of the marble inhabitants of the "metropolis of art." The contour of the head speaks of the lofty mind enshrined within it. The position was dignified, and the drapery appeared to fall in graceful folds around the form. It was my perfect ideal of the orator and statesman, and often did I return to gaze upon it, and to look on the figure of Cicero, and the bust of Mark Antony, the Minerva Medica, the group of the Nile, and the Mercury found in the Coliseum.

Of republican Rome, there was the tomb of Scipio, who was consul two hundred years before the birth of the Saviour. The reclining statue of Ariadne, although of colossal size, is admirable for its grace and ease of attitude. The well-rounded outline of the perfect form is delicately revealed through the folds of the marble drapery.

In the *Cortile of the Belvedere* are the richest treasures of ancient art. Around an octagonal court, from whose centre dart upward the waters of a lovely fountain, are small pavilions. Within these we saw the miracle of sculpture, the *Apollo Belvidere.* It is in truth most glorious—the embodiment of joyous beauty and triumphant pride. There absolutely seemed a life and a spirit in the faultless form, and we could readily believe, as we gazed upon the exquisite face, the legend of the hapless maiden, who died of passionate love, inspired by the marble God,

> "Which, if made
> By human hands, is not of human thought;
> And Time himself hath hallowed it, nor laid
> One ringlet in the dust, nor hath it caught
> A tinge of years, but breathes the flame with which 'twas wrought."

From the contemplation of this matchless statue we turned to the *Laocoon.* Startling was the contrast between them. Two thousand years ago Pliny described the fearful group of a father and his children enveloped in the coils of huge serpents, as superior to all other works, either of painting or sculpture. The terrific struggle of

> "A father's love, and mortal's agony,
> With an immortal's patience blending."

In the next pavilion was the *Perseus* of Canova, holding aloft the Gorgon's head, and the *Boxers*, with lithe and graceful forms; then *Antinous*, the noblest type of Grecian beauty, and the ideal of a hero of the land of which old Homer sang.

Along the "Hall of the Muses" are ranged Corinthian columns, brought from the villa of Hadrian, while the pavement is brilliant with mosaics of the olden time. The Muses and Apollo stand in the centre, and the seven wise men of Greece, besides many of her poets and orators. The noble Pericles and the bewitching Aspasia are placed side by side. Their marble forms awaken a thrilling interest, and a memory of those days when the inspiration of a woman's love animated the soul of Pericles, and was the source of his resistless eloquence and boundless power over the hearts of his countrymen. In the "Round Saloon" is the Porphyry Vase, more than forty feet in circumference, which was found in the Baths of Titus.

Then we came to the "Hall of the Greek Cross," luxurious and gorgeous in its architecture. On either side of the doorway are colossal statues of red granite. The floor is formed of glowing mosaics, the roof gilded and painted. Pillars run around the Hall, while vases, busts, candelabra, sarcophagi, and statues, are placed in all directions. In the centre are the tombs of Helena and Constantia, the mother and daughter of Constantine. They are of porphyry, carved from a single immense block, and are covered with sculpture.

Ascending a stairway, we came to the "Hall of the Biga," thus named from a marble chariot and horses. If Nero rode in it, his evening drives must have been vastly wearying.

The museum of Etruscan relics was exceedingly interesting. Buried beneath the lava of oblivion is the history of the race who fashioned all these beautiful objects of art. They were perhaps the first inhabitants of the country, or Phenicians, or Philistines from the land of Canaan. Although their tombs still retain their inscriptions, no linguist has ever been found learned enough to read them. In these tombs have been discovered nearly all the ornaments of gold and bronze—the vases of various forms and sizes, painted with illustrations from mythology, and with scenes from actual life.

The "Hall of Animals" was very curious. It seemed a menagerie of all descriptions of animals turned to stone. There were crocodiles, lions, serpents, wild boars, crabs, dogs, and centaurs. In truth, there seemed representatives of all the beasts of the land and all the fishes of the sea. Each was sculptured in its most characteristic attitude. Wonderful, indeed, were the resources of the Greek sculptors.

Not in one day did we see all the sculptured treasures of the Vatican, but, often returning, wandered amid the thousands of statues, finding ourselves, however, most admiringly drawn to those I have described. Never did we enter the vast halls and galleries without a thought of the grandeur of Rome in its days of pride and power, when these magnificent works of art adorned temple, palace, and forum. And these were only waifs saved from fire, from war, and time. The wealth of centuries, the gold of the African, and the Briton, are entombed beneath thronged streets and gloomy dwellings. The Tiber flows over many a richly carved figure and precious gem. Frequently, as we walked along, would we remark, as the foundation of a house, portions of an ancient building, with exquisite sculpture of noble and classic design.

Although the Gallery of the Vatican contains only a few oil paintings, they are all treasures of the art. First, then, among them is the *Transfiguration*, the last picture of Raphael. An almost divine power seemed to have inspired him, as he portrayed the history of human suffering, and of the soul's bright faith of a beautiful home above. Perhaps, as he toiled on, the portals of that home were open to his vision, and the voices of the blessed were stealing around him. Hence the heavenly radiance which beams from the face, and lingers around the figure of our holy Saviour. As Raphael eagerly painted and triumphantly gazed upon the realization of his wondrous conception, Death snatched him away. It was the last effort of his immortal genius. Often had I read those touching lines of Rogers, wherein he describes the mournful scene when the dead body was placed beneath that last great painting, whose colors were yet moist from the artist's brush. All Rome adored him, and Rome poured forth her noblest people to gaze upon the angelic face. The glory around the head of Christ seemed reflected upon the lifeless form. All wept,

> "When, entering in, they looked
> Now on the dead, then on that master-piece;
> Now on his face, lifeless and colorless,
> Then on those forms divine, that lived and breathed,
> And would live on for ages. All were moved,
> And sighs burst forth, and loudest lamentations."

This last picture of Raphael has called forth much criticism. Its purpose was two-fold—to give expression to human agony, in the form of the demoniac boy brought by the sorrowing mother to the nine disciples who stand around Mount Tabor, and who point upwards to the divine power, which can alone relieve. Floating in clouds above them is the figure of the Saviour, attended by Moses and Elijah, while the other three apostles are prostrate on the summit of the mountain, unable to endure the dazzling glory which beams upon them. In the same room is the *Madonna di Foligno*, another picture by Raphael, of wonderful beauty and exquisite delicacy of composition.

Next we stopped before the *Communion of St. Jerome* by Domenchino. It represented the dying saint as he receives the sacrament, and is a mournful and life-like picture. Then, passing on, we saw the *Madonna and Child* of Titian; the *Magdalen* of Guercino; *Christ* borne up on a rainbow, and encircled with angels, by Correggio; *St. Helena*, with the vision of the holy cross, by Paolo Veronese; the *Madonna* of Guido, and several others of great excellence, by Poussin, Perugino, and Andrea Sacchi.

We had seen the frescoes of the Sixtine chapel the day

when we listened to the utterance of the soul-thrilling *Miserere;* but again and again, during our roamings about the Vatican, we entered it. The *Last Judgment* is terrifically grand, and appeared constantly to us as illustrations of Dante's *Inferno*, although its purpose was said to be a history of God's dealing with man. I often thought of the remark of the French artist as I looked upon the countless figures which throng both the walls and roof: "I have seen Michael Angelo, and he is terrible."

The *stanze* (or chambers), painted by Raphael, are four in number, and each one is a noble monument to his genius. Every portion of the walls and ceiling is covered with frescoes, which occupied the last ten or twelve years of his life. He was only twenty-four when he was commanded by Pope Julius the Second to perpetuate in glowing pictures the "might and majesty of Rome" as the centre of religious faith and intellectual civilization. I could never look upon those radiant frescoes without remembrance of the toil and weariness of the poor artist to create them. The labor of painting them is incredible, especially those upon the roof. The plaster is placed upon the ceiling, and while yet moist, the painter, lying on his back, upon a platform, draws the designs, and then with his brush paints in the colors; as the mortar is wet, they mingle with it, and, when dried, become a portion of it. Thus forever do frescoes retain their brilliant hues. Only ten years after these were painted, Rome was captured, and the rude soldiers bivouacked in these *stanze*, building fires on the pavement. In spite of all these injuries and the touch of time, they are still exquisite in soul-touching beauty.

One chamber represents the "School of Athens," which is certainly among the most perfect productions of Raphael's mind. There are more than fifty figures, all in attitudes of graceful ease. Aristotle and Plato are standing upon the steps of a Grecian portico, engaged in argument, each holding a volume in his hand. Socrates is instructing Alcibiades; a group of other pupils are around him, listening with wrapt attention. Archimedes traces a geometrical figure upon a tablet; while the old cynic, Diogenes, listlessly reclines on the marble floor. Other Grecian philosophers fill up the fresco.

Next came allegorical representations of Theology, Justice, and Poetry. This last picture is delightful to look upon. Under the laurel trees crowning Mount Parnassus, are assembled Apollo, the nine Muses, and many Greek, Latin, and Italian poets. There is the graceful Sappho, seemingly addressing Corinna, Ovid, and Petrarch. The figure of Homer is grandly majestic; near him are Virgil, Dante, and Boccacio. Horace and the aged Pindar are side by side. In the midst of these Apollo is seated, playing upon a violin. The introduction of this instrument is often ridiculed, even by the admirers of Raphael; but why should there be such unpoetical associations attached to the violin? It is surely capable of giving forth divine melody, and possesses tones which dart rapidly like rays of light to the soul. All those who have heard the noble Norwegian, Ole Bull, must have felt the electric power of his music, when, like one inspired, he bent his head lovingly over the instrument, until his long golden hair appeared like a halo around it, as he drew forth those delicious and plaintive notes, thrilling the heart to its inmost depths.

From the soft and gentle shades of Parnassus we turned to the contemplation of the terrible picture of the *Expulsion of Heliodorus* from the temple by the avenging angel, who, mounted upon a fiery horse, with eyes of fearful vengeance, rushes upon the monarch, and dashes him on the pavement. The story is related in Maccabees, and the crime (not an unusual one in our days) was seizing the money laid up in the temple for the fatherless and widows.

In another *stanze* or chamber was *Attila* with his Huns, stopped as they were entering Rome, by the appearance in the heavens of Saint Peter and Saint Paul. Then the *Miracle of Bolsena*, and the *Deliverance of St. Peter from Prison.* The *Incendio del Borgo* (the burning of the environs of St. Peter's) is most admirable. In the "Hall of Constantine" there is an immense fresco, representing the battle between Maxentius and Constantine (the first Christian emperor), upon the *Ponte Molle*, near Rome. It is a magnificent composition, and a victory over the well-known difficulties of the subject. The figure of Constantine is grand, mounted upon a noble charger; triumph and power seem to animate his frame and flash from his eyes. The defeated usurper has fallen into the stream, whose turbid waters are just closing over him. In that fearful battle, the records of those times tell us, the Tiber was a river of blood, rushing furiously over the dead bodies of Roman soldiers.

Not far from this terrific painting is the apparition of the *Fiery Cross in the Heavens*, which appeared to Constantine before the battle. It is painted by Giulio Romano, the pupil of Raphael.

From the *stanze* we went into the *loggie* of Raphael, arcades around the courts. These frescoes are scenes from the Bible, beginning with the creation of the world. They are splendidly executed, and are full of grace and variety. The walls and ceilings are covered with arabesque paintings of figures, landscapes, temples, flowers, and scrolls. They are much faded by exposure to weather, but still sufficiently bright to give an earnest of the beauty of their early days. The *Tapestries*, or cartoons of Raphael, are also faded, but still showing the talent of the wonderful being who designed them.

How glorious was the imagination, and how inexhaustible the industry of Raphael! Although his career was so brief (he died ere he had reached his thirty-seventh year), his works are inconceivably numerous; and should we judge by them, we might say his life was long. In fact, its short span of years contained a lengthy existence of toil, suffering, sorrow, and triumph. Neither Byron, Mozart, nor Burns lived until they were thirty-eight. Like impetuous streams, they dashed madly onward, with heated brain and throbbing pulse, over that precipice beyond which is the dark abyss of death.

The printed books of the Vatican Library are about thirty thousand. They are closely locked up in cases, which, however, are opened for one, if a special permission is shown. The manuscripts are said to be the most valuable in the world. We saw a *Virgil* of the fourth century, with illustrations, and a picture of the poet; *Tasso's* autograph of "Jerusalem," and *Petrarch's* "Rome;" a *Dante* of the fifteenth century, and a *Terence* of the fifth; the illuminated Hebrew Bible, for which the Jews of Venice offered its weight in gold. There were seventeen letters written by Henry the Eighth to Anna Boleyn. These were singular treasures for an ecclesiastical library. They were letters written in the full bloom of his passion by the fierce Henry, breathing an eternal love. How strange that these records should have been snatched from the wreck of centuries, while so many grand effusions of noble minds have perished.

The rooms of the library are eighteen in number, opening one into another, and thus forming a long, long vista.

They are adorned with paintings, Etruscan and Malachite vases, columns, and frescoes.

The gardens of the Vatican are extensive and beautiful, and the palace is world-renowned, for its thunders once had power to make all Europe tremble.

CHAPTER XLIV.

M. D. had crossed the Atlantic expressly to see ancient, and not modern Rome; hence he was quite impatient at our oft-repeated visits to St. Peter's and the Vatican, and gladly welcomed the announcement of readiness to accompany him through the crumbling ruins of more than two thousand years. These ruins are as waifs cast up by the waves of the past, and left stranded upon the shores of the present. For weeks we spent long days, and the soft twilight hours, among them;

> "And the heart ran over,
> With silent worship of the great of old,
> The dead, but sceptred sovereigns, who still rule
> Our spirits from their urns."

Our first visit was to the Roman Forum, which certainly possesses more thrilling interest than any other spot of earth, unless it be the holy city of Jerusalem. Glancing over the wide space between the Capitoline and Palatine hills, it appeared a scene of perfect desolation, with here and there a lofty column, like a lone watcher amid the ruins of ages. Hour after hour we wandered around them, imagination filling up the ravages of time, and restoring many an attribute of its former grandeur. Several arches yet remain of the Basilica of Constantine, and eight pillars of the Ionic Portico, which adorned the Temple of Vespasian. Then the three columns of the Temple to Jupiter Tonans, erected by Augustus on the spot where he escaped a stroke of lightning. Not far away stands one lonely pillar of graceful Corinthian form; it needs no other history than the impressive words of Byron:

"Tully was not so eloquent as thou—
Thou nameless column with a buried base."

In the wall of the Temple of Venus at Rome we saw the niche where the goddess was enshrined. A richly variegated pavement is all that indicates the spot where stood the gorgeous Temple of Concord. It was there Cicero addressed the assembled Senate in language of immortal eloquence, denouncing the bold conspiracy of Catiline.

The Arch of Septimus Severus is wonderfully preserved from the inroads of decay. Beneath it runs the *Via Sacra*, leading up to the capitol. It is paved with huge blocks of lava, and is as smooth and broad as when Horace described it. The precise place was pointed out to us where grew the famous fig-tree, beneath whose widely spreading branches the wolf suckled Romulus and Remus, and the spot where the fathomless gulf opened, which the gods declared could only be filled by the richest treasures of the Roman people. Marcus Curtius, with heroic devotion to his country, leaped into the yawning abyss. It quickly closed forever, thus showing that good and true men are a nation's greatest wealth.

Churches are built up against the massive walls of the Temples of Pallas, of Mars, and of Antoninus and Faustina. Fragments of noble columns, of sculptured friezes, of entablatures, and capitals of pillars, are scattered around in wild profusion. The Romans delighted in the fresh and unconfined air of heaven; hence the Forum was their grand exchange, where all business, public and private, was transacted. Rostrums were erected within its spacious confines, where orators addressed the people, stirring up their bold passion for conquest, or exciting to internal strife. The wisest legislation the world ever knew, had there its origin. Statesmen and orators illustrated there its controlling and beneficial influence, and through long centuries it has descended a precious dower from the mighty minds of the olden time. The Forum was the centre of power,

> "Whence a mandate, eagle-winged,
> Went to the ends of the earth."

The Forum was like a great heart, whence the life-blood flowed to every portion of the vast empire.

Upon the wings of memory, far away into the dim labyrinth of the past, our thoughts were borne, and there, entangled in its mazes, we almost forgot the actual present. Soon, however, our wandering fancies were recalled by the necessity of escaping a large herd of cattle, and several flocks of goats and sheep, which, driven by the savage-looking and gaunt shepherds of the Campagna, came dashing down upon us. They certainly had the "right of way," for the Roman Forum is now a cattle-market—a kind of Smithfield, where buyers and sellers assemble.

Virgil relates in his Æneid a pleasant scene, where Evander and his guest Æneas are walking at evening along the Tarpeian rock and the Capitoline hill. In the vale below them herds of fat cattle, and flocks of sheep are grazing. That valley became the Forum. In the lapse of ages, the sacred spot where

"A thousand years of silenced factions sleep,"

has returned to the possession of its first occupants, "lowing herds and bleating flocks," and the grass springing from the broken pavement of the Temples of the gods is now their scanty and daily food.

We left the Forum, passing under the Arch of Titus, erected by the Roman Senate after the conquest of Jerusalem. The *bas reliefs* are very striking. They represent the Jews bearing away the treasures of the Temple. Among them, most conspicuous, is the "Seven-branched Candlestick," of colossal size. This was lost in the Tiber from the Milvian bridge, when Maxentius fled before the triumphant soldiers of Constantine. Josephus describes it in his history. We were told in Rome that even unto this day, the Jews avoid walking under the arch built to commemorate their downfall, and thus manifest their undying veneration for the "faith of their fathers."

Near the Arch of Titus are stupendous masses of brick, stone, and mortar. These are supposed to be the ruins of the Golden House of Nero, which Tacitus says "was the universal astonishment of the world." The palace was decorated with precious gems, with paintings, and Grecian statues. It had a banqueting room, whose ceiling was of ivory, and porticoes a mile in length.

Directly opposite to these ruins are the Baths of Titus, built upon the site of the house of Mæcenas. The walls of some of the chambers still retain their stucco, and are exquisitely painted.

"While stands the Coliseum, Rome shall stand;
When falls the Coliseum, Rome shall fall:
And when Rome falls, the world."

This prediction, made by the Anglo-Saxon pilgrims in the eighth century, has proved but the coinage of the enthusiast fancy. The Coliseum is crumbling fast away; Rome has fallen from her early grandeur; but the world progresses more proudly than ever, for that fair and glorious land beyond the broad Atlantic has been added to the treasures of time—that unrivalled land, the birthplace of Washington and of freedom, which seems, "Pallas-like, to have sprung from the head of Jove," with all the knowledge of departed centuries, and the experience of long-buried nations.

At the end of a soft and balmy day of spring, we first entered the Coliseum. Its immensity and desolation were overpowering. The lips absolutely refused to frame into words the emotions inspired by this grandest of ruins. So, to escape questions from our party concerning the impression made upon my mind, I stole away from them, and climbing up a mass of stone, I found a little nook, where I seated myself, and, free from interruption, gazed upon the wondrous extent of the majestic Coliseum. It is of oval form, and when perfect, the walls were one hundred and fifty feet in height. Now, the lofty rim around it is broken in all directions. The deep blue sky seemed to rest like a roof above the arches, which rose up tier over tier to the summit, where once floated an awning, as protection from the mid-day sun. It is built of *travertine* rock, whose coarse grain and porous texture afford a safe lodgment for the grains of dust. These soon become soil, whence spring myriads of flowers, and tufted bushes of dark green foliage. Nature appeared to have seized the ruin from decay, and hidden the ravages of the destroyer beneath a mantle of verdure, sprinkled with glowing blossoms, belonging to a flora unknown elsewhere save in ancient Rome. There were delicate vines clinging around enormous prostrate columns, while long tendrils, like garlands, were waving in the air. Along a terrace which encircled the arena, were still visible ranges of boxes, intended for the emperors and nobles. This was covered as though with a carpet, so various and brilliant-hued were the flowers growing upon it. Far up along the edge of the broken battlements was a fringe of green and shining ivy.

The Coliseum was commenced by Vespasian, and finished by his son Titus in the year A. D. 80, a few years after the destruction of Jerusalem. Twelve thousand captive Jews were compelled to labor incessantly in its construction, and when it was completed, for one hundred days gladiatorial combats were held within it, and thousands of Christians were torn to pieces by the wild tigers, lions, and leopards. During four hundred years the Coliseum was devoted to these fearful games, where gladiators met, or where savage beasts buried their claws in the quivering flesh of human beings. Seas of blood have washed over the broad arena, and myriads of martyrs to the faith of our holy Redeemer, have yielded up their souls to God within those circling walls. Hence, with all these memories crowding on the mind, I could readily picture the terrific scenes of those horrible days, when

> "The buzz of eager nations ran,
> In murmured pity, or loud-roared applause,
> As man was slaughtered by his fellow-man.
> And wherefore slaughtered? wherefore but because
> Such were the bloody circus' genial laws,
> And the imperial pleasure."

In the reign of Honorius these frightful combats were

abolished. The Coliseum remained perfect for many centuries, until it became a kind of quarry of stone and marble, with which many great palaces were built up. It is said that the nephew of Paul the Third asked permission to remove stone for only twelve hours. This being granted to him by his uncle, he employed four thousand men, who assailed the walls, and bore away sufficient material to build the *Farnese Palace*, one of the largest in Europe.

Pope Benedict, in 1750, caused a cross to be erected in the centre of the arena, and consecrated it to the martyrs who had perished within it. There are now rude altars, with paintings illustrating the progress of the Saviour from the prison to the place of his crucifixion. Just after twilight a long train of monks, with a linen mask entirely concealing their faces, went chanting around the arena. Great shadows falling from the walls above, seemed now and then to engulf them in dark caverns, as they passed along.

Even more suggestive of picturesque and wild grandeur was the Coliseum at night, when the bright stars were out, and the tender beams of the young moon were just disappearing beyond the ivy-crowned rim of the lofty walls. With that view ended our first visit; but often again did I see it. If Mont Blanc may be styled the "Monarch of Mountains;" the Coliseum may be justly hailed as the "Sovereign of Ruins."

During a long morning we wandered over the Palatine hill, amid the ruins of the palace of the Cæsars. It was Augustus, nephew and heir of Julius Cæsar, who first laid its foundation upon the site of the house of Cicero; although other emperors increased its dimensions, until it covered more than a mile of land. The central portion, however, interested me most, for it was there Augustus lived, with his tender and loving sister Octavia, whom he often proclaimed the paragon of her sex, and model of a Roman wife and mother. The gifted Octavia, still mourning the death of her husband, by the entreaties of her brother, was induced to give her hand to Mark Antony. This marriage, barren of love on both sides, was an act of policy with Augustus, to bind to him more closely and firmly the triumphant General of Julius Cæsar, who had so often led his legions to victory. In the great Hall of Reception, which adorned his gorgeous palace, the nuptials were celebrated, thereby dooming the noble Octavia to endless misery; for soon Mark Antony, ensnared by the wiles of Cleopatra, abandoned his virtuous wife for ever. Upon the terrace of the palace I lingered for several hours, with my thoughts full of the hapless fate of Octavia. In vain I strove to trace the outline of the building. Vines and ivy, wall-flowers and long wiry grass, are "massed and matted" so thickly together, it is only at rare intervals the marble columns or frescoes peep out. Gardens and vineyards cover a portion of the palace, while the neat and newly-painted villa of an English merchant occupies another.

"Behold the imperial Mount! 'tis thus the mighty falls."

The Baths of Caracalla are not far from the palace of the Cæsars. After the Coliseum, their ruins impress one more forcibly with the almost fabulous magnificence of Rome in its pride and prime, than any other we visited.

The Roman *Thermæ* were not only bathing-places, but comprised vast libraries, forums for debate, concert-rooms, saloons for eating and drinking, studios of pictures and Grecian statuary, splendid gardens, leafy groves, and immense chambers, whose floors were of exquisite mosaics. Amid all these enchantments of art and taste, the luxurious Romans passed days and nights in voluptuous pleasures. More than one mile in extent are the ruins of the Baths of Caracalla. They were covered with glowing spring-flowers.

Roaming hither and thither, I found myself quite alone in an enormously grand apartment. Having heard that beneath the vines and flowers there was the ancient floor, I tore them away, and removing the earth, came to a beautiful mosaic pavement. As I looked upon it, an eager fancy to take away a few stones as a souvenir seized me; and detaching some from the smooth mass, I carefully hid them in my pocket, for the voice of the old guardian was heard without; and casting back the crushed verdure, I quickly fled from his view, as it is not permitted to touch an atom of rock or stone.

We went through the ruins of many other *Thermæ.* In those of Diocletian one great hall was converted by Michael Angelo into the superb church of *Maria degli Angeli.*

Early one morning we started forth for the Campagna, and passing the Triumphal Arch of Constantine, whereon are sculptured in *bas relief* his numerous victories, we drove along the Appian Way, to the Tomb of Scipio. It is a winding labyrinth cut in the tufa rock, with many recesses, wherein were placed the bodies of all those who bore that name. They are all empty;

> "The Scipios' tomb contains no ashes now;
> The very sepulchres lie tenantless
> Of their heroic dwellers."

We went down into a Columbaria near by, where rest the ashes of the slaves of Augustus, and his sister Octavia. About two miles out upon the Campagna we came to the tomb of Cecelia Metella, erected by her husband Crassus more than nineteen hundred years ago. It is an immense tower, like a fortress, covered with ivy.

"Who was she, the lady of the dead,
Tombed in a palace?"

* * * * * * * *

"Alone we know,—Metella died,
The wealthiest Roman's wife: Behold his love or pride!"

It seemed the custom of the Romans to make the tombs of their dead along the great roads beyond the gates, that the remembrance of their ancestors might be the last thought in departing, and first when home-returning, of the sons of Rome. In all directions over the vast Campagna are great tombs, some converted into dwellings, and others into churches for the poor peasants.

Driving back to Rome, we entered the city by the *Porta Maggiore*, once an arch of the Claudian aqueduct. These aqueducts are wonderful evidences of the majesty of the Roman people. Far, far away beyond the power of vision they stretch over the green plain, their graceful arches broken at intervals by man or time. Passing the noble Basilica of St. John of Laterano, we went to the Mausoleum of Augustus, built by his command twenty-seven years before the birth of Christ. It was of matchless grandeur. The first person buried within it was the young Marcellus, son of Octavia, who was tenderly loved by his uncle, and intended by him as his successor. Marcellus was remarkable for his talent, beauty, and virtue. He died at the age of eighteen, almost adored by the Romans. Who that has read, can forget those thrilling lines of Virgil, wherein he bewails his untimely death, paying the tribute of tears to excellence such as Rome could never see again. Standing near that tomb, imagination painted the scene upon my mind—the noble retinue of Augustus, senators, and people, all clustering around the marble palace of the dead, into whose icy splendors the first occupant had just been placed; and Octavia, the wretched mother, bending over the beautiful form of her soul's idol, to take one last look of love, startled by the words of almost divine eloquence which burst from the lips of Virgil. For a time she listened, until the tumultuous waves of anguish swept away reason and consciousness, and she fell lifeless upon the bosom of the dead Marcellus. Years rolled on, and Augustus, his children, and Octavia, were all laid there too. Many of the bodies of the imperial family were burned in those days, and their ashes placed in urns. We saw the ashes of Octavia, preserved even until now, in a great vase of rock-crystal.

Many and many changes have come over the Mausoleum of Augustus. It has been a fortress, an amphitheatre for bull-fights, and is often used at present for fire-works and rope-dancing. But still, ever must it be a hallowed spot. The memory of Octavia, of Marcellus, and of Virgil, are as guardian angels to snatch it from the oblivion of time.

Crossing the long and statue-decorated bridge over the Tiber, we stopped at the *Castle of St. Angelo*, built by the Emperor Hadrian as his mausoleum, a hundred and thirty years after the birth of Christ. All the circular edifices of ancient Rome are well preserved. As they possess no salient points, time and the elements seem to sweep around them.

> "The Mole which Hadrian reared on high,
> Imperial mimic of old Egypt's piles,"

now serves as a fortress filled with French soldiers. A dashing and jaunty young officer was our guide in the crypt below, where once lay the Emperor's body. We also were shown the cell occupied by Benvenuto Cellini, the famous artist. From the summit near the colossal statue of the archangel Michael, with drawn sword, the view is magnificent. The young Frenchman was bitterly lamenting the stern necessity which compelled him to tarry in the Castle, while his comrades were " winning laurels of victory in the Crimea." Poor creatures! these laurels, alas! are too often strewed over their graves.

By the gate of San Paolo is the *Pyramid of Caius Cestius.* It is about one hundred and thirty feet in height, with walls of prodigious thickness. From the inscription upon it, we judged that Caius Cestius was a tribune, and one of the seven persons appointed to prepare the banquets for the gods.

Beneath the shadow of this tall Pyramid is the tomb of Shelley, that bright and erratic genius, so fondly loved and so truly mourned. Flowers were growing in profusion around his grave, green bay trees, and the wide-leaved cactus. There is only his name, and the words, " Cor Cordium," (the heart of hearts.) After he was drowned in the Bay of Spezzia, his body was burned on the shore, but his heart remained unconsumed; it was brought here, and buried by the side of his child, who had before been interred in this Protestant burial-ground.

> "Nothing of him that doth fade,
> But doth suffer a sea-change
> Into something rich and strange."

Thus runs the inscription on the marble slab.

Alone in a little green meadow was the grave of Keats; in death, as in life, he appeared isolated and neglected. Sad was the fate of the author of " Endymion." Even in his youth a shadow of despair hovered over him, and though at times his spirit, defying its influence, burst forth into song, where beauty, like his own oft-quoted words,

> "Is a joy for ever,"

too soon, alas! his noble heart, the home of every generous impulse, was crushed to death by cruelty and injustice. Upon his simple tomb is a single line, suggested by himself:

> "Here lies one whose name was writ in water."

CHAPTER XLV.

At the close of a beautiful afternoon we drove over the Campagna to the *Fountain of Egeria*, which derives such pleasant interest from the tradition telling of the meetings there of Numa with the Nymph. Livy and Juvenal both mention it in their works, but it is to Byron the fountain owes its greatest charm. He has thrown around it an enchantment of poetry which will outlast all the records of historians.

> "Egeria! sweet creation of some heart
> Which found no mortal resting-place so fair
> As thine ideal breast,—whate'er thou art,
> . . . whatsoe'er thy birth,
> Thou wert a beautiful thought, and softly bodied forth."

We seated ourselves within the grotto by the green hillside. A stream of sparkling water fell into a great basin of granite, and thence flowed away through the meadow, now a perfect parterre of spring-flowers. The grotto was covered with the most delicate and ethereal plant I ever beheld, called "Egeria's Hair." It is almost as thin and gauze-like as the spider's web.

Crowning the hill above are the ruins of the *Temple of Bacchus*, and not far distant the entrance to the *Catacombs.*

Into these we did not venture, as persons are often lost in their dark and gloomy caverns. Returning, we stopped at the *Circus Maximus*, the scene of the Rape of the Sabines in the days of Romulus. It is a mass of ruins, still preserving, however, the semi-circular curve of the terraces, upon which were the seats of the nobles and people. Then onward, we passed down to the *Ponte Rotto*, over the Tiber. Near this is the *Temple of Vesta*. It is quite small, and perfectly round, encircled with twenty columns of Corinthian marble. A young American artist from my native State (Georgia), had his studio in a house just upon the bank of the Tiber. From his balcony we had a most splendid view of St. Peter's, as the glowing rays of the setting sun tinted with golden light the majestic dome. As we looked, the golden hue changed to rose-color, then to purple, and at last darkness fell like a black mantle over it. We were quite charmed with our youthful compatriot, and with his genial manner and earnest appreciation of the beautiful. He has a noble gift of talent as an artist.

Augustus boasted that he "found Rome of brick and left it marble." Hence, in all directions, the grandest ruins were of monuments constructed by his command. The *Theatre of Marcellus* and the *Portico of Octavia* are near each other. It was evidently the delight of Augustus to do honor to his lovely and gifted sister, the uncared-for wife of Mark Antony. Her name he gave to this glorious portico. A magnificent double colonnade was roofed over, to afford shelter and shade to those who walked and talked within it. In the centre of the grand area which these columns enclosed, were marble temples to Jupiter and Juno. In the Portico of Octavia painters displayed their works for criticism or for approbation. It was likewise decorated with superb statuary. Pliny speaks of a Venus of marvellous beauty, sculptured by

Phidias, as one of its chief adornments. This famous statue is supposed to be the Venus de Medici.

The Theatre of Marcellus is now the palace of a Roman Prince, and the noble Portico of Octavia is converted into a *pescheria*, (fish-market,) in the midst of the Ghetto, a crowded part of the city, where all the Jews were forced to live, it mattered not how great their numbers. The Roman Jews are the descendants of the captive people brought by Titus from Jerusalem. There were gates to their quarter of the city, and at a certain hour of the night they were always locked in. When the present Pope came into power he abolished this severe law, and had the wall across the street and the gates thrown down, and permitted to the hitherto despised Israelites many withheld privileges.

Amid "the relics of nobler days and noblest arts," the *Pantheon* stands unrivalled for its simple and majestic architecture. It was built by Agrippa, before the birth of our Saviour; and although near two thousand years have pressed upon it, still, noble and erect, it springs from the hands of time—

> "Shrine of all saints, and temple of all gods,
> From Jove to Jesus."

The portico is admirable, with columns of the Corinthian order. The interior is a grand rotunda, above which rises a symmetrical dome. The Pantheon has no windows, but the light falls through an opening in the top, and appears to fill the whole space with a fresh brightness from the blue sky itself. The pavement is of porphyry and other precious marbles; and though yearly it is overflowed by the waters from the Tiber, and receives the rain through the aperture in the roof, it is still beautiful. The "divine Raphael" is entombed near one of the altars, (for the Pantheon is now a church.)

As I looked upon the slab which tells of his warm and generous heart and gifted mind, up rose to memory the grand pageant of his burial within this

"Pantheon! pride of Rome!"

As we drove down the Capitoline hill, we came to the *Mamertine Prison*, into whose dungeons we descended. They are cut out of the solid rock, and are cold, frightful places of imprisonment. No wonder the bold Jugurtha cried out when placed within this hideous cell, "The Thermæ of Rome are cold instead of hot." There he perished from starvation—the reckless soldier who had passed more than half his life beneath the burning suns of Africa.

In the Mamertine, St. Peter was imprisoned by the command of Nero. The old custode pointed out with great reverence the pillar to which he was bound, and the well of water which so miraculously sprung up. From it he baptized his jailers. Catiline and his companion conspirators were strangled in the same dungeon.

By the Arch of Janus we saw the *Cloaca Maxima*, a subterranean canal running under the city. It was the great sewer of ancient Rome, and is considered among the most wonderful monuments of antiquity. Although it has been built twenty-four hundred years, it is still firm and perfect. The blocks of stone are put together, like all the ruins of the Etruscan period, without cement. Tarquin, fifth king of Rome, caused it to be constructed, one hundred and fifty years after the foundation of the city.

Upon the summit of the Capitoline hill is the *Tarpeian Rock:*

"The promontory whence the traitor's leap
Cur'd all ambition."

It is now covered with miserable houses and consumptive-looking gardens.

Glorious memories crowd upon the mind at the sound of those words, the "*Roman Capitol!*" The great Tree of Power planted thereon o'ershadowed with its spreading branches nearly all the lands of the earth. Eagerly, and with throbbing pulse, we ascended the long flight of steps leading to the piazza above. In its centre was the bronze equestrian statue of *Marcus Aurelius*, unequalled by any modern work, it is said. So wonderful did Michael Angelo deem it, that he often was wont to stand before it, and call out, "Go!" there seem such life and spirit in the limbs of the horse. The noble rider appears to be bending in recognition of the acclamations of the populace. His handsome face beams with kindness and sympathy.

Along the balustrade are the colossal statues of *Castor & Pollux*, and other pieces of sculpture, dug from the ruins of Rome. The *Palace of the Senator* is erected upon the foundation of the temple of the tutelar gods of the empire, and is still occupied by a senator, who there holds his court. It was he who crowned with laurel poets and artists, in the midst of vast assemblages. Petrarch was crowned there, and Corilla Olympica, the only woman who ever was thus honored. She was a miracle of talent, gifted as a poet and improvisatrice, but neither young nor lovely. It is supposed that the incident of her coronation furnished a theme for the history of the beautiful Corinne of Italy, by Madame de Staël.

Besides the Palace of the Senator there are two others, the *Palace of the Conservatori*, (administrative officers,) and the *Museum of the Capitol.* These buildings, although designed by Michael Angelo, are exceedingly ugly, outwardly, though within they are rich in noble works of art. In the first are thousands of busts of the great of old, filling long lines of rooms. The colossal statue of *Julius Cæsar* is splendid, and is the only authentic one remaining. The *Bronze Wolf* is there, with the legs half melted by lightning. Cicero mentions the circumstance in one of his orations against Catiline, and Virgil also relates it in his flowing verse. The wolf has a starved look, and the twins, (Romulus and Remus) are rather poor specimens of children.

The picture-gallery has a multitude of paintings, but not many of rare excellence.

Crossing the piazza, we went to the Museum, wherein are gathered noble relics of the olden time. There we saw the world-renowned mosaic of *Pliny's Doves*. It is thus called from the description given of it by Pliny. It was discovered in Hadrian's villa. There is also another mosaic, representing Hercules conquered by love.

In a large oval room we saw the *Venus of the Capitol*, an exquisite representation of a beautiful woman, and near it the enchanting group of *Cupid and Psyche*, full of pure and child-like sweetness, of delicate gracefulness and fresh young love. In all the cabinets of sculpture we met *Leda and the Swan*.

Through grand saloons we passed onward. These were all tenanted by busts and statues of emperors and empresses, of philosophers, orators, poets, and historians. In the *Hall of the Faun* there is the tablet of bronze, from which Rienzi expounded to his followers the power of the Roman people. In the last room is the *Dying Gladiator*, a statue of such pathetic and surpassing interest, that we were riveted before it, as though turned to marble ourselves. I can only say of it, that the stanzas of Byron, (themselves a bright creation of genius,) are worthy of the theme: for ever are the two linked together. Every one has read those touching lines, so graphic and true a picture of this masterpiece of sculpture:

> "I see before me the Gladiator lie.
> He leans upon his hand his manly brow—
> Consents to death, but conquers agony,
> And his drooped head sinks gradually low;
> And from his side the last drops, ebbing slow
> From the red gash, fall heavy one by one.
> . . . . . . His eyes
> Were with his heart, and that was far away
> Where his rude hut by the Danube lay.
> *There* were his young barbarians all at play;
> *There* was their Dacian mother—he their sire,
> Butchered to make a Roman holiday."

We gave one long day to the ruins of Hadrian's villa, and to an excursion to Tivoli. Starting at sunrise, we drove by the *Forum of Trajan*, from whose centre rises a lofty column adorned with *bas reliefs*. A statue of the Emperor Trajan once adorned it, but the figure of St. Peter has replaced it now. Through the gate of San Lorenzo we passed out into the Campagna, no longer desolate in appearance, for spring had showered over it myriads of flowers, amid which were stalking, with stately strides, the great dun-colored cattle, with immense black horns, like polished ebony. Our road was along the *Via Tibertina*, still paved with its ancient blocks of lava.

Beyond the Anio, we came to the *Lago di Tartaro*, whose waters possess such petrifying qualities, that every substance thrown within them is converted into a stone called *travertine*. Of this material nearly all the buildings of Rome are constructed. The walls of the Coliseum, and the crumbling masses of the Palace of the Cæsars, were perhaps thousands and thousands of years ago held in solution by lakes of water like the one we gazed upon to-day. Our coachman stopped the carriage, and opening the door, gravely informed us we were near the "Tartarian regions." Of this we were quite aware, for the odor of sulphur was powerfully strong. Walking nearly one mile amid the curious petrifactions, we came to the heart of the lake, which is now contracted into a very small circle. Canes, branches of trees, and mosses even, were all rock. Some of these we gathered up and threw into the water. The gases thus disturbed caused it to "boil and bubble" like a vast cauldron.

Near by this lake are the ruins of the *Baths of Agrippa*, where Zenobia spent many years of her life, after she had graced the triumphal entry into Rome of the Conqueror of Palmyra. Not far off is the *Bridge of Lucano.* This view of the bridge, and of the mausoleum of the Plautia family, was seized by Poussin as the most admirable landscape of the Campagna.

Diverging from the main road, we visited the ruins of Hadrian's villa. This Roman Emperor, wearied with conquest, resolved to create for the joy of his declining years an earthly paradise. He therefore selected this beautiful portion of earth, with its rocky hills, its quiet valleys, its rushing streams, and forest-crowned heights. A space of ground was then enclosed, ten miles square. Thousands and tens of thousands of laborers were then set to work, and soon the ground was covered by imperial palaces, by libraries, theatres, academies, and miles of colonnades and porticoes. There was a miniature likeness of the Vale of Tempe, and groves resembling the Elysian Fields. We were fortunate in having a well-informed guide, who pointed out in an interesting manner the *locale* of the most famous buildings. The palace and its noble surroundings were just completed, when Hadrian was attacked with a violent disease, and died. In after years the treasures of art he had gathered went to enrich the temples of Rome. Forests of splendid trees are growing along the spacious corridors and the gorgeous saloons, and ivy and clematis cling along the walls in place of the pictures of their earlier days. In great profusion, every where, in the ruined *proscenium* of the Greek theatre as well as in the grove dedicated to the muses, we saw a peculiar and luxuriant shrub, with a bright and sweet-scented yellow flower. This the guide told us was brought from the East by Hadrian, and planted here by his own hands. Bronze, marble, and even adamant have perished, but this delicate flower, surviving all, still breathes its perfume on the air, as though its sweetness were a tribute to the memory of that emperor who transplanted it to these lovely glades, far more genial, it would seem, than the burning sands of its native Asia.

Through the midst of a grove of venerable olive trees we drove onward to *Tivoli*, a city of Greek origin, which existed hundreds of years before the foundation of Rome. It was the favorite retreat, during the existence of the Empire, of Augustus Cæsar, of Catullus, Horace, and Mæcenas. Now it is a miserable, squalid abode of poverty. Leaving the carriage, we went directly to the *Temple of the Tibertine Sybil*, a small circular edifice, with a graceful colonnade of richly-sculptured pillars. It is perched on the top of a high cliff, overlooking the valley of the *Cascatelle* (the cascades). This valley is a deep abyss, encircled by lofty mountains, which rise around it in the form of an amphitheatre. The river Anio leaps from a mass of verdure, and dashing madly over stupendous terraces of rock, plunges into a dark cavern, where it is lost to the light of day. The gulf is bridged over at times by beautiful rainbows, and then left in misty gloom.

From the Temple of the Sybil we descended a winding pathway, until we came to the *Cave of Neptune* and the

Grotto of the Syren. Through these dart rapidly downward streams of water. The entire river once passed along them, but in consequence of frightful inundations, and thereby great loss of life, the Pope ordered that a mountain-peak should be pierced by a tunnel, and thus draw off the vast volume of water which poured through the valley of the Cascatelle. Climbing over the huge rocks, we saw the deep chasms and caves worn by the rushing river in its ancient days.

Having seen all the wonders of the Syren's Grotto, we carefully stepped over the slippery stones, which form a dangerous-looking bridge amidst the foaming rapids of the Anio, ere it takes another leap, and swinging ourselves up by catching to the branches of trees, we reached the opposite side of the ravine. There we found donkeys awaiting us, and, mounting them, rode along the verge of the precipice for several miles. We passed the arched grottoes of the tunnel, and stopped to look into them. The water runs swiftly over the smooth floor of solid rock, and springing over enormous ledges of granite, disappears in the thickly wooded vale below.

Our ride was enchanting. Every turn of the path brought us to a new scene of beauty. There was the farm of Horace, which he loved so well, he often declared it would be rapture to pass an entire lifetime within its leafy groves. The foundation of the villa is still visible, and my donkey-driver, who was quite a classic scholar, (in a livery of rags,) quoting the poet's words in the original, asserted the olive trees were planted by the hands of the "immortal Horace." The *Villa of Mæcenas* deserves more the name of a palace, for it is of great size. It is made use of now as an iron forge, worked by the water-power of the Anio. Sheets of foam were gushing out from the vast windows, and the red glare from the fires flashed along the lofty arcades of the portico. The *Villa d'Este* is exquisitely situated. In truth, all the ruins are so picturesquely placed, it seems as though nature and art had purposely arranged them to delight the eyes of mortals.

We dined at Tivoli, in the portico of the Sybil's Temple, and drove back to Rome at night. The delicious twilight, with its purple hues, had long vanished into darkness ere we reached the walls.

The beggars of Rome! oh! they are really wonderful! as numerous as the legions of Augustus, and possessed of an eloquence as pathetic and overwhelming as the words of Cicero. It is impossible to escape them. They are every where—on the steps of palaces and churches, at the doorways of houses and shops, amid the ruins, and far out on the Campagna. At early morning, at mid-day, and even at midnight, they assailed us, in every form of expression and every tone of wretchedness. The maimed held up their crushed limbs to view; creatures legless and armless rolled themselves over and over across our path; beings almost entirely paralyzed, twisted along with a snake-like movement to our feet. Every variety of disease, deformity, and misery, appeared before us in our wanderings about the city. People told me, when I first arrived, that I would soon become indifferent to these touching appeals for charity; but, alas! I did not find it so. Often looking upon these horrid objects, had no power to blunt and dull the sharp pang which always struck my heart at the sight of them. With all this frightful starvation and destitution, we were assured, by persons of high and honorable distinction, that there were more houses of charity in Rome than any other city on earth of its population. The monks of the monasteries and the nuns of the convents feed multitudes of the poor daily. From the kitchen-doors of cardinals and bishops the poor are never sent away empty-handed. There are societies of noble ladies, and of the Holy Brotherhood, who clothe and give food to the wretched creatures. Still, with all these associations of charity, and the kindness of individuals, the beggars appear as innumerable as the sands upon the shores of the sea.

We were vastly amused by watching the assemblage of professional "models," gathered one bright evening on the immense steps leading up to the Trinita di Monti from the Piazza di Spagna. These models earn their "daily bread," by standing before artists and sculptors as originals for pictures and statues. There was a noble-looking old man, with a long white beard, whom they told us often served for "St. Peter," "St. Joseph," or "Moses." His little great-grandson, clad in sheepskin, was "St. John." A wild, fierce, dark-haired man filled the *rôle* of the "Brigand." A pretty peasant-woman, with a baby in her arms, was a good "Madonna;" and several young girls, with rich complexions, brilliant eyes, lithe and exquisitely moulded forms, were the "Psyches," the "Eves," and the "Venuses" of many a studio in Rome. These models seemed well-fed, and had a well-satisfied air about them. When any one looked very eagerly at them, they instantly fancied they were artists, and forthwith threw themselves into most artistic attitudes—the "Brigand" grasping his great knife, and twirling his long moustache; the "Madonna" looking down tenderly upon the infant in her arms; and the "Venus," springing into a *pose* of indescribable grace, glanced slyly at us through the lashes of her lustrous eyes.

The fountains of Rome are exceedingly numerous, and were always to me a pure delight. I cannot express what a joy it was to look upon their ever-flowing waters, so fresh, transparent, and bright. The Swedenborgians, I believe, consider the mention of water, when it occurs in the Bible, as typical of truth and purity, an emblem of the soul's regeneration. Our blessed Saviour has promised " living waters " to those who love Christ and come to him. Often did the various words concerning the revivifying element come over my mind, while standing by the fountains, where I passed a brief portion of time every day. Sweet as the notes of music was the sound of the falling waters, and bright as a happy thought the play of the perpetually-flowing stream. The *Fountain of Trevi* is the most majestic. It gushes from the base of the Palazzo Conti, and falls over rocks picturesquely placed. Upon them stands a statue of Neptune in a car, surrounded by tritons. In the Piazza of Navona there are three fountains in the midst of river-gods. During the summer these are permitted to inundate the square, forming thus a mimic lake, in which the people take an *al fresco* bath.

Near the church of *Maria degli Angeli* is the *Fountain of Happy Water*, adorned with a colossal figure of Moses striking the rock. The poor artist who made the statue died of grief, when he heard the ridicule it excited after it was placed upon its pedestal.

All the " seven hills of Rome," every square, every palace and villa, and many private residences, are embellished with fountains, whose sparkling rush of waters is constantly a refreshment to the mind and senses.

Soon after the Holy Week was over, Gaspar, the excellent young Spanish priest, (our travelling companion from Marseilles to Rome,) accompanied me one day to the *Propaganda Fide*, in the Piazza di Spagna. Our good friend, Bishop Portier, of Mobile, had given me a letter to Monsignore Barnebo, the secretary of the institution, who received me with warm and cordial kindness. He was a most charming person, learned and gifted. Many were the pleasant visits I made to him during our sojourn in Rome. We were always received in the great library of the college, where Monsignore often presented me to distinguished dignitaries of the church, cardinals and bishops. Rarely have I met more intellectual and accomplished men; and it is a delight even now to recall the recollections of the varied and interesting topics of conversation.

The library contained many valuable books and manuscripts, among others the writings of Mezzofanti, the greatest linguist the world ever knew. He was a native of Bologna, and in early life became remarkable for his facility in acquiring foreign languages. There were many anecdotes and incidents concerning him related to me. A man from the north of Europe came to him one day, and spoke a most difficult *patois*, which it was almost impossible to comprehend.. As the cardinal had never heard it before, he was peculiarly interested in it, and desired the man to come every day, and always to speak to him in that dialect, explaining the meaning of the different words through the medium of his scanty store of Italian. At length, to the utter amazement of the northman, Mezzofanti spoke to him in his own wild *patois*. "How could Monsignore have learned the language? for no other man in Rome, except myself, knows one word of it," inquired he. The cardinal laughingly replied, "It is yourself who was my teacher. I never forget a word I once hear."

There is a belief with many Italians, that his wonderful power to acquire languages was a divine inspiration. When he was a very young priest, he was summoned to confess two criminals who were to die next day. Going into their deep, dark cells, he found they could not understand one word he said. Discovering what was their native land, he retired to his room, and in one night acquired a sufficient knowledge of their language to receive their confessions, grant them absolution, and give them the consolations of holy religion, ere they were executed. From that moment he had never the slightest difficulty in acquiring any language. It would seem as though the noble and heart-warm purpose which urged on his mind during that weary night, had proved its own reward; and the earnest prayer for power to console two dying creatures, was miraculously blessed by God himself.

The Count Borromeo, cardinal and chamberlain to his Holiness, we met several times in the library. He is the son of the owner of that paradise of Isola Bella which we visited a year ago. In our conversations about the Pope, it was really charming to hear of the many acts of clemency and disinterested kindness which mark his daily life.

Cardinal Antinelli, who is deemed by every one to be the moving and ruling spirit of the government, is a most striking-looking man, with a lofty brow, and stern energy of expression.

The college of the Propaganda Fide was founded more than two centuries ago, as an institution for the education of youths from every portion of the world, as missionaries, to carry the Word of God to distant lands, and teach it to the heathens and infidels there. One morning, while I was visiting Monsignore Barnebo, the scholars started forth for their promenade. There was a curious assemblage of all hues and complexions—the Ethiopian and the Norwegian, the Persian and the American, the Turk and the Englishman, the Arab and the Frenchman, the East Indian and the Mexican, the German and the Spaniard, the South Sea Islander and the Cuban. Many were only lads, while others were well-grown men. They were all dressed in long gowns, and walked demurely side by side, while their teachers (all priests) attended them.

During the past winter there was a grand gathering in Rome of all the dignitaries of the churches of the whole Catholic world. They assembled, with great pomp and state, to discuss and decide the dogma of the Immaculate Conception. To commemorate this meeting and its decision, a splendid and colossal statue of the Holy Virgin is to be erected just in front of the Propaganda Fide. The workmen are now engaged in building the pedestal upon which it is to rest.

CHAPTER XLVI.

The palaces of Rome are exceedingly numerous; and as there is a great family resemblance between them, I need only describe a few. They are all built around a *cortile*, or court, which is encircled by balconies or colonnades of pillars. The lower story has barred windows, and usually serves for shops of mechanics. Great marble staircases lead to the upper stories. The rooms are of immense size, with very little furniture, but a vast wealth of pictures and glowing frescoes. These palaces have mostly been built by dignitaries of the church, who, having no sons or daughters to inherit their riches, have sought to perpetuate their names by the enduring creations of gifted artists, whose most precious works their gold could purchase.

The *Colonna* palace is perhaps the most splendid in Rome. Its vestibule has columns of alabaster, and its walls are covered with pictures and immense mirrors. Above the gilt cornice springs the arched ceiling, upon which is painted the Battle of Lepanto. For his noble deeds during that bloody day, one of the Colonnas received a public triumph at the capitol. There are many portraits of the princes of the family painted by Rubens and Vandyke. That of Vittoria

Colonna, the sweet poetess and friend of Michael Angelo, is very lovely. The gardens are extensive, and contain fragments of the entablature of the Temple of the Sun, which once crowned the hill in their centre. The ruins of the Baths of Constantine are within it, and used as granaries. We were told, as an evidence of the downfall of this once famous family, that within a few years past, the last princess of the house had married a man who made his fortune as a peddler in the square of the Colonna. Such even here was the aristocracy of wealth, that the princess and the peddler were deemed equals, and the descendant of the heroic prince, addressed by Petrarch as

> "The glorious Colonna, sole support
> And hope of the great Roman name,"

became the bride of the low-born peasant.

In the gardens of the *Rospigliosi* palace is a small casino, upon whose ceiling is painted the Aurora of Guido, surely one of the most exquisite frescoes in the world. Aurora seems floating before the chariot of the god of day, casting flowers beneath the horses' feet, while her attendant nymphs, types of the rosy hours, hover around her. The coloring is brilliant, and a golden hue tinges the whole picture, lighting up the landscape below, which seems just throwing off the shades of night.

In the Villa Ludovici we saw the Aurora of Guercino, another and bolder revelation of the loveliness of the rosy goddess. She is seated in her gorgeous car of day, and is scattering flowers over the earth below her. Before the spirited forms of the horses, the hours are flying, extinguishing with their delicate hands the stars of night yet lingering in the sky. The villa is said to be upon the grounds once the garden of Sallust. It is very difficult to obtain an entrance to its gallery. One of the courteous cardinals I met at the Propaganda, procured a permission for us to visit it. There we saw the colossal bust of Juno, a noble work of antiquity, and an illustration from the poems of Sophocles, representing Orestes as he recognizes his sister Electra. The gardens are formal and stately, like those of Versailles, with many statues and gushing fountains.

In the *Barberini* Palace we saw the original picture of Beatrice Cenci, said to have been painted by Guido from memory, after he had seen her on the scaffold. Her sad story, woven into the verse of Shelley, gives additional interest to the painting, which is in itself the history of a gentle nature crushed and driven to madness by fearful outrage. The loveliness of the young face is inconceivably touching. The tender and appealing look of the eyes appeared to haunt me for long hours after we had seen them. One day, in driving along a gloomy quarter of the old city, our coachman pointed out the Cenci Palace where the terrible scenes resulting in the death of the fair Beatrice were enacted. It is a stern, dismal-looking edifice.

In this palace we also saw the Fornarina of Raphael, considered by the world as the image of his earthly love. The painting is exquisite; the eyes large, bold, and bright; the bosom very fully revealed; and the arms of unrivalled perfection. There is an animal beauty about the face, but no soul or tenderness; and as I gazed upon it, I could not realize that the delicate organization of a nature like Raphael's could rest its sympathies upon a being so evidently sensuous as the Fornarina.

In the *Borghese* Palace there is an immense collection of pictures—among the most admirable, the Chase of Diana, by Domenichino, and Raphael's Entombment of Christ, and his portrait of Cæsar Borgia; the Danae of Correggio, and the Earthly and Divine Love of Titian.

The *Doria* Palace is of stupendous size, with long lines of rooms filled with fine pictures of great artists. In one of them we saw the portrait of Lucretia Borgia, by Giulio Romano. It is of a woman in the full bloom of life, with a warm, richly-tinted complexion, luxuriant auburn hair, full lips, and large brown eyes, expressing powerful energy, and intensity of passion.

The *Sciarra* Palace, on the Corso, has only a few, but choice pictures. Among the most valued is the Suonatore of Raphael (The Violin Player). This is supposed to be a portrait of the artist himself. It is wonderful for the life-like expression of the tender eyes. Then there is the Bella Donna of Titian. The ripe, warm glow upon her cheek is like

> "The dusky bloom upon the peach, which tells
> How rich within the soul of sweetness dwells."

At the *Corsini* Palace we looked with delight upon the Madonna and Child of Carlo Dolci. The mother's face is pure, holy, and serene. The infant Christ lies asleep in her arms, with the soft lips parted in a half smile, as though whispered to by angel-voices. In one of the rooms Christina, Queen of Sweden, died. This palace was her residence. After her conversion to the Catholic religion, she never quitted Rome.

The pride of the *Spada* Palace is the colossal statue of Pompey, which has been the source of so much controversy as to its identity with that at whose base "great Cæsar fell."

> "And thou, dread statue! yet existent in
> The austerest form of naked majesty;
> Thou who beheldest, 'mid the assassins' din,
> At thy bathed base the bloody Cæsar lie,

Folding his robe in dying dignity,
An offering to thine altar from the queen
Of gods and men, great Nemesis!"

It is related that when the French were masters of Rome, Voltaire's tragedy of Brutus was performed in the Coliseum, and the statue of Pompey removed there. During the last act, the Brutus of the play was slain at the base of the statue. They were compelled to saw off one arm of the statue to accomplish this great dramatic effect. It has since been restored.

The *Farnese* Palace, built from the stones and marble of the Coliseum, is full of relics from the ancient ruins. There is the Parian marble sarcophagus taken from the tomb of Cecelia Metella, and which contained her ashes once; granite basin from the Baths of Caracalla; vases, columns, and other fragments. The ceilings are of frescoes by Annibale Caracci, and represent subjects from heathen mythology, nearly all illustrating the passion of love.

The *Farnesina* Palace (belonging, like the Farnese, to the King of Naples) is a palace of wondrous interest, from the frescoes of Raphael, representing the story of Psyche and Cupid, and the Triumph of Galatea: both paintings of matchless grace, and of delicious and delicate beauty. The great banker, Agostino Chigi, a man of incredible wealth, erected this palace in 1506, purposely to entertain Pope Leo the Tenth, his cardinals and ambassadors. So runs the story, at least. At one of the banquets of this modern Mæcenas, this Amphitryon of Rome, he had fish served up brought from Spain and Constantinople, and parrots' tongues from Africa. All the golden dishes were thrown into the Tiber after the repast, that no other hands should ever profane them.

The *Quirinal* is the summer Palace of the Pope of Rome. It is upon a peak of the Quirinal hill, on the square of Monte Cavallo, thus called from the colossal group of Castor and Pollux holding their horses. They seem as fresh and perfect as when they came from the hands of Phidias and Praxiteles, the immortal Grecian sculptors, near twenty-four centuries ago. We ascended long marble stairways, and passed on through great rooms, with draperies of crimson and gold, and adorned with the pictures of noble artists. We went into the Pope's library and to his bed-chamber. A very cold, dreary-looking chamber it was, destitute of all furniture save a bed, a chair, and a cushion before the *prie-dieu*, where he knelt for prayer. The dining saloon was also very cheerless in aspect. There he dines for ever alone. No one ever eats at the same table with the Pope.

The gardens are a mile in circuit. The trees are cut into long aisles, into arches, grottoes, and vast colonnades. Statues of nymphs, of fairies, and of satyrs, peep from out the verdant foliage, and surround the numerous fountains, which dart up from marble basins in all directions.

In the Quirinal assemble the conclave of cardinals, to elect a new Pope, when the old one expires. They are shut up somewhat after the fashion of our jury until their verdict is rendered. An interesting story was told me of the election to the pontifical chair of Mastai Ferreti, the present Pope. When Pope Gregory died, the sacred college assembled to elect his successor—each cardinal seated on a kind of throne in the chapel, all equal, since any one of their number might be chosen as the supreme ruler of the Catholic world. Lambruschini, minister of the former Pope, was deemed the probable choice of the cardinals. Mastai Ferreti called out the names when the ballots were opened. There were fifteen votes for Lambruschini, and thirteen for Mastai. As his name was uttered by his own lips for the last time, a white dove flew in at the window, and fluttered around his head. Thirteen members only of that august conclave knew the virtues and honesty of Mastai. Far away from the court and its factions, he had passed his life in the exercise of his ministry, to comfort, to cheer, and save the erring, to uphold the sinking heart, and sustain the courage of the faithful. He had no ambition for power, no desire to possess it. Again and again the ballotings continued. Each time they were opened, Mastai had gained an additional vote; and with trembling lips he announced his own name, until the last ballot was about to be opened. Then he implored the conclave to depute some other person to read them. This could not be, and they begged him to wait until he was more calm. Pale and almost speechless from the before unthought-of responsibility now resting upon him, he opened the last ballot, and pronounced his name for the thirty-sixth time, (the number of votes required to elect him.) One loud cry of acclamation resounded through the chapel. Mastai, unheeding it, sank upon his knees in devout prayer. So touching was the humility and meekness of his attitude, and the saint-like expression of his face as he knelt, forgetful of all around, and in earnest communion with his God, that tears burst from every eye, and all felt they had named as their supreme pontiff, an honest, true-hearted, and noble man.

From the balcony of the Quirinal it was announced to the countless throngs which surrounded, and their shouts of triumphant joy floated far over the wide Campagna, and even crept down to the dark dungeons, where for years had languished the weary and the wretched prisoners. All hearts throbbed with exultation, and for days and days Rome was almost mad with joy. Many a dungeon-door was opened, and the prisoner permitted to take in at one glance the light of heaven, and the light of loving eyes. Often did the Romans tell me of those glorious days, when the hope of a brighter future dawned upon them. Then, with a dark look, they would add, " But the French have darkened our lives again."

Just without the walls, near to the Porta del Popolo, is the entrance to the Villa *Borghese*. Ere its grounds were devastated by the Roman Republicans, in 1849, it was said to have been a paradise of smiling glades, quiet dells, long avenues, broad plains, thick groves, and sparkling fountains. A sad air of neglect and decay now hangs over it.

In the Casino (principal building) there are many works of art, modern as well as ancient. Upon the upper portion of the wall, opposite the entrance, is a colossal group in *bas relief* of Marcus Curtius leaping into the gulf of the forum. Then another, by Bernini, of Apollo and Daphne, which represents the transformation of the flying nymph into the laurel, just as the god is about to seize her. The hands and fingers are already leaves and stems, and around the legs the bark is formed and the foliage springing out. It is a very curious and remarkable work. In another apartment is Canova's statue of La Venus Victorieuse, for which the Princess Pauline (sister of Napoléon the Great) sat as a model. It is very beautiful. The figure is Eve-like in costume, save a slight scarf thrown over the form. From the absence of all drapery arose the question by a friend to Pauline, " How could you endure such exposure ? " The Princess quietly answered, " It was not in the slightest degree unpleasant, the room was so well warmed ;" thus accepting her friend's inquiry as a question of personal comfort, and not of delicacy of feeling.

The Villa *Albani* is very lovely, and its collection of sculpture is ranked next to that of the Vatican. As the friend and librarian of Cardinal Albani, Winckelman lived many years in the Villa, continuing his researches, which have given so much delight to thousands.

The Villa *Pamphili Doria* has more extensive grounds than any other near Rome. They are many miles in circumference, and are filled with gardens, with lakes, groves, avenues, and terraces.

The Villa *Madama* is on Monte Mario, and once belonged to Margaret, daughter of Charles the Fifth, and the wife of a Medici. It has many rich frescoes by Giulio Romano, and objects of art.

Besides the villas I have mentioned, there are many others, of rich adornments, and picturesque and embellished grounds. There is never the least difficulty in obtaining entrance to any of these villas. Only say, "I am a stranger," and at those magic words the doors fly open. The gold of strangers is the great revenue of Rome, and therefore as a matter of policy, as well as hospitality, they are always courteously treated and permitted access to studios and galleries, when even the inhabitants are excluded.

CHAPTER XLVII.

The churches of Rome, it is said, are equal in number to the days of the year. Of this I am not quite sure, but there are certainly many hundreds. Of course, after looking upon St. Peter's, they appeared as feeble shadows compared with that wonderful structure. However, in all we visited, we found precious works of art, statues and pictures, monuments and rare mosaics; chapels with costly vases and sculptured columns from the ancient temples. The portals of the churches were always open. No one stood at the door as keeper, to decide, from his apparel, where the person entering should be placed. In the spirit of our blessed Saviour, those long aisles always seemed to me to hold out an invitation to the weary and sorrow-stricken to come in and rest. The deep silence, the cool, calm atmosphere, and the kneeling figures always met within those churches, disposed the mind to meditation and the heart to purer influences, lifting the thoughts above the eager cares which are constantly dragging us from the spiritual to the material of existence. Never did I enter these sacred buildings, but a soft and gentle quietude stole over my soul, refreshing my spirit as though in a bath of purified emotions.

One day we drove to *Mount Janiculum*, to the church

and convent of San Onofrio. There Tasso died, and is buried beneath a simple marble slab. He came to Rome to be crowned at the capitol, but was seized with a fatal malady. He went to the convent, and calling for the monks, exclaimed, "I have come to die among you." They nursed him with tender care. At times he revived, and would seek the shade of a venerable oak, whence he looked over Rome. But his heart had been crushed by many sorrows, and his frame aged before its noon-day prime. In peace, and without a struggle, he expired, after a few weeks' sojourn in the convent. We saw the cell where he died, and the mask, in wax, moulded from the face after death. The features, though sadly emaciated, were still noble, indicating the glorious intellect of the poet. In a storm, some years since, the oak, called "Tasso's Oak," was blown down; but shoots are now springing up from the broken trunk.

San Pietro in Vincoli was built to preserve the chains with which St. Peter was bound. It has two splendid rows of marble columns along the aisles, and contains the grand statue of Moses by Michael Angelo. It was intended by the artist to form the centre of a group, which, however, was never completed. The figure has a majesty well befitting the leader and lawgiver of his people.

To the *Trinita de Monti* I went one Sunday afternoon with Gaspar, the young Spanish priest, who was often my guide amid the churches of Rome, interesting me always by his earnest narration of incidents in the lives of the saints. Long shall I cherish a pleasant memory of this dear little priest, so pure and saintly in his character, so enthusiastic in his love of the church. He carried me to the Trinita that I might hear the *vespers*, in which the voices of all the young girls of the "Sacred Heart" so sweetly mingle.

Gaspar also took me to the church of *San Clemente*,

which stands upon the site of the house of Clement, who labored with St. Paul in the conversion of souls to the true faith; and then to the church of the *Cappucini*, which possesses the picture of the archangel Michael, by Guido. It is a wonderful picture.

Basilica is the term applied to the seven great churches of Rome. This term is derived from the circumstance that the first churches of the Christians (when they dared openly to announce themselves as such) were the public tribunals, or courts of justice, called *basilicæ*. The basilica of *Santa Cròce in Gerusalemme* was founded by Helena, who placed in it a piece of the true cross, and earth brought from Jerusalem. Beyond the walls we drove to the basilica of *St Paul*. It was the most magnificent church, after St. Peter's, and was erected by Theodosius in the fourth century. It was burnt thirty years ago, but is now almost rebuilt by the enormous contributions of sovereigns, princes, popes, and nobles. It is of marvellous grandeur, with porphyry and alabaster pillars, and almost countless columns of marble, and brilliant mosaic pictures of the saints, fresh from the great manufactory of the Vatican.

I will cease my descriptions of churches, and turn to the house of Rienzi—

> "The friend of Petrarch—hope of Italy—
> Rienzi, last of Romans! While the tree
> Of freedom's withered trunk puts forth a leaf,
> Ever for thy tomb a garland let it be."

It is near the temple of Fortuna Virilis, and is a curious structure, covered with fragments and strange monuments. There are long inscriptions over the door-way, which have puzzled the antiquarians immensely. Then we saw the house of Poussin, and the *Palazzo degli Convertiti*, where Raphael died.

One day we gave to the studios of modern sculptors and another to modern painters. In the studio of Crawford we were delighted, and there saw many noble works, which would have joyed the heart of even the sculptors of the olden time. The monument for Virginia is magnificent, and the pediment for the capitol, representing the progress of civilization, a most suggestive and admirable design. The artist himself is a fine, intellectual-looking man, with a frank and self-possessed manner. He was exceedingly courteous and kind, and obligingly showed all the treasures of his rooms. The Virginia monument, or rather the Washington monument, is to be sixty feet high, crowned by an equestrian statue of Washington. Below this will be placed the statues of six of the great men of the " Old Dominion." Two only were completed, Jefferson and Patrick Henry. The contrast between the two is very striking. Jefferson stands in an attitude of absorbed thought, while Henry is represented giving expression to an outburst of eloquence. Crawford's Flora is sweetly graceful and classic in form. He displayed to me the group of the " Babes in the Wood." A lovely and touching impression it left with me.

In the studio of Ives we saw his Ariadne, and in that of Gibson, many of his own works, and the Medusa's Head, by Miss Hosmer, an American woman of decided talent. The Archangel of Tenerani is really a sublime statue. The wings are half folded, and the dread trump is resting on the knees, as though waiting for the signal to sound forth the fearful doom. Then his dying Psyche, so exquisite. She has just opened the fatal vase sent by Venus, and has inhaled the poison contained therein, and her pure life seems passing away.

In the studio of Page we saw several pictures painted after the fashion of Titian, with almost the same warm and glowing hues which characterized that remarkable colorist. I was exceedingly pleased with the remarks of Page upon the art of portrait-painting. He seeks to know his sitters well ere he commences the picture; and as revelations of mind or soul are brought forth, he marks their shadows or their brightness on the features; and seizing the noblest, transfers them to the canvas. It was a deep regret to us we could not tarry long enough, that he might paint the portrait of Octavia—he would have made such a charming picture of her, now that she is in the fresh spring-time of life, with all the innocent hopes and beautiful emotions of youth clustering around her heart, and giving their own bright radiance to her face.

Mr. White is likewise an admirable artist. In his studio were many bewitching pictures.

Brown, (a landscape-painter,) displayed along the walls of his room many gorgeous and brilliant representations of Italian scenery, along the Alban hills, by the sea-shore, and far out upon the desolate Campagna.

The Carnival of Rome is famous for its merriment and variety. Persons to whom we brought letters often regretted we had fallen upon the "dull season," when balls, parties, and operas had ended; but to me it seemed a mockery to think of the usual gaieties of fashionable life in Rome. Rome is truly the "City of the Soul," inspiring a grandeur of thought by its thousand spells of association and memories of the "undying past." Rome absolutely magnetized me, enchaining every emotion, and filling each hour with some precious remembrance of classic or historic interest. Therefore, to me, quadrilles, polkas, or redowas, would have been a sad intrusion. To one delightful *réunion*, however, we did go. It was given by an intellectual woman of our own country, Mrs. Edward Bill, who lives in elegant style in the *Via Gregoriana*, with one most lovely, fair, and gentle daughter, and her adopted son, an exceedingly clever young man. They kindly assembled many pleasant people to meet us—Americans, Romans, English, and Germans; among them artists, sculptors, musicians, authors, and poets. I was warmly interested in a son of the celebrated Mrs. Hemans, to whom Mrs. Bill presented me. He is a man of intellect, and has become, since his residence in Rome, an ardent and enthusiastic Catholic. To him, in succeeding interviews, I was vastly indebted for valuable information concerning Rome and its present institutions of learning and of charity; and for invitations to visit libraries and private studios. At this party we also met Lehman, the German artist, who painted that enchanting picture of Graziella, from Lamartine's touching and graceful story of the same name.

CHAPTER XLVIII.

I AM persuaded the best description I can give of our interesting interview with his Holiness, will be to transfer to these pages the letter written by me, warm from the heart, to dear Mamma, a few hours after we left the Palace of the Vatican.

"ROME, ITALY, *April 19th*, 1855.

"I cannot sleep to-night, precious Mamma, until I have written, and told you of the delight we experienced in being presented to the Pope of Rome, and of the affectionate and captivating kindness with which he received us. A cordial letter from our excellent Bishop Portier introduced us to Monsignore Barnabo, to whom we were indebted for the favor of this private audience.

"Yesterday morning a charming note came from Count Borromeo, informing me that his Holiness would gladly receive a visit from us at four o'clock this afternoon. Hence at that hour we drove to the Vatican (the winter residence of the Pope), attired, according to the etiquette of the court, in deep black, with long black veils thrown over our heads. Passing a group of Swiss Guards at the foot of the marble stairway, we were conducted by an officer along corridors, and through great apartments, to the ante-chamber. The walls of this room were glowing with the radiant pictures of Raphael, of Murillo, Titian, and Guido. As we stood admiring these masterpieces of painting, Monsignore Talbot (an English Bishop) joined us, and we then proceeded to the reception room, which was a long saloon, with exquisitely frescoed ceiling, but no adornment of furniture.

"Near a table, at one end of the room, his Holiness was seated. He arose when we entered. Monsignore Talbot presented us, and immediately retired. As we approached him, he held out his hands, and in a sweet voice said, 'Welcome to Rome, my friends.' I knelt before him and kissed his hand, with the earnest reverence I would feel for an honored parent. At once we glided into conversation, and were soon completely charmed by his genial manner, so honest and truthful. He is an exceedingly handsome man, about sixty years old, we were told, although he appears much younger. His features are fine, and his eyes beautiful. The expression of his mouth is indescribably sweet, and his smile possesses a magnetic charm which draws to him all hearts. Every word and look revealed the generous and sympathetic nature, which, were it within his power, would gladly shield every human creature from sin, suffering, or sorrow.

"He spoke of our country, and its onward progress, with deep and warm interest, calling it the 'noble land of Washington.' The New World, he remarked, had always been very dear to him, for the early days of his life as a priest had been passed in Buenos Ayres, South America. Its vast pampas he had traversed, and crossed over the Andes to the Pacific shore of the continent. During his residence in Chili, Pope Gregory had recalled him to Italy, and soon after named him Bishop of Imola. Oh! Mamma, it was a perfect enjoyment to listen to his descriptions of those far-away lands, and of the sublime scenery of the lofty mountains whose summits are nearest heaven.

"We conversed at first in French and Spanish (English, the Pope said, he could never learn); but fearing it might be some effort to his Holiness to speak them, I begged he would address me in Italian, which, although not so familiar to me as the other languages, I could understand exceedingly well. How glad I was afterwards this thought came to me, for his utterance of the Italian was as soft and melodious as the strains of music, so rich, full, and sonorous. The orations of Cicero, and the verses of Virgil, were worthy of a language harmonious like this; for, though the Italian is somewhat changed, it is still the daughter of the Latin, and has all the exquisite grace of expression and flowing elegance of the parent tongue.

"Then, the dear Pope dwelt with touching eloquence upon the goodness of God, which had so miraculously saved him from a terrible death, during the accident at the Convent of St. Agnese. He related to us the incidents of that frightful scene. Some catacombs had been recently discovered near the church, and his Holiness went to visit them, accompanied by a large suite of cardinals, bishops, and foreign ambassadors. After they had explored the subterranean home of the dead, they proceeded to the convent near by. In a great, old room of the building, long unused, the monks had prepared a collation. The Pope was seated in an immense oaken chair, with a high back and enormous arms. Before he commenced partaking of the refreshments, a number of boys from a neighboring school were brought in to receive his blessing. He had just given it to them, and had commanded the servants to bring him some of the delicacies to distribute among the children, when a fearful crash was heard, and the floor sank into a vault below, thirty feet deep. Shrieks of terror, and appalling cries of the wounded, resounded through the convent. The crowd without, rushed along the corridors leading to the banquet-room. The walls alone were standing. Far below there was a mass of rafters, and stones of the paved floor, and crushed and bleeding bodies. "Save our Father! save his Holiness!" was the first thought animating the hearts of the throng around. Through the vaults below, they found their way to the scene of disaster, and removing tables, chairs, and mangled forms of men and children, at last they reached the great oaken chair, which had fallen over the Pope, and thereby preserved him from serious injury, perhaps from instant death. They raised it, and to their joy the good Pope was unhurt. His hands were clasped in prayer for the suffering creatures around him. He seemed to have no thought of himself.

"'Oh! how frightful must have been your emotions, when you felt the floor sinking beneath you,' I exclaimed, as I listened. He looked at me almost reproachfully, as he said, 'No, my daughter, I was calm; for in that fearful moment, I felt I was in the hands of a gracious God, who would save me, if it were his divine will; but my heart was pierced with agony, as I heard the screams of the innocent children, and I thought of the poor mothers rendered desolate by this horrible accident; for I then believed many were killed, and that others would die of their wounds. However, the result has proved less severe than I imagined, and, with the blessing of the Almighty, I trust all may recover.'

"The Pope asked O. her name, and she replied, 'Octavia;' while I added, 'She bears my name, your Holiness, and I was called after the Roman Octavia, whose character my mother greatly admired.' Whereupon his Holiness uttered a most charming panegyric upon the character of my illustrious namesake, saying, 'You should be proud of that name, for the Roman Octavia possessed every virtue and grace which should adorn a woman. Even now, in Rome, you will find an undying remembrance of her noble and generous qualities, and many monuments to her memory.'

"Thank you a thousand times, Mamma, for giving me the name of *Octavia*.

"I wish I could repeat to you all the words the Pope said, they were so genial, sparkling with intellect, and warm with kindness. After one hour's interview, we bade him farewell. But ere we left him, he gave me his benediction. As I knelt before him, he placed his hand upon my head, saying, 'May the blessing of God descend upon you, and his Holy Spirit guide you into all truth; may God's providence protect you and yours, and bring you in peace to the world of the redeemed.' The tones of his voice were so solemn, so full of affectionate feeling, tears of gratitude burst from my eyes, as I eagerly, and with the utmost veneration, kissed the hands he extended to raise me up. Then I asked him to bless my child; and she, kneeling before him, likewise received his benediction, and we withdrew. M. D., as well as your two Octavias, was deeply impressed with the honesty, the truth, and nobleness of the Supreme Pontiff, and with a sincere admiration of his kind manner and cordial reception of us.

"In the ante-chamber we met again Monsignore Talbot, an extremely intelligent man, who had spent some years travelling in the United States. He accompanied us to our carriage, and after a little pleasant conversation we drove away. It was a bewitching afternoon, and the grand colonnade of St. Peter's was bathed in a golden flood of the sun's parting rays. The fountains were joyously casting up their bright waters, and 'earth and air seemed in a holiday mood.'

" It is impossible for me to tell you, Mamma, how happy I was, thinking of the sweet visit to his Holiness, and looking upon the grandeur which encircled me. The blessing and the prayer of that saintly man will be forever precious to my soul, and dear to me as the memory of the loved and the lost.

" I will write soon to Bishop Portier, and tell him of the message from his Holiness which he charged me to deliver. It is very kind, and manifests how deep an interest the Pope feels in the spiritual welfare of his distant children.

" Octavia has been long asleep, and I am quite weary, for it is past tho midnight; but I care not for the lateness of the hour. I have faithfully given my darling Mamma a picture of the scene, and a true history of the incidents of our interview; and I will now knock at the 'golden gate of dreams,' first asking the good God to bless Mamma, and dear little Netta, for the sake of their loving

" OCTAVIA."

CHAPTER XLIX.

April 21st.—Awaking at dawn, and remembering that I had never seen Rome from the Monte Pincio by the soft light of morning, I quickly made my toilette, briskly walked up the terraced hill, and seated myself by the balustrade overlooking the grand old city. Very often before, at evening, we had been here, to watch the gorgeous sunset. Then the gardens on the summit were filled with thousands of people, and the drive beyond it with hundreds of equipages. Now, save a few artists with sketch-books in hand, I was alone, to enjoy the glorious scene.

The cross, springing heavenward from the majestic dome of St. Peter's, was wrapt in a gauze-like drapery of snowy mist, while the vast Basilica, the Vatican, the Pantheon, the lofty column of Antoninus, obelisks, spires, and cupolas, were glowing in the brilliant rays of the morning sunlight. The freshness of Spring was expressed in every tree, shrub, and flower, and bright-winged birds were singing amid their green foliage. Never was the joy of existence greater to me than during those three hours of the young day, spent upon the Monte Pincio. It was not a bright, gay happiness, but a deep, serene, sublime feeling; a gratitude to God that I had seen Rome, whose glory even in my childhood had been as a halo around me. Like the fabled wand of the magician, the very name of Rome had possessed an electric power, darting along from century to century, and calling up visions from the great past, which fired the imagination while they thrilled the soul. The dream of my youth was now a reality. I was looking upon that noble city, once the queen of nations, and the home of heroes, patriots, poets, and philosophers. Other cities, however vast their extent, are only capitals of countries; but Rome seems the metropolis of the world, appealing to the hearts of all civilized people, as the birthplace of the noblest arts, and the spot whereon had been enacted the most thrilling incidents in the mighty drama of human life.

I gazed upon the spectacle before me with reverence, even as though I were in a hallowed presence. In scenes like these, the past so mingles with the present, we are scarcely aware how we cross the gulf which separates them; and almost unconscious of its utterance, I found myself murmuring, "May not men some day gaze upon St. Peter's and the Vatican, and marking their ruins, say, 'These things were?'" Truly has Byron called Rome the "Niobe of Nations," for no object more touchingly awakens our sympathies, than the mother bereft of her children; and thus it is with Rome, lonely and desolate; our hearts cling lovingly and with tender enthusiasm to the remembrance of her departed glories.

The day was far advanced ere I could tear myself from the contemplation of the scene, and return to the hotel, where all was prepared for our departure. There is an ancient superstition of the Romans, which says, "Whoever shall drink of the waters of Trevi, the last hour of their stay, shall surely come again to Rome." Thinking of this, and having a brief space of time to spare, I jumped into a carriage, and bade the coachman drive quickly to the fountain of Trevi. There, kneeling by the sparkling waters, I caught them in my hands, and drank earnestly to my return to the "City of the Soul."

By twelve o'clock we were out of Rome, driving rapidly along the Campagna. Near by Albano we stopped to look back upon its undulating surface, like a great green lake around the city, isolating it from all the world beside, or like an emerald setting enclosing an antique gem. By night we had reached the Pontine marshes. A fine road, bordered with trees, runs through them, while beyond this embankment it was a drear and darksome swamp. It was brilliant moonlight, and we saw distinctly the loneliness of the "Foro Appia," where the friends of St. Paul met him as he journeyed on to Rome. When daylight came I was ill (for the first time since I left my home) with a violent cough and headache, and was compelled to close my eyes until we were near to Naples, when I opened them to charge the courier to find us an hotel where we could look constantly upon Vesuvius. He took us to the *Hotel de Rossie*, in the Santa Lucia; and now we are in Naples, for several weeks at least. So with that comforting thought, I threw myself on the bed, perfectly exhausted, and slept profoundly.

CHAPTER L.

[As the letters addressed by me to dear Mamma contain a full and free account of our experiences and observations during the residue of our wanderings, I shall give them in preference to the more elaborate form of description observed in my journal, and which I have hitherto followed.]

NAPLES, *April 25th.*

THERE is a Neapolitan adage, "See Naples, and die." I assure you there is not so much national egotism in this as we imagined; for unrivalled is the situation of the city, and myriad are the charms which surround it. Our apartments are directly on the incomparable bay, and our immediate *vis-à-vis* is hot-headed Vesuvius.

It is just dawn as I write, yet the first light of day tinges the atmosphere with a rose-hue indescribably lovely. The bay before me is a placid lake, and the mountains, villas, and villages, are mirrored on its glassy surface. Only one look it was my purpose to take, and then again address myself to slumber. But now it is impossible to sleep amid the enchantment of a scene like this. As Octavia's enthusiasm is far less intense than mine, I will not awaken her, and thus am alone in my delight, dearly wishing that you, Mamma, could share it with me. As this cannot be, I have drawn my table to the open window, where I am alternately gazing upon the beauty before me, and writing, so that my descriptions may come fresh and new to the eyes of affection.

The view is enrapturing. I cannot leave the window one moment, and am dressing myself by snatches, far too absorbed for the niceties of toilette matters. There comes a knock at the door—" Breakfast is ready, Signora ! " Ah ! what an interruption are the necessary actualities of life.

April 26th.—We have just returned from Pompeii, and most enchantingly the day has glided by. Just at sunrise we drove along the shores of the bay to Portici, where we visited the palace, most charmingly situated, but not equal in magnificence to those of Genoa or Rome. In one room were the portraits of Napoléon and Joseph, of Murat and his wife, and Mme. Letitia, the mother—splendid paintings, and said to be wonderful resemblances. Thence we drove to Herculaneum, and descended seventy-five feet below the town of Portici. The exhumed city that perished so many centuries ago, is far more perfect than the mummies of Cheops and his illustrious successors.

We visited the silent theatre of the élite of Romans in Rome's most palmy days. It seemed in a perfect state, or at least all its marked portions have been cleared of the burying lava. The orchestra yet retains its music stands; the stage and corridors are clearly revealed. We were all provided with candles, so we lighted up the house. As we could not act one of Terence's comedies, we contented ourselves by fancying we saw before us *Roscius*, just from the " Eternal City " on a starring engagement.

Climbing up again, we went to the houses of the city, which have been opened to the light of day. It was an impressive view, but we hurried away from this mute city of a forgotten people, to visit another of a similar kind.

Strange and intense feelings moved me as I wandered

through the grand and silent Pompeii. The dwellings of the antique race who once inhabited this city, amidst the collected luxury and elegance of all existing refinement, are as tongueless orators. The mosaics and frescoes are as brilliant now as they were two thousand years ago. Every room is opened to the bright sky, as though some Asmodeus had indulged his power in unroofing the entire city, so that for our sakes nothing should be longer concealed within it. There were the halls, with their marble floors; the walls, with their glowing frescoes; the windowless bed-rooms, like closets, small but lofty. The light and air must have entered them directly from the heavens above. All the apartments opened on the court, or atrium, which was entirely encircled by a colonnade of richly sculptured marble pillars, and adorned with exquisite statues and voiceless fountains.

We saw the house of Glaucus, passing an hour in the court where he received the beautiful Ione, and where the blind Nydia tended his flowers; then the house of Sallust; the villa of Diomede, where Julia dwelt; the temples of Jupiter and of Isis, of Venus and of Mars; the forum, and the amphitheatre. Pompeii is like a vast museum, or a collection of curiosities, with the roof taken off. For hours we passed along through narrow streets, amid noble columns, and vacant shrines, fit for the wonder even of modern man.

"How long by tyrants shall thy land be trod,
How long thy temples worshipless, oh! God!"

We partook of a collation on the cliff overlooking the ruined city, and during our moon-lighted drive back to Naples, our imaginations were busy picturing the happy lives of the buried Pompeians. Oh! Time, time, time, and thy changes!—Good night, and bless you.

April 27th.—Congratulate me, dearest Mamma, for I

have ascended Vesuvius! and that, too, on my own feet, instead of being carried up in a *portantina* (a kind of sedan chair), as women usually are. I am proud of my achievement, and Octavia is quite as much so. But the ascent was the funniest thing imaginable. We absolutely laughed until tears poured in a stream from our eyes. Remembering the words of dear grandmother, "Begin, my child, at the beginning," I will tell you, we left Naples by six o'clock, and drove merrily through the city. Our road lay among groves of fruit trees and vineyards growing amid the masses of lava. At the hermitage we all left the carriages, and mounted donkeys. M. D. would go no farther. He declared he would not ascend the mountain, and had only accompanied us thus far, to be at hand to set an arm or a leg, should they be broken in the frolic. My donkey rejoiced, as a good donkey should, whose master

"Stuck a feather in his head,
And called him *Macaroni.*"

At the foot of the cone we left the donkeys. Then came a noisy quarrel between the guides and the bearers of the sedan chairs, who should have possession of us. We, however, cut the difficult knot of debate, by resolving on a pedestrian trip, so we could look about us; and thus we started. Just picture to yourself a giant haystack, with a parcel of ants climbing up and slipping down, then trying again and again. The cone was very steep, about one mile in height, covered with masses of lava and *scoriæ*, or ashes. I had no less than four assistants. A man held each arm. Around my waist was a leather band, with a long strap passing over the shoulder of the third, who pulled me up all the way, while the fourth came behind me, and gave now and then a strenuous push in the back, or caught me up when I slipped. In the front walked the guides to show us the best road. All talked, laughed, gesticulated, and shouted, in ceaseless medley. It was well for me I was thus supported, for so uncommonly ludicrous was the appearance of those before me, I could not have walked for the merriment they excited. As it was, I had only to raise my feet and put them down again, while my chattering crew bore me upwards. By promise of *buona mano* (a fee), they permitted me to stop very often, and enjoy the view. Oh! it seemed a vision of enchantment! The noble bay, the glittering city, the beautiful islands, the deep blue sea, and far, far away the *Cape of Circe*, where Ulysses filled his sailors' ears with wool, to prevent them from hearing the voice of the Syren, luring them to destruction. (There was no cotton in those days, I believe, or it might have proved as efficacious as those famous bags at New Orleans to keep off danger.)

Our old friend Morris was with us, and a splendid young officer from the Saranac (Lieut. Daniels); Dr. Parker, of Richmond, a charming acquaintance we formed in Rome; Mr. Thurber, of Detroit, our pleasant *compagnon du voyage* for many weeks. Mrs. Thurber was an invalid, and therefore was compelled to tarry at the base of the cone; but she had rare fun in laughing at our ridiculous attitudes in ascending. Thus we were a party of six, with twelve guides, and sundry assistants. Two old men, with baskets filled with wine and oranges, made the whole ascent, with the hope of selling a few carlinas' worth. We were more than two hours going up, and when we reached the summit, we all gave three cheers for America! The very clouds seemed to favor us, for just above our heads one veiled the hot sun from us, while the whole world below was flooded with glorious radiance. The sea was like a silver mirror, and the islands like sapphires set within it.

The new crater was smoking and hissing like some enormous engine. Over the hot lava, we passed around to the extinct crater (as they termed it); but when a stick penetrated the coating of lava, out rushed a stream of smoke. The old crater was magnificent; and down, down, down, a thousand feet below, boiled the great cauldron of Vesuvius! Clouds of sulphurous smoke were arising from it, and almost suffocating us, as we stood on the edge to catch a glimpse of the mighty flames of those mysterious regions of eternal fire. How grand was the spectacle! How solemn the silence, broken only by the throbs of the great mountain's heart, which fluttered and struggled as though in its wild, last agony! The cliffs around the crater were covered with incrustations of sulphur, of a bright yellow or delicate pink, or pale green hue.

We lingered until four o'clock, when our guides counselled us to retreat, as the wind, blowing over the snow-banks, lying even then near the fiery mouth, was keenly cold. The descent was by a path through the ashes and cinders, and we plunged up to our knees in them at every step. The going down is the matter of only a few moments, and is managed by holding one's self back, and allowing the guides to bear one along. At times we would strike a loose lava-stone, which would go thundering down, terrifying those before us. My obliging guides permitted me to stop occasionally, that I might gaze around me. Once, while seated on a mass of lava, I heard a deep, crashing sound, like thunder, in the mountain beneath me. With the sound darted out a small column of white smoke, which wound around in the air as though it were a shadowy serpent, and quickly vanished. With the regularity of the heart's pulsations came the subterranean thunder, and there issued from a crevice of the mountain the snow-white smoke, as the steam from the safety-valve of an engine. Calling Beppo, (my guide,) I asked him if he did not think the mighty powers below were preparing a grand eruption. He answered quite sadly, " Ah, no, Signora; it is these cursed openings in the mountain which let off the heat of the fires far down yonder, and so we have not been blessed with an eruption for these five long years." " What!" exclaimed I, " do you call an eruption a blessing?" " Yes, a thousand times a blessing. It brings *forestien* (strangers) with their money, and we eat macaroni."

All the party had reached the base of the cone before me, and were loudly calling for me to come. So away I rushed down, swift as a flash of light. I absolutely sighed when we reached the plain of the extinct crater of Monte Somma (whence flowed the fiery deluge which overwhelmed Pompeii and Herculaneum,) and thought there was one inspiring and tumultuous pleasure less for me in life.

Mark the date of my letter, and you will see it is the anniversary of *our fête* of last year. Have not singular events mingled with the current of my existence since then? I must not forget to tell you, we drank your health in *Lacrima Christi,* (a wine made from the grapes growing amid the lava-fields,) as we stood on the rim of the great crater-bowl of Vesuvius.

Mounting once again my macaroni, we passed over the lava which is here like enormous waves of the sea turned to stone, and reached the hermitage. M. D. was amazed to find us safe and " sound of limb." Amid a locust-throng of beggars we entered our carriages, and drove down the mountain, stopping, however, to see the " Witches' Cave," which Bulwer has made so famous in his peerless novel, " The Last Days of Pompeii." What think you! In the house of Glaucus, seated on the rich mosaic floor, I read to Octavia the description of those scenes of passionate love between the gentle Ione and the noble Pompeian. Even the exquisite language of Bulwer caught from the classic surroundings a new beauty and a greater charm.

Oh! with what joyous spirits we dashed along, meeting at every moment some singular and characteristic spectacle; now a *calesso*, drawn by one horse, and holding thirty-five persons above, around, and beneath it—young, old, middle-aged, priests and sucking babies; then the handsome equipage of a high-born Neapolitan woman, who luxuriously reclined on the soft cushions, while a gallant youth reined in his prancing steed by her carriage, looking most energetic love upon the fair occupant; now a lot of beggars, some without legs, some without arms, some on crutches, some shaking with palsy, and many poor creatures quite blind. These, above all others, awakened my sympathy. Great God! what a misfortune to be blind in Italy! where both earth and air are filled with beauty; where the spirit of loveliness has brooded longer than over any other portion of earth!

As the sun went down, the whole west seemed covered with flaming banners, which rose higher and higher, until the atmosphere was glowing with a rosy light. It gradually enfolded the city, and rested upon the waters of the bay. At last it reached Vesuvius, and wondrously beautiful was its aspect. Over the summit hung a cloud of smoke, which was turned to banks of rose-leaves by the magical hue, and every rock and tree was blushing in the radiance which streamed upward from the couch of the setting sun. We stopped the barouche, and watched the enrapturing glory of the sky, until it vanished in the approaching night, and then drove quickly to Naples. As soon as we reached our apartments,

I ran out on the balcony, and waved a proud salutation to Vesuvius, with whom I could now claim acquaintance.

So, dear Mamma, good night.

April 28th, twelve o'clock.—Although it is so late, I must tell you of the busy, merry day we have had. In spite of the unusual exertions of yesterday, we awoke this morning fresh and bright, unwearied and happy. As we sat at breakfast, Octavia was wishing she could hear the Neapolitan song I so often sang to her in her baby-days. As she uttered the words, in the street below our window we heard a few chords of the guitar, and then the same little romance,

> " Io ti voglio, bene assai,
> Ma tu non pensa a me."

We ran to look out, and a fantastically dressed minstrel, fluttering with rags, was singing, playing, and jumping about in a sort of " Jim Crow " manner, while a large audience of beggars were around him, not listening, but gazing up at us with hungry eyes. We seized all the breakfast from the table, and threw it down to them. What a scramble for it there was, to be sure! Presently our waiter came in, and seeing all the dishes, plates, and sugar-bowl empty, he gravely inquired, " Will the *two* signoras require more breakfast ?"

At eleven o'clock we went on board the *Saranac*, a fine American steamer, commanded by Captain Long, a gallant officer. We were delightfully entertained. There was a collation and dancing, and a *réunion* of all the Americans then in Naples. We met among them Major and Mrs. Van Buren, and Miss M'Duffie, a most charming young woman; Mrs. Sherman, of New York, and Mr. and Mrs. Whales, of Boston; and the daughters of our friend Thompson Brown. If we had only finished our visit here, we should accept the kind invitation of Captain Long to take passage with him to Leghorn.

Coming home from the Saranac, we went to the *Grotto of Posilippo*, a tunnel nearly half a mile in length, cut through the mountain, by whom or when there is no record. It is lighted by lamps, and a constant stream of travel flows through it. Above the Grotto, on a high peak, is the tomb of Virgil. We ascended *five hundred* steps to reach it. The prospect thence is bewildering in its variety, and glorious in its matchless loveliness. The tomb in which the body of the poet once reposed is a kind of temple, built of brick, now covered with ivy and other creeping plants. The old *custode* told us they had often planted laurel trees there, but eager tourists tore them to pieces, to bear away as souvenirs. As he said this, he looked triumphantly upon the linden tree which now overshadowed it. The branches were far above the reach of the rude invaders. Having promised a dear good friend to bring him a sprig from this very tree, I waited until the guardian had gone with Morris and M. D., to show them some very remarkable vegetables; and then I climbed up the jutting points of the tomb, holding on bravely to the vines, till I reached a limb of the tree, whence I broke a nice little branch, and jumped down just in time to escape the sharp eyes of the ancient guardian of the Grotto.

At nine we went to a party at the house of the American Minister, Mr. Owen. This intelligent and well-informed gentleman we found vastly agreeable and most kindly courteous to us. There were a number of Americans, and many gay and pleasant Neapolitan people present, and we passed a charming evening. Every moment of our life here is an enjoyment.

But gathering mists from the "world of sleep" are floating softly around me now, and I must end this letter. Good night.

Sunday morning.—As the fête of *San Gennaro* is near at hand, all the theatres are closed, and we feared we should not see the *San Carlo*, the rival of *La Scala* of Milan; but Mr. Daniels most obligingly obtained permission of the manager for us to see it. The theatre is of stupendous size, with six tiers of boxes, all glittering with gold and hung with rich silken draperies. The royal box, fronting the immense stage, is almost large enough to serve as a theatre itself. Pretty little saloons are attached to all the private boxes, where the persons occupying them receive their visitors.

After spending some time in the San Carlo, we went to a great number of churches, none very remarkable. Mass was over, and the streets were filled with the merriest, noisiest crowd we have seen in Italy. They were singing and acting on impromptu theatres; dancing the *tarantella*, and eating *polenta* (small cakes of corn-meal, cooked by being dropped into a pan of boiling grease). Around every group was a fringe of beggars, rapping their chins and crying out, "morte di fame" (dying of hunger). Indeed, this seemed true, for many were skeletons, with that look of starvation so fearful to behold. Every day more and more I thank God for being born in America, where spectacles such as these rarely come between us and happiness. The Roman beggars are very pathetic; but the lazzaroni of Naples (all beggars) the most mirth-provoking, with their curious signs and funny gesticulations. They have a jaunty air about them, as they implore charity, which would make a miser laugh. The Roman beggar, amid all his wretchedness, has a certain dignity, telling of the noble race whence he came.

Passing through many of the thronged streets, we came to

the *Chiaja*, which terminates in the *Villa Reale*, a public promenade, and one of the brightest and loveliest in Europe. It is about one mile in length, divided from long rows of handsome houses on one side by a street, and bounded on the other by the broad bay. It has groves of orange trees, avenues of the lemon and citron; myrtle-shaded walks; labyrinths of the acacia and oleander; gushing fountains, cool arbors, and myriads of statues and vases. Multitudes of gaily-dressed people were pouring through it, or standing on the parapet wall, whence they could see the whole extent of the varied scene.

The afternoon was delicious, and so we resolved to drive to the *Castle of St. Elmo*, overlooking the city and guarding it by its numerous guns. Our road was through the heart of Naples. The streets are wider than those of Rome, and cleaner, too. The houses are brighter and whiter, and we passed some lovely villas, half hidden by the groves of orange trees. They appeared the fit abode of delight, and should be the favorite home of "deep and passionate love."

There is certainly a magical charm in this climate. To breathe the air is a joy. In that far-away island of the tropics, Cuba, I have felt the same rapture of mere existence, but never elsewhere.

After seeing the Castle, we sought a little vine-covered arbor on the verge of the lofty cliff, whence we could look over the entire surroundings of the city, which lay directly beneath us. Beautiful Naples! Earth does not possess another gem like Naples! It is the Kohinoor of cities! It has every variety of scenery—mountains and islands; valleys and the noble bay; magnificent promenades and classic ruins; splendid streets, palaces, and churches. Then Vesuvius, presiding over all, and forming a portion and part of every vision of beauty.

Although often implored by Luigi (our courier) to leave our leafy nook, we could not withdraw ourselves until it was almost dark. Upon reaching the city, we were several times stopped by religious processions, and thus did not arrive at the hotel until very late, and found a large party of friends awaiting us, all alarmed at our prolonged absence.

As this letter goes at dawn to-morrow, I shall now say good-bye, dear Mamma.

May 1st, Tuesday.—Very early yesterday morning, dear Mamma, we left Naples for Capri, an island at the entrance of the bay, and distant twenty-five miles from the city. There were about forty or fifty persons on the wretched little steamer, among them the Count and Countess de Moulins, Spanish exiles now, whose magnificent house we saw in Madrid; then a young son of Queen Christina, borne rapidly on to death by the fell destroyer, consumption; and the old Spanish grandee, father of our dear little priest, Gaspar.

About twelve o'clock we anchored near an immense cliff, some thousand feet in height. Just where the waves broke against the rocks, we saw a small opening in them, and soon after, entering a *barciolina* (little boat), we rowed towards it. As we approached it, our boatman called out, "Lie down in the boat." Obeying his command, we soon felt ourselves carried quickly onward upon the crest of a great wave. For an instant, the darkness was intense, and a sharp pang of fear assailed me, but in another we seemed to have entered a fairy land of mystery and dazzling light. We seemed floating in the air. The water was deeply blue, and the atmosphere of the same color. A vast arched roof rose above us; beneath it, stretched far away long corridors and aisles, whose pavement was a rich turquoise blue, as smooth and calm as though it were indeed stone, and not living water.

From the roof hung multitudes of stalactites, around which was playing a clear blue flame, like burning spirits of wine. The fish swimming below us were as blue as the jay birds of our forests, and the walls and broken rocks seemed carved from a quarry of lapis lazuli. It was wonderful, unique, and the fit abode of sea-nymphs, which the people of Capri say still inhabit it, while the Neapolitans call it the "Witches' Cave." The depth of the water is about eight fathoms. Near the centre of the grotto there is a landing-place, leading to a corridor, which, after a few feet, is found closed up by a great stone. In the time of Tiberius it no doubt served as a bath for the luxurious monarch; and the subterranean passage led from his palace on the cliff, far, far above it.

Of course, you will eagerly ask, "What causes this luminous light?" It is said to be produced by the sun's rays interpenetrating the sea, and refracted and reflected through the blue waters, thereby giving to every object this remarkable azure hue.

A boat came through the aperture while we were within the grotto, and quite filled it for an instant; but there was no change in the radiant light. The echo is wild and singular. We rowed under the arches, and beneath the aisles, enraptured with the peculiar beauty of the sea-cavern, when the boatman informed me the water was rising, and said, "You must go out very quickly, for the waves will soon close the doorway, and then you must stay till they go down again." You can well imagine we did not tarry much longer, but soon passing the aperture, we were out on the open sea, looking back upon the dark entrance to the azure grotto.

Our steamer next proceeded to the village of Capri, where we took donkeys and rode up (I may say climbed) to the ruins of the Palace of Tiberius, about eighteen hundred feet above the quai where we landed. From a perpendicular cliff it was the custom of the cruel and bloody monarch to cast his victims into the sea. A tower is built upon it, and the view from it was of boundless extent, stretching even unto the ruined temples of Pestum.

We spent many hours upon the island, which is famous for the healthfulness of the climate and for the Capri wine. My donkey (named Angiolina) was the property of an old woman, who was his driver also. It was really saddening to see the aged woman climbing up the steep mountain-paths, and holding me securely on the donkey's back when we passed near the edge of a dangerous precipice. She was very chatty and amusing, and gave me all the wild legends of the *grotto azzura*, which she firmly believed was inhabited by spirits. To confirm this, she told many thrilling stories of those who had entered it, but never came out again. Then she pointed out the ruins of the Palace of Augustus, and of his daughter Julia; of the Temple to Jupiter, and of Venus. She described to me the terrible poverty of the people, and the frequent occurrence of death from starvation. The little donkey was all the worldly goods she possessed, and she expatiated upon his merits, in which I joined her heartily; for it was indeed a sure-footed creature.

A signal from our steamer recalled us, and we hastened on board to find a sirocco was blowing; so we steamed away as rapidly as the miserable engine could move us. You may think, in the tossing waves, how I suffered from sea-sickness; but I endured it all with calm philosophy. We had seen the azure grotto, with its gleaming vault and turquoise pavement, and no shadow could dim the brilliant impression it left with me.

It was very late when we reached the quai. There we found several persons waiting for us, who assured us it was the opinion of the sailors about that our old steamer would go down ere she reached Capri, she was so unseaworthy. Thus you see, dear Mamma, guardian angels are always hovering over us, and in safety we are again within our own apartments. The sirocco prevailed with wild fury all night, but to-day the beauty of the Italian sky and climate have returned. Visitors are coming in, so I will end this letter when they leave me.

CHAPTER LI.

Tuesday night, twelve o'clock.—Glorious news I write you, glorious news indeed! Vesuvius is in full eruption! During the morning several Neapolitans told me an eruption would soon burst forth, as the dark clouds above the crater had been tinged with a crimson light just at midnight on Monday. This had been the herald of the fire-fiend since the days of Pompeii. Hence I was not surprised when I received a message from our courier, begging us to hasten from the dinner-table, as the flames were already visible from our balcony. Away we flew up the stairway, as though we imagined that, like a flight of rockets, they might vanish ere we could see them.

The night was calm—not a wavelet disturbed the mirror-like surface of the bay. The moon, high in the heavens, was casting a long train of radiance over its waters. Parallel with the moonbeams fell the crimson light from the volcano, while between them lay a space of deep, deep blue, like a pavement of sapphire. How strangely beautiful was the scene! Palaces and domes, spires and churches, ships and little boats, were all touched with a silvery light, or glowing in the crimson rays of the "fiery mountain." Along the mole were clustered hundreds of Neapolitan fishermen, urging the passers-by to embark with them for a row across to the base of Vesuvius, their dark, gipsy-like faces singularly wild by the gleams of the red light.

But the mountain! It was perfectly wonderful! blazing and flaming like—but to what shall I compare it? In truth, it was like Shakspeare's Richard, "itself alone." Down the side poured a cataract of lava, while from the crater sprang up at times great blood-red stones, which seemed poised in air for a few seconds, then fell crashing down below. Although we were eight or ten miles distant, we heard the "voice of the mountain" above all other sounds of earth or air. Clouds of smoke hung in festoons around the highest peak of Vesuvius; and though there was no wind, they were constantly changing into most fantastic forms, now presenting the appearance of a lion, then an eagle with a scroll of fire in his talons, or a procession of monks with black cowls, or palaces, or castles, all tinged with a crimson hue.

It is now four o'clock, and I have passed the entire night looking upon the burning mountain, and at intervals, when my delight must have expression, running to the table, and writing down for your dear eyes a description of the dazzling scene. The enthusiasm of M. D. and Octavia faded away by two o'clock, so they retired to sleep. But for me there was an enchantment which absolutely forbade repose, and it was only when daylight came, and half the majesty of the eruption had departed, that I was enabled to close my window.

Not content with our distant view, we resolved on Wednesday afternoon to approach nearer to the wonderful spectacle. At five we left Naples in an open barouche, drawn by three strong horses, and drove rapidly through Portici, and up the mountain to the Hermitage, passing through the vineyards from whose grapes the *Lacryma Christi* wine is made. The road was thronged with carriages, horsemen, donkeys, and pedestrians by thousands. It was an exquisite evening, and the very heavens seemed to rejoice in the universal happiness; for an eruption of Vesuvius is a benefaction to the Neapolitans. Smiling joy was pictured on every face. The beggars even ceased to rap their chins and to cry "morte di fame." The lame hobbled along merrily, and the blind stretched out their hands, as though to feel the happiness they could not see. There were crowds of handsome peasant-women, with sparkling eyes and ruddy cheeks, hastening up. Even the poor little infants many carried, were laughing in spite of being wrapped up like Egyptian mummies, and tucked under their mothers' arms as though they were great loaves of bread.

At the Hermitage, midway to the summit, there was a scene precisely like a race-field in America. Hundreds and hundreds of carriages were all crammed together, while the drivers were swearing and gesticulating furiously. We gladly left our barouche, and hastened down a pathway through a grove of young chestnut trees, which brought us, after a brisk walk, to the verge of the lava flood. It poured from the crater far above, and formed a stream many miles in length. It was a deep burning red, with here and there a little island of black, caused by the cooling of the surface of the fiery river. From this ravine we climbed up the heights above, and approached nearer the crater. There we encountered our guide Beppo, who made the ascent with us. The instant he perceived us, he cried out, "*Bene! bene!* Signora! You remember three days ago, when I allowed you to stop on the side of the cone, and you asked me about the little serpent of smoke that burst from the lava, when the great mountain thundered,—*bene!* that was the mouth of the crater, and the fire was trying to open it. You see what it has done now. *Grazie a Dio!* we shall eat *macaroni* to-night!"

Precisely true were the words of Beppo. Just where I had gathered up pieces of hot lava, and heard far, far down below a wild, fierce murmur, almost like the utterance of human agony, a new crater had opened its flaming mouth, whence came a torrent of lava, sixty or seventy feet in width, flowing down the very path by which we had ascended. It did not dash rapidly along, as does the water, but moved slowly and majestically. It was only when a rocky barrier stayed its progress, that it would swell up into grand waves of fire, and madly dash over it. Imagine Trenton Falls, with every drop of water turned to flame, pouring over ledge after ledge of rocks; or the Anio a river of fire, rushing wildly over the heights of Tivoli, and some faint idea may be formed of the lava-cataract of Vesuvius.

As we descended the mountain, after midnight, we met the King of Naples, who had been lured from his close retirement in the Palace of Caserta (twenty miles from the city), to ascend the mountain. We stopped for him to pass us; and the transient view I had of his face, revealed a stern, hard, and cruel-looking person. His carriage was encircled by multitudes of soldiers and mounted guards.

When we reached home, it was impossible for me to sleep, so intense had been the excitement of the visit to the fiery mountain. Therefore I concluded to occupy the hours in describing the glorious eruption, ere the occupations of another day should chase from my mind one attribute of its sublime grandeur. The blue light of the early morning is stealing through the latticed window, and I will say, Heaven bless my mother and my child, and so "woo the blessing of sleep."

CHAPTER LII.

Thursday night, May 3d.—This morning we visited Major Thompson Brown's family. They have been here all the winter for his health. Five years he remained in Russia as engineer, building the railway from St. Petersburg to Moscow. At length his cough became so serious, his family brought him here; but alas! he is still fearfully ill. When he heard my voice in the parlor, he sent for me to come in; and the physician who was present gave me permission to see him for a few moments. Was it not very strange? He had never seen me since I was fifteen years old, and yet he knew me at once, though several ladies entered his chamber at the same moment I did. Poor Brown! He was a living skeleton, though his eyes were bright and sparkling. He could only speak in a whisper, and with that faint voice (almost like a voice from the tomb), he sent to you many messages of love, and grateful remembrance for your kindness long, long ago. Then kissing my cheek, he said, "Heaven bless you, Octavia!" just as he had so often said in the days of my childhood. I could not repress my tears or check my sobs, as I looked upon the wreck of that noble and gifted man; so I ran out of the room while his feeble tones were still entreating me to stay. M. D. then went in to see him, and says death is very near, and that a few days is all he has of life. A dark cloud seemed hovering over me for many hours afterwards. I am almost sorry I have written you about the sad interview. But such are the shadows of the bright picture of yesterday.

Saturday night, May 5th.—For two days we have been so unceasingly occupied, it was impossible to write, dear Mamma.

We have made a long visit to the classic shore where Virgil laid the scenes of his Æneid. In the days of the empire, it was the abode of emperors, poets, historians, and philosophers; and they adorned and decorated every hill and vale with palaces, villas, and temples. For this luxurious class of people Virgil wrote, and more deeply to thrill their satiated fancies, he peopled every glen with nymphs, every cave with mysterious sybils, and every stream with nereids.

Near the ancient Cumæ we saw the Temple of Apollo, where Dædalus came down to earth after his flight from the Island of Crete. Then we entered the cave of the Cumæan Sybil, where Æneas consulted the oracle. At. Baia were masses of ruins, some most grand and majestic. The Temple of Venus is just by the shore; there, in a niche where once stood the statue of the goddess, we had our breakfast spread out; but ere we could begin our repast, a flock of beggars encompassed us, and with their piteous cries of "Datemi qualche cosa," and their famished looks, quite destroyed all appetite; so we gave them every thing we had. This, however, was but as a grain of corn to a hungry flock of turkeys, and they clamorously begged for more. M. D.'s heart, usually as hard as adamant to their entreaties, melted at the sight of their misery; so he sent our courier to buy from a little *cabaret* near us some of the bread of the country. And such bread! It was almost black, made of coarse wheat and crushed chestnuts. It absolutely seemed to require the strength of a Vulcan to cut it. M. D. attempted it, but finding it impossible, he called up a stout beggar, who took it in hand. Oh! Mamma, it was a fearful spectacle to see those poor wretches, men, women, and children, climbing up on each other's shoulders to reach a piece of this disgusting looking mixture they called bread, and devouring it with an eagerness only starvation can manifest.

We found a very curious antique lamp discovered in this temple, which we bought for our friend Tom.

In the harbor of Baia the whole Roman fleet often assembled. It was there Octavius Cæsar (usually called Augustus) and Anthony were entertained on board the magnificent galley of Pompey. During the banquet, Pompey's admiral whispered to him, "Shall I cut the cable, and make you master of the world?" But Pompey's word was pledged, and he could not violate the rites of hospitality though the Roman empire were his recompense; therefore he cried out, "No!"

The Temple of Mercury is a circular building, with a dome like the Pantheon. It has a most clear and remarkable echo, repeating not only the last syllable, but the whole word or name. A group of girls gathered around us, and for a consideration danced the tarantella. Their agile and graceful movements would have made the fortune of an American manager, could he have presented them on the stage of one of our theatres.

At Lake Fusaro we tasted the oysters for which it is famous. They do not compare in excellence to those of Mobile bay. This lake was the renowned *Styx*, where old Charon was the ferryman, and beyond it were the *Elysian Fields*, a most dreary, desolate waste now. On a lofty eminence we saw the ruins of the Villa of Augustus, where he spent the summers with his much-loved sister Octavia. It was to that lovely retreat Octavia retired after the death of Marcellus, and there Virgil cheered the dark hours of her grief by his exquisite poems, in which were mirrored the virtues and noble gifts of her dead son.

Of the once celebrated city of Pozzuoli, nothing remains but a few miserable houses, and the stones which the sacred feet of St. Paul first touched when he landed upon the Roman shore. The Temple of Jupiter Serapis is there also, and its vast ruins speak of the mighty grandeur of its prime. Its great columns bear evidence of the conflicts between land and sea.

A nice little donkey carried me safely over and all around the crater of the *Solfatarra*, where sulphur vapors were rising, hot and suffocating, from the burning soil. We saw the stone upon which San Gennaro was beheaded, and which, the legend says, turns red upon the anniversary of his death. We passed the Villas of Lucullus, of Cicero, of Agrippina, (mother of the tyrant Nero;) then the Monte Novo, thrown up by a great convulsion of nature in a single night. Although it is several centuries old, it has rather a *parvenu* look, and not the true dignity of a mountain. The entrance into Tartarus, (the same path, I suppose, by which Virgil's Æneas descended into Hell,) is dark, abrupt, and gloomy. Seated upon the shoulders of the guide, one is compelled to go down through splashing water into immense black chambers in the mountain. After viewing the dismal place for a few moments, an escape from it is rather a pleasant emotion.

We drank the Falernian wine, so loved and praised by Horace, just by the shore of the bay, where, looking down beneath the clear lucid waters, we saw marble columns, capitals of pillars, and pavements of houses. By the frequent convulsions of nature, these temples and palaces have been entombed beneath the waves.

Oh! inconceivably delightful was the drive by twilight along the noble bay. At times we stopped to see the people playing the *Lotteria*, which signifies taking tickets in a lottery, and watching the drawing of the chances. The Neapolitans adore this game. The crowd around the table of the "public writer" was also very peculiar. As very few can write, they employ this person, who sits in state, before a miserable little stand, and listens to and puts down the outpourings of the heart, or the fierce reproaches of the forsaken; the tender words of the loving mother, or the stern commands of the father to the absent child.

The window of my chamber opens directly upon Vesuvius, and often, for hours of the night, I lay awake, gazing upon the ever-blazing fires, and the crimson river flowing down the dark mountain. Even my dreams assume a wild and fantastic form, and sleep is not a respite from thought. It only seems to transport my spirit to a world more beautiful than this, where it revels in joyous delight, amid scenes of gorgeous splendor. I am almost tempted to believe it is the influence of the volcano, to which an old superstition of the Greeks attributes "a strange power over the mind and the soul, filling both with visions of joy or wild scenes of horror." Thank Heaven! only the first have been my portion, and I really love the "fiery mountain" for the spell it has cast over me.

We have passed many hours in the Museum, looking upon the objects of art brought from Pompeii and Herculaneum. They occupy rooms innumerable, and defy rivalry, for to none other in the world can they be compared. The ashes and lava of the volcano, in place of destroying, have preserved (as though hermetically sealed) all these evidences of the "inner life" of the Pompeians. There are wonderful varieties of jewels and ornaments, of cooking utensils, of vases and bronzes. There are loaves of bread, with the baker's name upon them; jars of figs, corn, rice, and nuts; oval mirrors of silver, and pots of paint for the face; surgical and musical instruments; tickets for the theatre, and dice for the gambling tables,—in truth, every thing pertaining to life (luxurious life, too) that can be imagined, all blackened and hardened by the awful destruction of that fearful day, but still revealing the perfect form of every article.

The frescoes from the walls of the houses uncovered in Pompeii have been skilfully taken down and brought here, until recently, when an order has been issued to leave them as they were discovered, protecting them from the weather only. From these frescoes it would seem the heathen ideas of existence were to crowd the brief space with all the fascinations of sweet flowers, of music, of wine, of feasting, dancing, and loving. Death must have appeared to them an eternal night and a chaos of everlasting darkness. Along the walls were exquisite forms, some with a light drapery floating around them, and many quite nude. There were dancing girls, and bacchantes crowned with grape-vines; then fauns and centaurs; nymphs, and groups of the gods and goddesses. All these were painted upon a ground of azure hue or golden color. Every object that met the eye was suggestive of mirth and delicious pleasure, of joyous life and present happiness.

Many of the bronze statues found there were admirable; above all, those of Mercury, of Venus, and of Psyche. The statue of Aristides, found in the theatre of Herculaneum, is one of the noblest works of Greek art I ever beheld. Intellect, power, and dignity, were never more eloquently expressed in marble. The busts of Caracalla, of Alexander the Great, of Scipio Africanus, (whose tomb we saw by the shores of the bay of Baia,) and of Seneca, are exceedingly fine. Then we saw the Farnese Bull, found in the Baths of Caracalla at Rome, and brought here. It represents the story of Dirce, who won the heart of Antiope's husband, the King of Thebes. This queen, joined in her revenge by her two sons, is binding Dirce to the bull's horns, when she relents, and commands them to release her. The sculptor has seized the moment when the youths are striving to restrain the mad animal by throwing cords around him, while Dirce, prostrate on the earth, gazes up with wild horror upon them.

But days and days, even weeks, it would require, to see all the wonderful works of art enshrined in that vast building.

We visited the King's palace, a fine residence, but too modern for my taste. Then we saw the church where Massaniello issued his first proclamation, when, from a poor fisherman, he became king, for a time, of Naples. Short was his career, and miserable his end. Auber, in his opera of that name, has made him a hero, and as such we delight to regard him.

How often, in my drives along the gay streets of Toledo and La Chajia, have I thought of our dear little Giuglio, and wished I knew the house in which he was born.

At six this evening we went to the church of *Santa Chiara*, to see the "Miracle of San Gennaro," which consists in the liquefying of his blood, caught by a pious woman when his head was cut off, near Baia, two thousand years ago. This saint, according to tradition, was exposed to be devoured by lions in the amphitheatre of Pozzuoli, but they became gentle at his approach. After this, the proconsul of Diocletian had him beheaded, and it was then the blood was preserved and brought to St. Severus.

San Gennaro is the Patron Saint of Naples, and protects the people from the "burning mountain" So important is the "Ceremony of the Liquefaction," that all the most important personages attend it, beginning with the King. The church was crammed with a dense crowd. Great numbers were praying aloud, with vast energy, and all faces expressed eager anxiety that the miracle "should be made," as they termed it. About six o'clock, accompanied by Mr. Townsend, we forced our way up near the altar, where a pretty Neapolitan gave me a place on the base of a column. There was a crowd of women just before me, praying very loudly. These, they told us, were the relations of San Gennaro. A priest walked to and fro with the vials in his hand. They seemed filled with dark, congealed blood, or some substance like it. Inquiring of the people around when the "miracle" would take place, they answered, "When God pleases, Signora." Thus we stood, watching the singular scene and the intense emotion revealed in the faces around us, until a little bell rang, and thousands of voices cried out, "Il miracolo e fatto!" (the miracle is made.) A universal thrill of joy seemed to dart through the great throng, who fell upon their knees, and held up their hands towards the vials which the priest displayed, now filled with fresh blood, as though just drawn from human veins. A splendid orchestra and many magnificent voices poured forth triumphant strains of music, mingling with the murmurs of delight and the fervent prayers of the multitude. Then came a procession through the church with San Gennaro, borne on a platform (a statue of him in silver), thickly incrusted with precious stones. The cannon were fired at St. Elmo, and a general joy prevailed.

I must not forget to tell you that the blood liquefies while the priest is holding it up to view. Thus none of the unbelievers have been able to account for it, though they all insist it is some kind of legerdemain.

After leaving the church, the procession returned to the cathedral of San Gennaro, where the vials are kept in a tabernacle, of which the city authorities keep the key. This is the great *festa* of Naples, and we were happy in seeing it.

You must be wearied reading such long letters, so good night.

CHAPTER LIII.

[Letter to a friend.]

May 7th.—Often in our wanderings amid the antiquities of Rome, and along the peerless bay of Naples, have we thought of you, and earnestly wished you were with us to enjoy these classic and beautiful scenes. Speaking of you this morning, M. D. said, "I wish you would write to our friend. I know the letter would delight him." Trusting his words may be prophetic, I gladly send you the record from my journal, which I style, "A Day in Pompeii and a Night on Vesuvius."

[*May 6th.*]—At early morning we went along the seashore to Pompeii. The atmosphere was filled with the blue light so peculiar to Naples, which rendered distant objects incredibly near. Thus Capri, Procida, and Ischia, the triune isles of beauty, seemed almost at our feet. We passed through Portici and Resina, the roof to buried Herculaneum, then through Torre del Greco and Annunciata, each so near one to the other as to appear quite a continued village, linked together by verdant vineyards.

From near Castellamare, the ancient Stabiæ, we walked through an olive grove to Pompeii, entering by an avenue of tombs. The long narrow streets were paved with lava, and the deep track of the chariot-wheels was still there, with the rust from the tire yet remaining. In the centre of each house was a large atrium, or court-yard, which was adorned with statues, fountains, and small parterres of flowers. From this there were doors opening into the sleeping apartments. These were exceedingly small, no larger than the state-rooms of our ocean steamers, and without windows; so light and air must have reached them by means of the wide open space of the atrium, over which it was said at mid-day there always floated a silken awning. All the floors were beautiful mosaics, and the walls painted in light colors. Upon this glowing surface were the figures of nymphs, of bacchantes, and of dancing girls, indescribably perfect in drawing and radiant in color.

In the house of Sallust we saw a fresco of *Diana and Acteon*, of most wonderful expression. In another the *Death of Adonis*. The form and face of Venus were represented in all the luxuriant beauty of the sea-born goddess, while grief seemed to cast a delicate veil over the full perfection of her charms. In her white arms she held Adonis, while her long brown hair mingled with the short curls which clustered around his noble brow. His dying eyes were fixed upon her face, with an expression of "love stronger than death." Cupid had fallen at his feet, his arrows scattered and his bow broken. It was really one of the most pathetic pictures I ever beheld. The hues and tints of coloring had all the richness and warmth of life. This fresco was in one of the recently uncovered houses, where now the treasures of painting and statuary are permitted to remain. All the first discoveries were taken to Naples.

Happy and prosperous indeed must have been the life of the Pompeians, in their beautiful city spread out on the plains, between the loveliest bay on earth's surface and the lofty Vesuvius, which for many centuries had been quietly sleeping. Gardens and vineyards, and smiling fields of grain, covered its gentle slopes, while forests crowned its summit; not, as now, furried and seamed with great wrinkles, and strewed with huge masses of black lava.

All day long we wandered through the silent streets, or lingered in the ruined temples of a dead religion, or, seated within the roofless houses, yielded ourselves up to the contemplation of Pompeii in its days of pride and power. We went down into the cellars of Diomede's villa, and saw the *Amphoræ*, wherein the ashes have displaced the rich *Falernian*. Near the doorway is the impression of a female form, of well-rounded proportions. Upon the skeleton arm was found a gold bracelet, with the name of "Julia" engraved upon it.

We visited the Forum, and the Temples of Jupiter and Venus. The theatre is so perfect, a drama might even now be acted therein. The amphitheatre is an immense structure, and in excellent preservation. Around it trees are growing, and grape-vines, whose long branches bind them together with garlands of fresh green foliage.

As I stood in the Temple of Isis, and looked up at Vesuvius, which seems to rise from the end of every street, sad and mournful feelings possessed me, increased by the silence, the intense silence, unbroken by the sound of footsteps or the song of birds. Pompeii was not destroyed by the lava flood, as was Herculaneum, but by showers of cinders and liquid mud, which penetrated to every portion of the houses, and formed a coating, which is readily removed. Thus we saw the gray wall of ashes and gravel, where a few men were working, and the marble facing of the doorway of a house they had just reached in their excavations. Upon it was carved the name of the owner. We dined in a green arbor, just without the walls, and ere the sun went down, bade farewell to Pompeii, and returned to Resina; thence ascended the mountain. Thousands, I may safely say tens of thousands of people, were climbing up in all directions, while a long line of carriages reached from the village almost to the Hermitage.

The eruption of Vesuvius is, in truth, the grand carnival time for Naples, and most quaint and curious specimens of humanity met us at every turn. As no stones were thrown up, we could approach to the very edge of the crater without danger. There appeared a strange fascination about the volcano, which absolutely invited and urged a nearer approach. The eruption had greatly increased since our first visit. Eight fiery mouths had opened, whence were pouring perfect rivers of lava. Its resemblance to Trenton Falls, or the Anio at Tivoli, had vanished. It was like Niagara on fire, rushing over the Horse-Shoe falls. Down, down rolled the ceaseless current. At the foot of the precipice, it flowed away in a slow stream, through the gorge, and into the plain below, overwhelming several small villages, and desolating the smiling valley far beneath us.

I have endeavored to place the sublime spectacle before you, but I feel there is no drapery of words in which I can clothe the "image in my mind," and present it to you as it appeared to me. This description is but the shadow of the wondrous reality.

We passed many hours upon the mountain, and then seated ourselves upon a cliff overhanging the cataract of lava, and supped by the red blaze of the volcano. Have I not told you of glorious scenes to remember? A day with Pompeii the *Destroyed*, and a night with Vesuvius the *Destroyer!*

Farewell! ever your friend.

CHAPTER LIV.

SAINT AGATA, *May* 8*th.*

AH! Mamma, we have left bewitching Naples, but I can't say I am ready to die after having seen it; rather would I wish to live, that I may remember its enchantments.

A pleasant little incident attended our departure, which I must tell you. Last night, until after two, we were upon the mountain, and as we came down, it was very dark. A little boy about ten years old, clothed in rags, ran before the horses to light up the road. After passing the "Witches' Cave," there was no more danger of "toppling o'er the precipice," and we directed the courier to take the child in the barouche, and stow him away under the feet of the coachman; whereupon both courier and coachman declared it was needless to do so, as a lazzaroni boy was accustomed to all kinds of fatigue and hardship. By the expiring flame of the torch, I saw the wearied face and appealing eyes of the little creature, and commanded them to take him up. They reluctantly did so, muttering at the mistaken kindness of the Signora, which they deemed sadly wasted upon such an atom of creation.

When we reached the hotel the child was asleep, and the coachman threw him out as one would do a little puppy, while he shook his rags, and prepared to run off. M. D.

called him, and gave him a five-franc piece, when he turned to me, saying, "Please, good Signora, tell me what this is; I never saw so much money before." There was such a look of intelligence in his countenance, that, after he was gone, I questioned the coachman about him, who looked incredulously at me, that it was possible to feel an interest in a vagrant like him. However, as I asked, he told me that many years ago he had discovered this child was in the habit of creeping into his stable, and sleeping upon the hay every night. Catching him there one morning, he inquired where he came from, and the boy answered that he had never known a father or mother, and his first remembrance was crawling about the streets near our coachman's stable, and after dark stealing in there. His only food had been bones thrown to him by the other beggars, who passed him from successful forays upon the neighboring kitchens. As he had no name, he gave him that of *Rafaello*, and permission to sleep with the horses; and when the child grew larger, he permitted him to rub the horses, and to hold torches for the carriage, when he drove up the mountain at night.

"Poor little being! no human creature to care for him!" I involuntarily cried. The coachman shrugged his shoulders as he said, "Bah! Signora! why should you care?—it is the fate of these lazzaroni. They are born in the streets, they live in the streets, (never sleeping under the roof of a house during all their lives,) and they die in the streets; then are thrown into a deep hole, like a dog."

The lustrous eyes of Rafaello really haunted me all night, and his pitiable story was often in my mind. Immediately after breakfast we entered our *vettura*, and drove away from the hotel. As we turned the corner, we heard a voice calling out, "Stop! Stop!" Supposing we had left some of our property in the apartments, we stopped; when little Rafaello ran up to the side of the carriage, exclaiming, "Pray, Signora, make them open the door." This was done, when the child sprang up on the step and said, "Please let me kiss your hand; you are the first and only person who ever spoke one kind word to poor Rafaello." Then seizing my hand, he kissed it several times, and pressed it to his little throbbing heart, then jumped down, and disappeared from our sight in an instant.

You may well imagine how this affected me, and how the tears poured from my eyes, as I vainly called him back. Never to *have heard but one kind word!* and that only the common expression of sympathy, that I would give to a dog or a cat I saw trampled upon and abused. And the child too, Mamma, was beautiful, as I looked at him standing on the steps of the carriage. His features were classically regular, his mouth exquisite, and his jet-black hair matted in close curls around his head. The glowing and radiant expression of soul and feeling which lighted up his face, can never be forgotten. I am sure this child is of noble blood, possibly the offspring of an unhallowed love, too fervid and daring for the conventionalities of the world, and whom the fear of shame and disgrace has actuated to this cruel act of inhumanity, in yielding up the creature of their passion to a living death.

Away through the streets we drove. The entire population appeared luxuriating in the sunbeams, which brightly tinged the little images of the Virgin over the booths of the water-vendors. The shops of the macaroni-sellers were surrounded with eager customers. There was the same dancing, acting, gaming, singing, and begging, as usual. No one was at work. No one followed the example of Vesuvius, who was constantly laboring and casting up great columns of smoke, and pouring forth rivers of lava.

For miles and miles from the walls of Naples we passed along roads hedged in with immense trees, wrapped around with grape-vines. It was a fête-day, and the peasants were out in gala costume—the women with red bodices laced up, and white shirts and sleeves, and the Neapolitan head-dress of square folds of linen; the men with velvet breeches and short jackets, with a bouquet stuck jauntily in their hats. The children were almost without clothes.

St. Agata is a pretty village, shut in by an amphitheatre of mountains. I find my eyes constantly drawn as though by a load-stone towards Vesuvius. So long have we been looking upon it, in sunshine and in storm, at mid-day and at midnight, at early morning and by the blaze of its volcanic light, that a portion of our existence will seem to leave us when we no longer behold it.

I am very tired, and the neat bed has a most repose-inviting aspect; so good night, dear Mamma.

Mola di Gaëta, May 9th.—We have stopped here for a few hours, in the *Villa Cicerone*, built upon the foundation of Cicero's house. The Apennines here come down always to the verge of the bay, leaving only a small valley, which is entirely covered with orange, citron, and lemon trees. We have had a delicious walk through the groves, now in full blossom, while the limbs are bending beneath the weight of the fruit. The view from the terrace where Cicero was wont to sit and hold his conferences with Pompey, is ineffably lovely—the shores around glittering with white villages, and rendered picturesque by old ruined towers. It was at this place the Pope lived for some months after he fled from Rome.

Evening at Terracina.—After leaving Gaëta, we passed the tomb of Cicero, a great round tower erected upon the spot where he was killed by the minions of Augustus. Then we came to the mountain region, wild and desolate. It was there the famous brigand *Fra Diavolo* made his haunt, and from the caves darted forth upon the unsuspecting traveller. Then we came to *Fondi*. There all the inhabitants were beggars. Many held their hands out of the windows, too lazy to come down and ask for charity. As we drove through, a loud chorus rang out, "Bread, bread, bread; we are all starving." Soon we reached the immense rocks of Terracina, crowned by the ruined arches of the Palace of Theoderic.

Our inn must be the very one famed in robber stories, for the corridors are dark and long, and the rooms dismal and insecure (quite without locks). We have a chamber opening to the sea, and I fell asleep to the music of the dashing waves. At dawn I awoke, and ran to the window to look out. The sea was calm, and the atmosphere filled with that blue light so peculiar to Italy. Like a *mirage*, it presents far-distant objects distinctly to the eyes. I clearly perceived the islands of Ischia and Procida, and Vesuvius with its coronet of smoke, looming up in the distance. As soon as the sun's rays touched them, they seemed to melt into air, and were seen no more.

Driving off shortly afterwards, we passed what I had fancied was an enormous haystack: what was my amazement to find it the "local habitation" of a woman, three children, and a man. Then over the Pontine marshes we rattled briskly along upon an excellent road, as perfectly shaded as the *Allée Verte* of Brussels. May had thrown its loveliness over the stagnant pools, covering them with myriads of flowers of a bright golden color. We dined at the *Fero Appia*, the chosen abode of *Malario;* and then to *Velletri*, the town where Virginius was encamped with the army of Coriolanus when the messenger reached him, telling of the seizure of his daughter as the child of a slave-woman. We saw the Volscian hills. The indomitable people who inhabited them were the fiercest enemy Rome ever had. We stayed all night at Velletri, and reached *Albano* in the early morning. There we took a small barouche and drove to the lake which fills the crater of a volcano. It is oval in shape, the waters of a deep blue, encircled by tall cliffs covered with splendid trees. High above the lake is *Monte Calvi*, with its ruined Temple of Jupiter. We passed the spot where Hannibal pitched his camp, when he looked with such longing eyes upon Rome. A charming drive through a deep wood, once the grove of Diana, brought us to *Nemi*, another gem-like lake, once the crater of a volcano also. Near it are the ruins of the Temple to Esculapius, and the tombs of the Curiatii and Horatii, the crumbling villas of Domitian and Pompey, and the Tomb of Ascanius, the son of Æneas.

From the Alban Mount we looked our last upon the Mediterranean, that historic sea along whose shores we had wandered with such deep delight for several months. Afar off was Rome, with the majestic dome of St. Peter's, and the broad Campagna, like a waveless lake of green. In a few hours we were again in the grand old city. The quietude was almost as profound as the repose of a grave-yard. What a contrast to the joy, the sunshine, the bustle, of Naples! The Romans are a handsome race, but they almost invariably have an unhappy expression about their great black eyes.

So still and silent were the streets, the rattling along of one carriage produced a stir among the idlers on the sidewalk. We tarried near one week in Rome, revisiting the antiquities, and spending one long day in St. Peter's. To-morrow at dawn we depart; therefore I will dispatch this letter from here. So good-bye, dear Mamma.

Civita Castellana, Sunday night.—It was really a grief to me to leave Rome, and an indescribable sadness pressed heavily upon my heart as we drove through the Piazza del Popolo. The square was filled with great flocks of goats, driven around by the shepherds from the Campagna to be milked at the doors of their customers. Along the tomb-environed Via Appia we passed for many miles, until the coachman called out, "Take your last look at Rome." The first object which met our eyes as we approached Rome was the glorious dome; so it was the last upon which they rested as we bade it farewell.

Civita Castellana, with its deep ravine, its aqueduct, and ruined fortress of Nepi, was exceedingly picturesque. During the day we had passed through the country of *Etruria*, where lived the skilful Etruscans, a people who had attained a high point of civilization, and were in their *décadence* ere Rome was founded. Many of their tombs were by the wayside; the inscriptions upon them are clearly cut, yet none can read them.

May 14th.—At dawn we were *en route*, and after a few miles came to

> "The woody Apennines,
> The infant Alps."

The scenery was really enchanting, each turn of the winding road revealing a new landscape, beautiful as the pictures of Claude Lorraine or Salvator Rosa. There were valleys of emerald green, and deep dells of forest-trees, groves of olive-trees, rising from the plains, even to the highest peaks of the mountains, and covering them with quaker-drab foliage, solemn and grave as a widow in half mourning. They formed a strong contrast to the yellow green hue of the grape-leaves. The vines are not trained in prim regularity, as in

France; but each seems wedded to one tree, (as a woman to her heart's love,) around which it twines its tendrils, enclosing it as though in a delicate network. Often we saw long branches which had caught to neighboring trees, thus binding many together as though it were a family group. The rich verdure of the wheat-fields was smooth and even as a velvet carpet. The towns were usually on the tops of the mountains, so we often saw them for hours ere we reached them. They really appeared as aerial cities built in the skies. (I must confess, when we attained them, they were any thing but heavenly, in sights, sounds, and odors.)

At mid-day, when we were on the very summit of a lofty mountain, a violent storm came on, thus revealing to us the Apennines in another phase of grandeur. The clouds rolled over and over like vast waves, while the lightning darted down into the dark gorges, and the thunder echoed from peak to peak.

We stopped some hours in the dear little village of *Narni*, which seems to cling to the side of a precipice. It is not far from the Bridge of Augustus, a splendid structure, with several arches perfect.

Terni, four o'clock.—We hurried rapidly on to Terni, that we might see the Falls this afternoon; but, alas! the rain is falling, and we cannot go. After reading to Octavia for some time, I fell asleep, with the pattering sound of the rain-drops still in my ears. Just at daylight the courier knocked at our door, with the pleasant tidings that the morning was clear. So we quickly dressed ourselves, jumped into a funny little carriage, with a postillion nearly lost in his enormous boots, and away through vineyards and olive groves to *Peperino*, perched like an eagle's nest on a peak of the mountain. Thence descending on foot, we entered the deep ravine, leading to the Falls of Terni. Perpendicular cliffs shut it in, while through the centre rushed with arrowy swiftness the river Velino. Imagine our amazement to find there the most noble grove of orange trees, in full flower. They had all the luxuriance of tropical climes, in the deep bosom of the Apennines. Then we entered a forest of old oaks, gray with age, and walking on for a mile or so, caught sight of the white mists, amid which rainbows were playing. Soon we began the ascent of a mountain-path, up which we clambered like goats, until we reached a little green arbor just opposite to the Falls. They are not grand, like Niagara, but still have a wild, picturesque beauty, worthy of the graphic power of Byron. We read his description of them as we stood with their spray falling over us. The circling mountains seem to shut in the sound, making the roar of the waters even more terrific—"the Hell of Waters," hissing, boiling, and rushing madly down from the heights above. The drops of moisture upon the huge rocks seem "the sweat of their great agony," pressed out by the torture of the resistless river. It would appear as though an artist had arranged the scene for an especial picture, so admirably appropriate are all the objects surrounding it—the steep cliffs, the ruined hermitage on their topmost peak, the well-placed trees, the shining evergreens, and falling waters, like liquid snow in rapid movement. Down the side of the mountain, in front of us, poured the swift Velino, in a sheet of white foam some hundred feet in length. A vast basin of rock received it, where the troubled stream seemed to repose for a second, then dashed wildly down into the abyss below.

We remained two hours, perched like birds upon a jutting point of the precipice, so great was the fascination of the spectacle. It was almost an act of heroism to leave it. We however were compelled to scramble down the dangerous pathway, and retrace our steps along the gorge. In a dark aisle of the oak forest, we heard the note of a bird, which quivered and swelled about the noise of the dashing waters. It was the song of the nightingale, from the green grottoes in the dense foliage of the little isles strewed amid the rushing waters of the Velino. The notes of this bird are not joyous and gushing with melody, as the song of our mocking bird, but a sad, mysterious, plaintive sound.

It was a delicious excursion to the Falls of Terni, and we were well repaid for leaving our pillows so early. The air was cool and fresh, making every breath a delight. As the mists rolled up like curtains, we saw the deep dells and the shining villages, all with "heaven-pointing spires," and the green valleys. An extra *buona mano* brought us soon to the town, where we breakfasted, and then set forth again. Our ascent of the mountains to-day was very slow for M. D. and Octavia, but far too rapid for me; for I would willingly have lingered days about the scenery which constantly met our eyes. At times our road was through verdant glades, then along the edge of fearful precipices, or between walls of rock. When the ascent was very steep, we had enormous dun-colored oxen to aid the horses in drawing us up. In these regions, as every where else in Italy, "the skeleton at the feast" was before us, in the shape of wretched and hideous beggars, following us for miles and miles. I cannot give to all, and thus they sadden my spirits very often. But beggars are M. D.'s *bête noire*, and the only thing he has found to vex him in this classic land. He curses them in *English*, and orders them to "get out" in *Indian.*

At *Spoleto* we saw the gates of Hannibal, and a short distance beyond it the tiny temple, mentioned by Pliny, dedicated in olden times to the river-god *Clitumnus;* then *Trevi*, built around and around a mountain, with a lofty church on its summit. At *Fogliono* we slept, and ere sunrise were up and away, passing through a more level country to *Assissi*, one of the most lovely cities of the Apennines. The grand Gothic church, with its noble colonnade, is like the gorgeous palace of a Roman emperor.

Leaving Assissi, we stopped at a magnificent church, called "Mary of the Angels," (built to enclose the little chapel of *St. Francis*, when he founded the order of Franciscan friars.) It is decorated with fine frescoes by Overbeck. St. Francis was a native of Assissi, and by his pure and beautiful character exercised a vast power over these impressionable people. His memory is even now revered, showing clearly that the remembrance of good deeds can never die. During the day we often met soldiers guarding carts, wherein were manacled prisoners. They were taking them to the prisons of Rome. They seemed to be all young peasants, and among them were many noble and classic faces, as perfect as the features one remarks in the frescoes of Pompeii. Our vetturino told me a great number were driven to crime by starvation.

We saw *Perugia* for hours before we attained the summit of the high mountain upon which it is situated. It was an Etruscan city, and bears evidence of having been extremely populous. We drove through the Etruscan gateway, which yet remains in good preservation. In the churches we saw the paintings of Perugino, and of his pupil Raphael. The entire valley of the Tiber was embraced in the view we saw as we descended to the plain. Along this we passed to the lake of *Thrasymene*, by whose shores the battle between Hannibal and the Consul Flaminius was fought. The Carthaginian had evidently the advantage. He occupied the heights, while the Romans were along the edge of the lake, and could not see far beyond their lines, in consequence of a thick mist. Hannibal rushed down upon them with his Africans and Spaniards, and so fierce was the conflict, so utterly absorbing, that an earthquake occurring during the battle was unfelt and unheeded by the rival armies! The Consul was killed, and thousands and thousands slaughtered, ere the horse of Hannibal completed the victory. The *Sanguinetto* (stream of blood) was a crimson river, tinging the pure waters of the lake for a vast distance out.

How calm, lovely, and quiet it was as we drove for miles along the shore to *Pasignano*, where we tarried all night, then by dawn proceeded again over the battle-field, and along the base of the mountains, which so gracefully rise from the verge of the waters. Green islands dotted the mirror-like surface, and here and there a ruined tower added a greater interest to the scene.

About mid-day we passed *Arezzo*, the birthplace of Petrarch. Crowds of peasants were out, for it was the *Fête of the Ascension*, (when the good Pope blesses his people from St. John of Laterano.) We were now in Tuscany, and the appearance of the people was quite different from the more southern portions. The women were fresh and handsome, with splendid black hair, elaborately plaited and twisted around the head in the shape of a basket. The men were strong and robust. In fact, all had a happy, well-fed look, quite refreshing to one's eyes.

At *Poggio Banolo* we stayed the night, and were fortunate in seeing a glorious sunset on the Apennines. A small black cloud was resting on the summit of a high mountain, when long rays of light streamed up from the west, and turned the dark cloud-bank to hues of golden radiance, while above it the sky was as intensely blue as the Azure Grotto of Capri. " Night and day seemed contending for supremacy." Along the east were fleecy clouds, like white sail-boats, wafted slowly onward by a gentle breeze. A violet-colored mist enwrapped the valley, and perfectly did I acknowledge the truth of Byron's description, as I gazed upon the changing beauty before me.

> And now they change; a paler shadow strews
> Its mantle o'er the mountains; parting day
> Dies like the dolphin, whom each pang imbues
> With a new color, as it gasps away,
> The last still loveliest, till 'tis gone, and all is gray."

I lingered long at my window, till the stars came to keep me company. From a grove of trees near by stole out the soft, sweet song of the nightingale, the only sound breaking the silence of the still night.

Before the "sun was over the mountains," we had entered the *Val d'Arno*, and were driving gaily along its fertile plains. At the small town of *San Giovanni* we stopped to see the skeleton of the man in the wall of San Lorenzo, an old church built many long centuries ago. It is only some years since workmen were making repairs, when they came to this skeleton. It is that of a tall man. The arms are tightly pressed across the breast, the knees bent inwards, and the toes overlapping the stone beneath. The attitude and the open mouth indicate death by suffocation. The man was evidently placed in the aperture, and the wall built up, while he was yet alive. There is no legend or story concerning it, but, what intensity of deadly hate must have raged in the hearts of the actors in this horrible scene! What ages of suffering must have passed through the soul of the victim, as stone after stone was cemented, and nearer and nearer came the frightful pang of such a death. An immense frame of glass is now placed before the skeleton, to preserve it, and over that a great door, which is only opened by paying a considerable fee.

At the neat town of *Fioretta* we breakfasted, and there a pretty young girl (*Annunciatia* by name) showed us the silk-worms, and explained to us the manner of feeding them, and told us how much care they required. Valuable little industrials! how much the world is indebted to them.

Our road was always along the Arno, and a far distant valley was pointed out as the famed *Vallambrosa*, which has caught a halo of interest from the names of Milton, Dante, and Ariosto. All of these poets loved it, and have immortalized its beauties in glorious verse.

At evening, when near the summit of a mountain, the vetturino called out, "Ecco Firenze la bella!" There indeed was *Florence the Beautiful*, in a valley shut in by an amphitheatre of mountains, upon whose highest peaks the snow still lingered. As we descended, by the road-side were long lines of blue lilies, through their midst flowing crimson rivulets of poppies. At the gateway our passports were examined, and then we drove through the narrow streets, over the river, to the "Hotel of Great Britain," where we have charming apartments, looking out upon the Arno, a wide, yellow-tinted stream, rushing and roaring against the piers of the bridges which traverse it. An embankment cased with stone confines it within its time-worn channel, passing directly through the centre of the city. Four bridges are built over it, and on one there are shops of jewellers, precisely like the Rialto of Venice. Above another is a long covered way, where the Grand Duke can pass from palace to palace without entering the street.

It is seven o'clock; dinner is served, and the courier waits to take my letter to the post, which goes to-night; so good-bye.

CHAPTER LV.

"Of all the fairest cities of the earth,
None is so fair as Florence. 'Tis a gem
Of purest ray. Search within,
Without, all is enchantment. 'Tis the past
Contending with the present, and in turn
Each has the mastery."

FLORENCE, *May 26th.*

I SENT off a very long letter the night we arrived here, dear Mamma. Since then a week has passed, and such a week of delight! Bright and glowing are its impressions upon my memory. I must describe some of them to you, and thus make you rejoice with me in the beautiful days which have blessed us in Florence.

The streets are rather gloomy, from the sombre shadows of the stupendous buildings rising on either side. These great palaces are constructed of huge rough stones, with walls of fabulous thickness, small windows with iron bars before them, and each house strong enough to serve as a fortress in time of need. In the heart of the city is the Piazza of the Grand Duke, with an immense fountain, and the statue of David by Michael Angelo, (one of the most inferior works, however, of the great sculptor.) Fronting the square is the *Loggia di Lanzi*, an open colonnade, wherein are seen the celebrated group of the "Rape of the Sabines" and the "Perseus" of Benvenuto Cellini.

In the *Uffizi Palace* we saw the "Venus di Medici." This "wondrous statue that enchants the world," was found in the *Portico of Octavia*, and more than three thousand years ago was deemed a miracle of beauty, sculptured by Phidias. The *Tribune*, now the home of the goddess, is of an oval shape, with a rich mosaic floor and a gorgeously frescoed dome. The statue is placed in the centre of the room, and near it are the "Knife-Grinder" and the "Wrestlers," both remarkable works of art by unknown sculptors. The statue of Venus appears much smaller than the forms of European women. It reminded me of the little, graceful figure of a very young Creole girl, and the chin and mouth are strikingly like my little Cara Netta. We were all impressed with this resemblance the moment we looked upon it. The statue is not the form of a voluptuous beauty, "to win whose love men would peril life and soul." It is rather of a refined and spiritual loveliness, delicate, pure, and tender.

On the wall near the statue hang two pictures by Titian. They both represent Venus in different attitudes, radiant with sensuous beauty, and glowing with the most gorgeous tints of color, as fresh, full, and bewildering as the undraped form of a perfect woman. Titian's "Bella Donna" and "Flora" are here too. His "Flora" charmed me, it is so soft, sweet, and loving in expression; then the "Virgin," "St. Joseph and the Infant Christ," by Michael Angelo, (one of the few easel-pictures he ever painted,) and several by Raphael; the "Sybil" of Guercino, and the "Madonna" of Correggio. In truth, dear Mamma, we spent hours and hours amid these galleries, gazing upon countless multitudes of pictures. The "Medusa's Head" of Leonardo da Vinci is one of the most fearful things and the most impressive I noted among them.

One room is devoted entirely to "Niobe and her Children." The figures seem starting from their pedestals, as though flying from the arrows of Apollo. Niobe is a majestic statue. Upon her face is portrayed the overpowering and hopeless agony of the mother's heart, as she sees one after another of her offspring dying before her eyes. These marble forms told such a story of the soul's anguish and desolation, that I was compelled to leave the hall quite blind with tears.

Within this palace are galleries of statuary, cabinets of bronzes and medals, and great cases filled with precious stones and rare jewels. The long hall containing the "Autograph portraits of Painters" is exceedingly interesting. The picture of Raphael pleased me most, for it was so like my ideal of the divine artist.

Leaving the Uffizi, we crossed the Arno, and drove to the studio of Powers, to whom Col. John Preston and Edward Everett had given me letters. He is a plain, unpretending person, perfectly a western man in his frank, cordial manner. He has wonderful eyes, luminous as stars, from which glance forth, as he speaks, rays of light. He presented me to his wife and children; and during our sojourn here, has invited us to his house, where we met a most charming circle of Americans. But in Powers' studio I revelled in pleasure. Oh! what forms of beauty has he created, almost equal to those of Praxiteles and Phidias, the sculptors of Grecian fame. There was the model of his "Greek Slave" and his "Eve"—the Eve of Milton,

> "God-like, erect, with native honor clad
> In naked majesty."

In her face we see the struggle between desire and fear,

while the serpent is coiled around a tree by her side, watching the influence of his words. The form of Eve is larger than the Venus di Medici.

Then we saw the statue of "America," for the capitol at Washington. Beneath her feet are the chains of tyranny, while one arm is raised, with the hand pointing westward. "California" is represented by a beautifully formed woman, a divining rod in one hand; in the other, which she conceals behind her, is a "bunch of thorns." A bust of "Proserpine" was exquisite. It rises from a capital of acanthus leaves. Sweet and lovely is the pure young face.

Next we went to the studio of Buchanan Read, the poet and painter, whose pictures, both in words and by the artist's pencil and brush, are so enchanting. We had known each other in bright days "long ago," and imagine his amazement to meet me here, when he believed me quietly at home in the far-away South. He was earnestly glad to see me, and showed me many very bewitching ideal pictures. There was the "Fall of the Pleiad," and "Sir Hildebrand and Undine;" then "Excelsior!" with the rose-hued light of the sky of Naples, and several illustrations of Shakspeare. As we sat merrily talking, Read remarked, "What a joyful meeting it will be between Mrs. Kinney and yourself!" Then he told me she lived here in Florence, having made this her home since her husband's appointment as Minister at Turin had ceased. You remember it was Mrs. Kinney who first presented Read to me. "So we three shall meet again," I cried, running down the stairway, and driving rapidly to the *Casa del Bello*, where he told me she resided.

Oh! Mamma, how truly happy I was to embrace this dear, precious friend! and her delight quite equalled my own. Italy has done wonders for her. When we parted, seven years ago, she was almost dying with bronchitis, and as thin and pale as a shadow. But now she is splendid; her eyes bright with joy, her cheeks glowing with health, and her arms and bust as exquisite as those of Canova's Venus. Then her genial manner, her sparkling and *spirituelle* conversation, so bewitched me, I quite forgot M. D. and Octavia waiting my appearance to dine. It was night ere I reached the hotel.

Thus, dear Mamma, I have written you the record of *one* day in Florence, and you may well judge how charming it was. Good night.

We have received several visits from the Duke of Casigliano, Minister of Foreign Affairs. Our kind friend, Mr. Manzoni, gave us a letter to him, and he called, directly upon our arrival, to welcome us to Florence, and has been exceedingly courteous and polite. We have visited his palace, where we saw two or three original paintings by Carlo Dolce, and a full-length portrait of Nicholas of Russia, taken while he was the guest of the Prince Corsini, (father of the Duke;) besides many great rooms hung with the finest pictures of the old masters as well as modern artists.

The Duke is an extremely agreeable man, conversing with spirit, animation, and intelligence. He related to me many interesting incidents concerning his own family, and many of Florentine history. He inquired particularly about Edward Everett, whom he had known in his youth, saying his father, the Prince, entertained for Mr. Everett the highest admiration and respect. When we were in Rome, we had gone through the Corsini Palace, containing splendid works of art. It belongs now to the Duke.

The Pitti Palace is a vast structure, built by Lucca Pitti, the opponent and rival of the Medici family. It has a glorious wealth of pictures and statuary. The rooms are divided into halls, and bear the names of the heathen gods and goddesses. The floors are smooth mosaics of wood, and the ceilings all painted in frescoes. Vain effort would it be for me to attempt to tell you of a hundredth part of the treasures of this storehouse of art. In one of the galleries we saw the *Madonna della Segiola*, by Raphael, one of the most lovely of his conceptions; the "Judith" of Allori, and the "Death-scene of Cleopatra;" also the "Venus" of Canova.

Then we visited the Cathedral, with its great dome, and beautiful Gothic tower just by its side, built by Giotto, and designed to surpass any structure of ancient architects. Both are inlaid with marble slabs of white, black, and red. The baptistery has wrought bronze doors of enormous size. There in the pavement is a square, called the "Stone of Dante," where he was wont to bring his stool, and sit in contemplation.

We saw, too, the house of Michael Angelo, still in the possession of his descendants, and religiously kept precisely as he left it, when borne to his last resting-place.

In the church of San Lorenzo is the mausoleum of the Medici family, built by Ferdinand the First in 1600. It was said that he intended it to contain the Holy Sepulchre, which he proposed taking from the church at Jerusalem, and had a fleet upon the coast to receive it, and bring to Florence this most precious relic of the world; but his design was discovered and frustrated. Then he converted it to a mausoleum for the ducal family. The walls are entirely lined with *pietre dure* (hard stones) of lapis lazuli, jasper, chalcedony, agate, and others even more precious, and the lofty dome richly frescoed. The tomb of Lorenzo di Medici, by Michael Angelo, is magnificent.

Both art and science are greatly indebted to Florence, and their light beams forth from galleries, libraries, and palaces. In the Museum of Natural History there are preparations in wax, commencing with seeds, leaves, plants, and small animals, and then constantly ascending through all the organs of the human frame, until the whole structure is revealed, from its germ to the full perfection of strong and healthy life. Then come the aspects of various diseases, death, and the sad appearance after the spirit has left the mortal tenement. Of course, these were of deep interest to M. D., but to us they were a solemn and unpleasant spectacle.

The Laurentian Library has many treasures in manuscripts and illuminated missals. It was founded by Cosmodi Medici, who, in these vast collections, possesses a monument as imperishable as bronze or marble. From all portions of the civilized world he obtained valuable works. His great wealth and his mercantile influence rendered these acquisitions exceedingly easy. There was the letter of Dante, in which he rejected the permission to return to Florence under the conditions imposed; and the sonnets of Petrarch to Laura, with their portraits. Then there was a copy of Virgil, among the first ever made, and the *Pandects*, captured at Amalfi by the army from Pisa, as early as 1100, and fragments of the writings of Tacitus and of Cicero.

The Tribune of Galileo consists of two apartments, with a noble statue of the great astronomer. The frescoes represent in vivid colors the discoveries of Galileo and other philosophers. Large cases with glass doors contain the instruments he used; among them, the first telescope he constructed—a simple wooden tube, with a double convex lens. We visited Galileo's house, where he received Milton, and one lovely afternoon drove up to his tower, whence at night he read the wonders of the starry world, and in the moon's orb "descried new lands, rivers or mountains." In my youth, you recollect, Mamma, how passionate was my love for the study of astronomy, and how often during long hours of the night I watched the heavenly bodies. Reading of the fierce trials of Galileo, my heart always swelled with sad emotion, or thrilled with delight, at his exultant exclamation (when forced to kneel and recant his belief in the earth's motion), "*E pur si muova!*" (still it moves.) Think, then, what a joy-invested thought it is to me, that I have looked upon the stars "from the top of Fiesole," standing on the very same rock of the battlement once pressed by the feet of Galileo!

We have seen the house where Dante was born, and the house of Americus Vespucci, and the Strozzi Palace, like an enormously strong fortress, and the *Palazzo Vecchiò*, with its overhanging battlements, its great tower, and massive staircase. In one of the faded saloons is a Portrait of Bianca Capello, and upon the walls are recorded the triumphs of the Medici in the wars with the Florentines.

The churches of Florence are numerous, but none of them seem finished. In Santa Croce (the Westminster Abbey of Florence) are the magnificent tombs of Michael Angelo, of Galileo, of Alfieri, and many others, great and immortal by the divine gift of genius. Truly has Byron said,

> "In Santa Croce's holy precincts lie
> Ashes which make it holier, dust which is
> Even in itself an immortality."

We visited many of the cloisters attached to the churches and convents. They are long colonnades built around an open court, and are intended as promenades for the monks, where, in seclusion from the eyes and the noise of the world, they may walk and meditate. To these besides are attached infirmaries, and shops where medicines are given to the poor by apothecary priests. We were often told of a society called *Compagnia della Misericordia*, which included in its ranks men of the highest nobility, even the Grand Duke himself. It is their office to attend the sick, to console the wretched, to befriend the erring, and in all cases of accident, to bear the wounded sufferer to a hospital. They never accept money for their services, or are permitted to eat or drink in any house they enter. A certain number of the *Compagnia* are detailed for a stated period, and at a moment's warning are summoned to their duties by the tolling of the bell of the tower. An Italian nobleman told me he had seen the Grand Duke, when entertaining a large dinner-party in his palace, rise up, and, without a word, withdraw to obey the sound which called him to deeds of mercy and charity.

In an old monastery there has lately been discovered a "Last Supper" by Raphael. It had been covered over by a whitewash of lime, and was by accident discovered. It is a touching picture, and the face of Christ is angelic, yet seemingly touched with a human feeling of tenderness, as he entwines with his arm the form of his "beloved disciple," who apparently has fallen asleep with his head resting on his Master's bosom.

In the *Palazzo del Podestá* we saw the portrait of Dante, by Giotto, which within the last twenty years has also been rescued from the whitewash. Our countryman, the gifted poet and scholar, Richard H. Wilde, united with several other persons, and induced the Government to permit them to remove the covering of lime at their own expense. After many difficulties they accomplished their purpose. It is the resemblance of the poet ere sorrow and injustice had stamped their wrinkles on his face. The face is handsome, the brow noble, and the expression of the eyes singularly intellectual.

CHAPTER LVI.

The topic of this night's *tête-à-tête* with you, dear Mamma, must form a letter apart from the excessively long one written yesterday.

I have spent the evening at the *Casa Guidi*, with Mr. and Mrs. Browning, whose poems we have read with such earnest pleasure at home. We have mutual and dear friends in England, and soon after my arrival, we called upon them, and have found in their acquaintance another link of enchantment to bind Florence to memory forever.

During all the years of her early life, Elizabeth Barrett was an invalid, shut in from society, and often even from the conversation of friends. While a close prisoner in her chamber, she wrote beautiful and noble poems, which have made the delight of many a household beyond the Atlantic, and the joy of her compatriots. Robert Browning, himself a poet, a man of rare talent and great personal attraction, read these outpourings of her pure and gifted mind, and loved the unseen authoress. After many weary months of entreaty, he was allowed to visit her, as she lay upon the sofa of her boudoir. I need not tell you, the sight of her sweet and gentle face, and her beaming, soul-lit smile, completed the conquest her genius had commenced. He married her, and brought her immediately to Italy, where they have ever since resided. Although her health is still delicate, and requires the unceasing watchfulness of love and friendship, she becomes every year stronger in this delicious clime, and is the happy mother of a lovely little boy.

Robert Browning is an admirable man, frank, cheerful, and charming. He is said to be the most captivating conversationist on the Continent; (however, I think there are some in America quite equal to him.) There is a genial warmth, and a sparkling merriment, in his words, which made us friends at once. Then Mrs. Browning I loved directly. Oh! she is indeed a precious gem! With all her varied and profound learning, and high poetic gift, she is as simple and unassuming in manner as a child. What a visit of joy it was to me, in their love-sanctified and art-beautified home. Their union seems perfect in happiness, the mind as well as the heart having met its own affinity. When we parted, after some hours of delightful conversation, wherein the bright and tender nature of Elizabeth Browning shone like soft beams of light, I felt as though years of pleasant acquaintance had passed between us.

Dear Mrs. Kinney, our own sweet poetess, has been most cordially kind and affectionate to us. In her apartments we have spent several evenings of true enjoyment. She has presented me to a number of distinguished people who live here, Florentines, English, and Americans; among them an exceedingly handsome couple, the Count and Countess Cottrell, and two brothers of Tennyson the poet. We met there, likewise, Hart, the sculptor, who is modelling the statue of Henry Clay for the ladies of Richmond. He tells me the work is nearly completed, and other persons say it will be a most noble and majestic monument to America's greatest statesman.

During an agreeable evening we spent with Mr. and Mrs. Powers, we met many of your old friends. There was Mrs. Page (wife of Capt. Page, of the Navy), Mr. and Mme. Soulard, from St. Louis, and Mr. and Mrs. Edward Center, of New York, who have been living many years in Europe. Mrs. Center tells me, that her pretty little sister, Cora Withers, who is so remarkable for her superb voice, has married a Russian, named de Wilhorst, and gone with him to Switzerland.

There are numbers of Americans here for the education of their children, and several young women studying music, to become opera singers.

When breakfast was over, an elegant barouche was brought to the door, in which we drove to palaces, galleries, and studios, spending long hours amid the glorious creations of genius, and amid the relics of the past. Returning to our hotel at three o'clock, we found an excellent dinner, and luscious dessert of fruit and confectionery awaiting us. At five we started forth for our afternoon drive, and then ended the day by passing the evening with my sweetest of sweet friends, Mrs. Kinney; with the intellectual Brownings; and at the hospitable house of Powers; meeting every where refined, cultivated, and appreciative people. I like the Italians. They are kind-hearted, agreeable, and social, and we have constantly received from them cordial attentions and graceful courtesies.

One beautiful feature of Florence I have not described to you yet. It is the drives about its environs. They are enchanting. To Fiesole we went one afternoon. It is a lofty hill, with massive ruins of the Etruscan city, once crowning its summit. The view from the broken ramparts is really a picture of beauty. The valley of the Arno was beneath us, with Florence in its midst, and stately hills, "infant mountains," rising from its green depths, while white villages and neat villas nestled amid the groves of oak and elm. Roads wound around every eminence, lined with hedges of roses and oleander, and the river, smooth and calm, gleamed like a silver ribbon spread out upon a pavement of verd antique. In the words of the Italian poet, I could almost exclaim,

> "This region surely is not of earth;
> Was it not dropt from heaven?"

Other afternoons we drove to *San Miniato*, then to the heights of *Bello Sguardo* (beautiful view); then to the Monastery of *La Certosa*, to the *Poggio Imperiale*, country palace of the Grand Duke, where he was then residing, and to *La Petraia*, (another palace,) where there is a "Venus" by John of Bologna, in bronze. It adorns a fountain, and the goddess wrings the water from her hair. It is very fanciful, and a pretty design. From all these places the view was equally as lovely as from Fiesole and from the tower of Galileo.

As a *bonne bouche*, I have reserved for the last the *Cascine*, and the *Boboli Gardens*. These are different, since they are the fashionable drive and promenade of the Florentines. We always ended our excursions without the walls, and on the heights encircling the city, by driving in the Cascine, very near the city, or walking in the Boboli Gardens, attached to the Pitti Palace. They are deemed the most splendid gardens in Italy, (but not to me half so beautiful as those of the Villa Pallaricini, near Genoa.) There are long aisles, like those of a cathedral, cut through masses of foliage, and lofty, smooth walls of verdurous green, grottoes formed in huge rocks, with fringes of creeping plants, half concealing their dim and cool recesses; parterres of flowers and shrubbery; and amid acacias, Italian pines, and laurel trees, are statues of marble and of bronze, the workmanship of Michael Angelo and of the famous sculptor, John of Bologna. At the base of the hill in these gardens is a little lake, with an island covered thickly with orange trees. There at evening, along its pebbly margin, assembled hundreds of children, while the avenues and walks were thronged with well-dressed people.

The Cascine is a drive a mile or more in length, just without the walls of the city. It combines the attractions of Hyde Park and the Champs Elysées, for there are multitudes of pedestrians, and many splendid equipages of the Florentine nobility, likewise of the noble and wealthy English people, who are very numerous, making this city their permanent abode. The Cascine (signifying the Dairy Farm) belongs to the Grand Duke, and is opened and embellished by his command for the pleasure and happiness of his subjects. It is a level tract of ground, bounded on the one side by the Arno, and on the other by the Apennines. Two carriage roads run through thick forests of fine trees, which are shut in by low hedges of laurel, myrtle, and laurestina. Within these forests are the game preserves, and we often saw flocks of graceful pheasants running to and fro through the long grass. Then amid these labyrinths of trees are many delightful rides, which fair *equestriennes*, with their attendant chevaliers, seemed vastly to enjoy; and pleasant walks along shaded avenues, expressly fitted for the "loving and beloved." A kind of creeping vine, resembling the ivy, closely entwines every tree from the root to the summit, covering the bark so entirely, the trees appear like smooth green columns, and produce a charming effect, as the eye wanders through this vast cathedral of nature's own creation.

In a great square in front of the Farm House, a fine

band of music plays several evenings of the week. There all the carriages, filled with handsome people, foreign and "native-born," assemble for a kind of reunion *al fresco.* Gentlemen leave their horses, and standing on the steps of the different equipages, carry on merry and gallant conversations. Pedestrians move in and out among them, and I often remarked a sly flirtation going on between a bright-eyed Florentine and an elegant young officer, while two or three of his comrades occupied the attention of the still beautiful Mamma.

The Cascine is the resort of the famous *Flower-Girls of Florence.* They are the most pertinacious and determined creatures in the world. If you will not buy, they will give you exquisite bouquets, saying at the same time very pretty words, which seldom fail to bring forth a return in silver. Some of them were young, and really good-looking, but with a bold, impudent air. They were jauntily dressed, with immense Leghorn flats on their heads. There was one who appeared always watching for us, whenever we left our hotel. She would glide along with a swimming step, and with a most seductive smile, showing her splendid teeth, place a delicate bouquet in M. D.'s hand. Octavia and I had many a merry laugh at the way he received it, which was not complimentary to the Flower-Girl, and rendered very emphatic by the use of a few American oaths. M. D. declares foreigners understand *these*, if they can't speak English!

Oh! what an enjoyable place was this Cascine! What happy moments we spent there, sometimes in delightful conversation with the many agreeable acquaintances we have made in Florence, or driving through the green-aisled forests, or walking in the leafy labyrinths, or watching the radiant sunset and the purple glow on the mountains, which lingered long upon them after the sun had sunk behind the snow-capped peaks. Several times we tarried in the Cascine until after dark, and then the forest, and the velvet-like lawns, were glittering with innumerable fire-flies and glow-worms, darting like little stars amid the foliage:

> "Blazing by fits, as from excess of joy,
> Each gush of light a gush of ecstasy."

One morning at daylight we went down to Pisa; and as all its wonders are comprised in a limited space, we soon saw them. They are the Cathedral, the Leaning Tower, the Baptistery, and the Campo Santo.

The cathedral is really grand, in the form of a Latin cross, with long rows of Corinthian pillars. Above them is a curious gallery, where the women were all compelled to sit in ancient days. Every town in Italy is protected by some especial saint: thus Florence has San Giovanni; Rome, St. Peter; Naples, San Gennaro; Venice, San Marco; and Pisa, San Ranieri, whose statue is placed in the centre aisle of the cathedral.

The Campo Santo is an immense square, surrounded by a colonnade, roofed over, beneath which was placed the sacred earth brought from Mount Calvary by a pious bishop some centuries ago. The walls are painted in fresco by Orcagni, and portray the Triumphs of death. They are fearful to behold. Though much faded by the salt air, they still retain all their outlines, revealing the wild and almost satanic fancy of the painter. There are thousands and thousands of tombs, and many sarcophagi and noble statues brought from Egypt, Greece, and Rome.

As we were departing, we met a long train of priests in their dresses of ceremony, all holding lighted candles. They were going into the Campo Santo, to chant a requiem over the tomb of a person who had died five hundred years before this day. I followed them, and saw them gather around a plain marble slab, where their united voices swelled forth in a solemn dirge, deeply impressive amid the silence and desolation of the spot. An old priest told me it was often the custom, upon the anniversary of the death of one exceedingly loved, thus to renew the memory, by the contemplation of their virtues. There was something extremely beautiful to me in this remembrance of the dead, which defied time and its forgetfulness. Many and many are the heart-touching customs and ordinances of the Catholic religion.

The Baptistery is a circular building of white marble, with a singular pulpit, by Nicolo da Pisa. It has seven columns, which support it. One rests upon the back of a crouching figure, and the others upon lions, tigers, and griffins.

The Leaning Tower of Pisa, of which I have heard since memory made a record of objects described, is the *campanile* or belfry of the cathedral, and is the most graceful tower I have seen. It is all of white marble, perfectly fresh and snowy in appearance, although it was built about seven hundred years ago. It is one hundred and eighty feet in height. There are eight stories, each surrounded with a delicate colonnade of pillars. The view from the summit is widely extensive, reaching to the Mediterranean on the one side, and to the Apennines on the other. There can be no doubt, from the spongy nature of the soil, that the foundation sunk on one side as they were building it. Rather an unpleasant feeling seizes one while standing beneath it; every moment it seems ready to topple over.

We saw the spot where the " Tower of Hunger " stood. It was there Ugolino and his children were starved to death. Of their frightful sufferings, Dante has written in his " Inferno."

From Pisa to Florence the railway passes through a fertile and well-cultivated country. As it was a day of *festa* (holiday), we saw multitudes of the inhabitants. They are a fine, healthy-looking race of people, with fresh complexions The women are remarkable for their full busts and white teeth; they appéared very industrious, too, for even in the fields they held the distaff, and were constantly spinning.

When we reached our hotel, we spent some charming hours in the parlor of Mr. and Mrs. Whales, whom we had known at Naples. Mr. Whales, being blessed with great wealth, is enabled to purchase multitudes of splendid engravings and beautiful pictures, besides rare and precious old volumes of the Italian poets and historians. As he is a man of excellent taste and good education, his selections are really as admirable as they are valuable.

May 28th, twelve o'clock at night.—" All that is bright must fade," saith the poet, and thus our enchanting visit to beautiful Florence is ended. Although it is very late, I feel it will be a joy to me to tell you, dear Mamma, of the many pleasures which have occupied the hours of this our last day here.

By six in the morning we were awakened by the ringing of bells, and hearing it was the " Day of Pentecost," we hastened to the duomo (the cathedral), where a grand high mass was to be celebrated. The superb edifice was hung with rich draperies, and regiment after regiment of stalwart soldiery-looking men were marched in, until there were many thousands standing in long columns, as though they were gaily decorated statues, so still and motionless they appeared. At length a throng of priests entered, and a bishop or cardinal in gorgeous vestments. Then came a clashing of arms upon the marble pavement, and the Grand Duke appeared. He was surrounded by handsome officers, and his noble guard brought up the rear. He is not remarkable in appearance; is seemingly about sixty years old, with hair and moustache of snowy whiteness. He was dressed in uniform, and wore several stars of brilliants and orders upon his breast. He was soon followed by the Grand Duchess and ladies of the court, dressed in magnificent ball costumes, with feathers, and a profusion of diamonds. A tribune was prepared for them, in which they were all seated, and then the mass began. The music of the coro (choir) was delightful, the finest voices in the city having been engaged for the ceremonial. The Grand Duchess is a dignified woman, rather inclining to *embonpoint.* She has a kind, good-natured expression of face. Some of her ladies were decidedly pretty, and others of excellent style and *tournure.*

The tones of the great organ lingered among the lofty columns and within the immense dome, as though unwilling to depart. It was really a fine pageant, and the entire duomo, which is exceedingly large, was filled with a well-looking and well-dressed crowd of people.

After leaving the cathedral, I drove to the house of the Count and Countess Cottrell. They have a splendid collection of pictures. The Count is a good artist himself. The Countess, who is an Englishwoman, is a most engaging creature. She is just now mourning the death of a precious child. You can well know how my heart was drawn towards her, and how truly my sympathies were awakened for the sorrowing mother.

A friend of mine lived in a modest little villa, without the walls; and driving out there to say farewell, a sudden turn in the road brought us near the whole Royal party, who were just returning to their present home, in one of the palaces in the environs of Florence. Of course, our coachman stopped, while the splendid carriages of the court passed by. In one of them the Grand Duke and the Duchess were seated, talking very merrily. They both gave me a most gracious salutation (which is always their custom when they meet persons evidently strangers.) I returned it quite as gracefully, and then drove back to the city, making numerous visits of adieu, until dinner; after which, accompanied by pretty Louise, the step-daughter of our excellent and learned friend, Mr. Willis Hall, (who is now here,) we went to the Cascine. It was glorious this evening. The day of *festa* had summoned forth every body. All were in handsome toilettes, and there were perfect regiments of officers. The band "discoursed delicious music," and a sunshine of pleasure and contentment rested upon the faces of "peer as well as peasant." The gleaming white villages and noble villas sprinkled along the heights of *Val d'Arno*, were still glowing in the rose-hues of evening, when we left the Cascine.

Going to our hotel, we quickly made our evening toilette, and drove to Mrs. Kinney's, where she had assembled a large party to do honor to my last evening. It was a perfect bouquet of notabilities, of poets and poetesses, of sculptors and painters. In truth, there was not a single uninteresting person in all the gathering. We were truly sorry to miss seeing Mr. Buchanan Read. He was ill, but his sweet wife, with the two children, came down to see me. (They live on the floor above Mrs. Kinney.)

Mr. Kinney was for many years editor of the Newark Advertiser, and so ably did he conduct the paper, that when General Taylor became President, he made him Minister at Turin, where he was highly appreciated and respected by the Sardinian government.

I quite neglected to tell you Judge Carleton and his wife, a charming person, are also here.

An enchanting evening we spent, you may suppose, amid such genial, refined, and cordial people. Mrs. Browning, who rarely ever goes out at night, paid me the compliment of coming on my account. I cannot tell you how pained I was to part with these kind friends; it seemed as though I had known and loved them always. But the sad moment came at last; and with tears, and earnest blessings, we separated.

As we drove home, we stopped upon the Bridge of the Trinitá, to see the long rows of gas-lights mirrored in the Arno, producing a dazzling effect upon the swiftly-rushing river.

In the quietude of my own chamber I am now seated, and as "sleep comes not at my bidding," I write you my last letter from Florence. Like my entrancing visit, it is now ended; so, precious Mamma, good night.

CHAPTER LVII.

BOLOGNA, *May 29th.*

AT six this morning, with a deep sadness upon our spirits, we left "Firenze la Bella," as its inhabitants most appropriately style their beautiful city. For one who has "elegant leisure," no place in Europe can be a more charming residence than Florence Its vast treasures of painting, statuary, science, and literature, are free and open to all, the lowly as well as the high-born. Its environs of exquisite loveliness, its joyous Cascine, its admirable hotels, its delightful society, and (what is very attractive in our utilitarian age) its remarkable cheapness of living, render it a desirable home either for weeks, months, or years.

Twenty miles on a railway brought us to Pistoja. There we took the diligence, and soon after began the ascent of the "woody Apennines," which we crossed by the *Pass of La Collina.* How slowly we crawled up you may imagine, when you hear we had two large oxen added to the six horses already attached. I had no idea, apart from the Alps, there was any scenery so grand in Italy. The mountains swelled up around us as though they were great undulating waves of the sea, some bearing on their surface pretty villages and farm-houses, and fields of grain, rendered so small from our vast height above them. They were as toy buildings and mimic gardens. Had little Cara Netta been with us, she would have realized her childish wish, so often expressed, of being " in the clouds; " for, as we stepped upon the topmost peak of La Collina, suddenly the clouds gathered above and below, quite shutting us in, and rolling and surging around us like the volumes of smoke within the crater of Vesuvius.

Casting off the oxen, we quickly descended, gladly leaving the " region of mists " and passing frequently between two great mountains, upon which the road above us (we had already traversed) seemed no larger than a mark of white chalk upon the rugged rocks.

At *La Porretta*, celebrated for its hot baths, we dined, then accompanying the noisy Reno, a brisk mountain-stream, we drove on to Bologna. Long ere we reached it, we saw far up on the lonely height of *Monte Guardia* the church of the Madonna of San Luca, containing a black image of the Virgin, said to have been brought hither by a hermit from Constantinople, in the eleventh century. A covered way, consisting of hundreds and hundreds of arches, like a portico, leads from the city to the summit of the mountain.

As Bologna was Luigi's birthplace, we gave him liberty to spend all the time with his relatives, and engaged an excellent cicerone, who conducted us to every point of interest. Of course, M. D. went first to the University, whose halls once numbered ten thousand students, and whence beamed the light of science over the entire Continent. He saw the very room where the first dead body was dissected, and the one in which the first experiment in galvanism was made. We were also deeply interested in seeing the platform whereon Novella d'Andrea often lectured on the canon-law, occupying the chair of her father. So striking was her beauty, that the professors were compelled to have a curtain placed before her, that the students might not see her face, and thereby be distracted from the subject of discourse.

> "A veil drawn before her,
> Lest, if her charms were seen, the students
> Should let their young eyes wander o'er her,
> And quite forget their jurisprudence."

Many other women at different periods occupied professors' chairs. Even within a few years Matilda Tambroni was teacher of the Greek in these halls. Cardinal Mezzofanti, the learned linguist, who was a native of Bologna, succeeded her.

The libraries are numerous, and filled with a vast wealth of learning. The churches are many, richly adorned with pictures. The two leaning towers of *Garrisendi* and *Asinelli* (near neighbors) appear bowing to each other, and are very curious. They are supposed to have been built by two families, between whom there was a deadly feud. They each resolved to erect a monument to perpetuate their rank and glory. Thus side by side the structures went up, and like the tower of Babel, the end of their ambition seemed the clouds; but death closed the career of one of the rivals, and the other ceased the work. Probably to make them more remarkable, they were erected in defiance of the accepted rules of architecture.

Guido Rene was born in Bologna, and it is only here he is seen in the plenitude of his fame. We saw whole galleries of his pictures. His "Crucifixion" is a solemn and fearful painting, a more dignified rendering of that awful scene than any we have ever looked upon. The "Madonna della Pieta" is an immense picture, filling an entire portion of the hall The Saviour is lying dead upon his bier, while the Madonna stands near him, her face turned away, and her eyes raised to Heaven. The expression of her beautiful features shows the deepest agony of the soul, mingled with a divine resignation. Then we saw Guido's "Sampson," and his "Murder of the Innocents," and the "Saint Cecilia" of Raphael; and many pictures of Caracci and Domenichino.

In an old church we saw Guido's tomb. Within it was buried, also, his favorite pupil, Elizabetta Sarani, a very wonderful woman. She was a painter of rare excellence (as her "Magdelene" attests), a sculptor of admirable talent, and a poetess. To all these gifts she added most seducing beauty,—and yet she died at *twenty-six*. What, think you, caused her death? Why, disappointed love! An Italian writer, speaking of her, says "she succeeded perfectly in every thing she attempted, save in winning the heart of the man she adored." After Pope Clement crowned Charles the Fifth in Bologna, he tarried some days there; saw Elizabetta, and looked upon her remarkable works; and, appreciating her genius, offered to take her to Rome. But she refused, and was found dead on the pavement of the church where she often went to pray. It was surmised she ended her life by poison. Was it not supremely ridiculous thus to cast away her beautiful existence for an ungrateful man—one who deserted her for another—far her inferior? If Byron had told her story, he would have made her live for *revenge*, which he declares "so sweet, especially to women."

The streets of Bologna are very pleasant. They have arcades, or colonnades, in front of every house, which give a delightful shade. In the public square is the fountain, with figures of Neptune and tritons by John of Bologna. They are considered miracles of sculpture by the inhabitants.

The afternoon we devoted to drives around the city, which are very lovely. From *San Michele in Bosco*, a palace and convent, we obtained a splendid view of the rich plains from the Apennines to the Adriatic; then afar was the shadowy outline of the Alps, and large towns, and villages, convents, and the cities of Ferrara and Imola; then just beneath us, Bologna, with its towers, domes, and spires. A purple haze enveloped every distant object, like a violet-colored veil of delicate lace.

The Bolognese speak a most barbaric dialect, harsh and disagreeable to the ear. They are a robust, energetic people, very famous for their love of liberty, and their efforts to free themselves from the trammels of Austria. The Legate of the Pope governs Bologna, but it is garrisoned by Austrian soldiers.

Ferrara, May 31st.—We left quite early this morning, and travelled over a level country, crossing the Po and the Adige in ferry-boats. Our road was upon an embankment, to raise it above the frequent inundations of these rivers. Trees were planted on each side, and thus, for miles before us, was a straight, shaded avenue. The people who inhabit these low regions are miserable creatures, suffering from ague and fever incessantly. So rapidly did we drive, that we entered the massive gates of Ferrara by three o'clock.

Ferrara! how many a story of impassioned love, of wild romance, and of terrible crime, are summoned to memory by the utterance of that name! A gorgeous and magnificent city was Ferrara some centuries ago, when a-hundred thousand inhabitants occupied the space within the seven miles' circuit of its walls. Then it was the splendid home of the illustrious family of D'Este, from which, they told us here, the present royal family of England is descended, through the house of Brunswick.

As our courier was occupied in having the everlasting passports *viséd*, he engaged for us a cicerone, who appeared as ancient as the old city. He conducted us first to the *Convent of Santa Anna*, where Tasso was confined for seven dreary years in a dungeon by the cruel Alfonso, caged as though he were a wild animal. We went down into the dark cell, and stood upon the spot where he made his bed during all that weary time, and saw the small aperture through which he looked so eagerly, fancying he saw the gliding shadow of Leonora's form as she daily passed. Then we read his scribbling on the wall, when paper was denied him to record the thoughts which stirred his great mind with a fierce passion allied to madness. Our cicerone related the story of Tasso's "infatuation," as he styled it, and when I exclaimed, "I do not believe he was mad; not even seven years of cruelty inflicted by his tyrant could make him so," the old man gravely shook his head as he answered, "Ah! Signora, it was madness to love so far above his own station in life."

The convent is still an asylum for lunatics, and several frantic women rushed to the windows as we walked along, and holding forth their skeleton-like arms, implored us to come in to them, and hear the story of their wrongs and griefs. Ah! what a pitiable spectacle it was! We quickly left this dismal abode of sorrow and suffering.

The house of Ariosto belongs to the government, and a neat old woman and her pretty little niece were its guardians. No article of furniture has been removed from the position it occupied when the "immortal poet" (as the Italians call him) lived within it. In his studio, upon the writing-table, the inkstand remains as when he left it, and the chair where he was often seated, writing those exquisite poems, still so dear to his countrymen. In this room there was a noble bust of Ariosto by Canova. He must have been an uncommonly handsome man. The forehead was gloriously intellectual, and the mouth sweetly expressive of tender feeling. His small garden, with its cool grotto and vine-covered arbors, appeared carefully tended.

As I remarked the watchful attention bestowed upon this house, I thought of Mount Vernon, the home of our own Washington. Why should not that sacred spot be the object of a love as unceasing? It should indeed be the nation's property—a Mecca, where pilgrims from all the vast regions between the Atlantic and the Pacific shores might come, and there, as at an holy altar, swear a new oath of faithfulness to that Union his patriotism created and preserved.

We entered the church where Lucretia Borgia is entombed, and saw a lock of her hair, preserved in a glass case. It was of a rich auburn hue. Then we passed the palace where she enacted those horrible scenes, perpetuated in notes of bewitching music, through the opera which bears her name.

The Ducal Castle is a great structure. Encircled by a moat, it stands aloof, like a giant above the common crowd. The dungeons of Parasina and Ugo were within its dreary walls, and from their thrilling story Byron drew his touching poem. The old custode showed us the very place where the ax fell upon their necks, and the marble pavement along which flowed the gushing streams of their life-blood, mingling into one crimson current, while their hearts, so fond and loving, grew cold together in the icy grasp of death.

All the afternoon we wandered through the silent, deserted, and grass-covered streets of forlorn and lost Ferrara. We looked into the uninhabited and decaying palaces. Up the marble stairways the ivy seemed the only traveller; while its shining green leaves were clustering around the head of a once lovely statue of Psyche, like a coronet of emeralds. Square after square we traversed without meeting a living form, and even our footfall sounded startlingly loud. Save in Pompeii, I have never beheld a scene so utterly desolate. Our garrulous old guide disturbed the profound silence, now and then, by apologetic words for its present state, contrasting it with the magnificence which invested Ferrara in the olden times. The stillness of the grave else rested upon the city. As Byron says,

> "There seems as 'twere a curse upon the seats
> Of former sovereigns, and the antique brood
> Of Este."

We are lodged in an ancient palace (now an hotel). Our chamber is a vast room, with windows about fifteen feet long, and heavy, dark curtains, precisely resembling the draperies before the tomb of a saint. Within cavern-like recesses are two beds, and curious old cases with black doors are scattered through the apartment. I am almost afraid to sleep; for in dreams I am sure Lucretia Borgia, Tasso, Leonora, and Parasina with her young Ugo, will visit me. But, alas! my candle is nearly out, (the luxury of gas is unknown here,) and I must write, good night, and bless my dear Mamma.

CHAPTER LVIII.

VENICE, *June 1st.*

HERE we are, darling Mamma, once again in the glorious "City of the Sea." At dawn we gladly left ghost-like Ferrara, and passing through Rovigo, came on to Padua. There we gave up our vettura. Sorry indeed we were, for of all modes of travelling through Italy, it is the most agreeable, by far. Seated in a railway car, (precisely like those in America,) we were quickly carried towards Venice, whose spires and cupolas were soon glittering in the evening sunlight. A gondola landed us on the marble stairway of the Mocenigo Palace, (now an hotel called the *Reale Danielli*, and the very one in which we lived when here before.) The servant conducted us to our apartments, and by a singular chance, they were the same we occupied during our first visit. We did not like them. They recalled so constantly the remembrance of our good Betsey, and our kind, affectionate R. So, to escape sad thought, we told Luigi to order a gondola, as we were determined to see Venice by moonlight. In all other aspects we had already seen it. He appeared quite amazed, and at last urged, "The Signora has forgotten how late it is—long past ten o'clock." But looking out, and thinking with truth "it was wronging such a night to sleep," we insisted the gondola should be brought to the steps. Our jaunty young gondolier, Antonio, removed the small black cabin, so there was no covering between us and the sky. And now, dear Mamma, behold your children, floating slowly along the wide laguna, leaning back upon the soft cushions, and luxuriating in the matchless beauty of the scene.

Three wonderful pictures have I beheld in Italy, which will hang forever on the "walls of memory." One was the *Illumination of St. Peter's;* another, the Niagara-like cataract of fire pouring from the *Crater of Vesuvius;* and the third is *Moonlight in Venice.* There is a glory about it here, never attending it elsewhere; the smooth streets of water receive its beams as though they were immense mirrors, and thence reflecting them upwards, fill the atmosphere with a light of such dazzling brightness, we constantly exclaimed, "This cannot be night!". It seemed a mingling of the soft tints of the early morning, and the tender radiance of the twilight. The air was warm and delicious, imparting a gentle languor to the senses, and lulling all troublous thoughts and cares to perfect oblivion. It was like a beautiful dream, where we seemed borne up by invisible wings, and wafted from joy to joy.

Along the Piazza of San Marco were multitudes of lamps, and their rays pierced the still waters as though they were glittering arrows of light. Every object was softened and rounded by the moonbeams, and its shadow singularly distinct in the watery surface below it. Thus there appeared two cities, one above and another beneath the Grand Canal, each with its Winged Lion of St. Marco.

From the open windows of a palace came the sound of merry, dancing music, while beneath another was a gondola with a serenading party. We made an entire voyage of the streets of Venice, passing under the "Bridge of Sighs," which for a moment or so shut out the moonlight completely. Then we glided by the Palace of the Foscari, and did not wonder the sad Jacopo was willing even to endure torture that he might look again upon it. Then we stopped under the marble-cased arch of the Rialto, and were shown the house in which it was supposed Shylock lived.

> "On such a night as this
> Did Jessica steal from the wealthy Jew,
> And with an unthrift love did fly from Venice."

"Slowly gliding ever," we passed all the landmarks of historic and poetic interest. Even Octavia, prosaic as she usually seems, was inspired by the scene, and talked with an eloquence quite bewitching. At length the great clock of the tower pealed forth the hour. It was two o'clock, and even then reluctantly we told Antonio to return to the Réale Danielli. My child was soon sleeping quietly, but I felt no weariness, no need of repose; so I crept away from her into our parlor, where the windows opened upon the broad laguna, and there again my soul was bathed in the delicious beauty of the enchanting scene. You must not scold me, when you read of "night-watching by the sea." You were always in my thoughts, and at intervals I have written this description. A moment since, leaving my pen to take another look, I found it was daylight; "thus indeed, good night."

June 4th.—We have spent several days in revisiting the wonders of Venice, playing cicerone for M. D. In my letters when here before they were all described, therefore I shall say no more about them.

To-morrow, we part with Italy, and I cannot repress the murmurings of regret which oppress my heart. I love the beautiful country, it contains so much to enrapture the fancy and to delight the mind. Ah! such happy days we have spent in its grand old cities, by the classic shores of its memory-haunted Mediterranean, and along its picturesque lakes. One must be insensible to the glories of the past, and to the charms of the present, not to love Italy. As the home of the greatest statesmen, the noblest poets, and bravest heroes of antiquity, it is invested with a soul-thrilling interest. As the land where the early Christians planted firmly the holy cross, emblem of our Saviour's love, it is truly sacred. Earth, sky, and air, possess here a beauty unknown in other climes. Every city, nay, every town even, has some treasure of painting, sculpture, or science. Each river, vale, and mountain, has its poetic or historic legend. In the forms and faces of its poorest inhabitants we often see the loveliness and manly grace which gave to Phidias and Praxiteles the models of the peerless statues of the Venus de Medici and the Apollo Belvidere. A mournful feeling of compassion for her present wrongs must endear Italy to the American heart, since from the skeleton form of her once glorious republic, we have seized the outline of the noble fabric of our own free and independent government.

In all our wanderings through this lovely land, we have never encountered one disagreeable incident, or met with look or word of rudeness or unkindness. The people have every where been cordial, appreciative, and thoughtful of our happiness and pleasure. There may have been times when we were uncomfortable and wearied; when we were greatly troubled by beggars, and annoyed by overcharging inn-keepers; but these were only trifles, like motes seen for a moment in the sunlight, then vanishing away. Hillard, whose admirable and eloquent book upon Italy we read last year in our dear home, says most truly, "It is only the hours of sunshine that are marked upon the dial of memory." Thus shall I only cherish the pleasures we have experienced here, and the remembrance of dear and kind friends.

It is long after midnight. I have just been on the balcony to bid farewell to Venice, as it glitters in the moonbeams, so soft and radiant. This letter I shall leave here, to be sent by the next post to America; and now, with many blessings for you, good-bye.

Trieste, June 5th.—We left Venice this morning. A slight rain was falling, and the weather quite gloomy, very like my own feelings. In six hours the steamer "Roma" crossed the Adriatic, and brought us to Trieste, a fine commercial city, with splendid quais and docks. The people seem brisk and busy, all but the "turbaned Turks," who sat quietly smoking in the cafés. As we passed along the streets we saw many varieties of costume, which rendered them bright and interesting. Handsome Greeks and dark-skinned Moors were quite numerous.

We had thought of going from Trieste to Athens, in Greece, and perhaps to Smyrna and Constantinople; but upon inquiry, M. D. found there was cholera prevailing in those regions, and he would not consent to make the voyage, as the season was too far advanced to venture without danger. We have therefore resolved to go on at once to Vienna, and thence I shall send this letter.

CHAPTER LIX.

VIENNA, AUSTRIA, *June 10th.*

WE have now been several days in the superb city of Vienna, so constantly occupied with "sight-seeing," and with society, that I have not written to you, dear Mamma, knowing well you would gladly excuse my silence when you read how happy we have been.

At five on Monday we left Trieste in a post-carriage. From the summit of the Karst mountains we had a magnificent view of the Adriatic, and the peculiar indentations of the Dalmatian coast. The city, with its multitude of ships, lay at our feet, and upon the calm and shining sea rested several dark clouds near the horizon's verge. They were the "Isles of Venice," and we looked lovingly and long upon them, until they seemed to mingle with the deep clear blue of the heavens.

We travelled all night over a rocky country, and by morning reached Laibach, where we took the railway, certainly the best and smoothest in the world. The cars (or carriages, as they call them here) were exceedingly comfortable, and we could read with pleasure, nay, even write, so entirely level was the road—no jolts or jars, but a pleasant gliding motion always.

The country, as seen from our railway windows, was highly cultivated, and afar off were the Rhetian Alps, their topmost peaks still covered with snow. The road appeared to follow the valley of the Save river, and often passed through wild chasms between high mountains, where the scenery was picturesque and grand. In the distance we perceived handsome cities, and lofty heights crowned with castles and fortresses.

We journeyed on all night, not so rapidly as we travel at home, but safely and surely, and the dawn found us near Vienna, an immense city of five hundred thousand inhabitants, spread out over a great plain, upon the banks of the Danube. I thought, as we crossed the river, of the song you so often sung to me in my childhood:

> "Alone on the banks of the dark-rolling Danube,
> Fair Adelaide hied, when the battle was done."

We drove to a hotel called the "Archduke Charles," where we have pleasant rooms. It is upon a narrow street, as thronged and noisy as Broadway. We sent our letters immediately to Col. Jackson, the American Minister. He soon answered them by calling upon us, and we have been truly delighted with him, and honestly proud that our country has such a representative at this court. He is a man of talent, of richly cultivated mind, of fine poetic gifts, and of refined and graceful manner. I cannot express to you all his kindness and charming courtesies to us, during the week we have spent here A record of them would quite fill this letter.

Think how fortunate we were to arrive here just in time for the fête of *Corpus Christi*, the great religious festival of Vienna. It occurred the day after our arrival, and every window along the streets through which the procession was to pass had been rented for fabulous prices. Col. Jackson obtained an invitation for us to the house of the Swiss Minister, which was directly opposite to the cathedral of St. Stephen, where the high mass was celebrated, and whence the procession started. It was indeed, Mamma, a most wonderful and splendid pageant, almost barbaric and oriental in its gorgeous magnificence. What think you of the hour? Half past six in the morning! That was perfectly barbaric too!

The Swiss Minister and his charming wife gave us a cordial greeting, and we were soon seated by the window, looking out upon the animated scene beneath us. At seven the Emperor, Empress, all the Royal family, and the Court, entered the cathedral. Thousands and tens of thousands of people thronged the streets, and gathered like flocks of birds upon the housetops, or clung to posts and chimneys. Regiments of Austrian soldiers, with glittering bayonets, were drawn up in double lines. In their rear were stationed the Hungarian Hussars.

About half past seven a whole army of workmen appeared, each bearing the detached portion of a platform of planks, which they quickly laid in the centre of the narrow street. Then came multitudes of other persons, who strewed it with green grass, and sprinkled over it a profusion of flowers. Soon a procession of monks issued from the cathedral, holding in their hands enormous banners, on which were painted scenes in the life of our Saviour. They were followed by the nobles of the empire; by the palatines of Hungary and Transylvania, in superb dresses, embroidered with gold and silver, and sparkling with precious jewels; then the generals of the army, among them Radetzky, so world-renowned for his severities in Italy. Although he is eighty years of age, he walked with a firm and stately step, his form erect, and his bearing that of a gallant soldier. Next were the cardinals and bishops, and the "host," under a golden canopy; and then the Emperor of Austria, (Franz Joseph.) He is a tall, well-formed young man, with a cold, stern expression of countenance. The Empress came after him, in full court costume. The dress was a white petticoat with flounces of gold thread, woven into a delicate web-like lace. Her train (seven or eight feet in length) was of pink velvet, heavily embroidered with seed-pearl and gold. Around her head was a dazzling crown of diamonds, of bewildering radiance, as it caught the morning sun-light. Upon her bosom, on her arms, and around her waist, seemed the wealth of a kingdom, in treasures of rubies, of sapphires, of opals, of emeralds, of pearls and diamonds. Two pretty boys held up her long train, while in her hand she carried a tall, lighted candle. The Emperor and all the Court likewise carried them.

The Empress is only nineteen. She is a lovely, fair-haired young creature, cousin to the Emperor. She was very pale, and seemed in delicate health; (her child is but six weeks old.) We were exceedingly interested in her sweet and graceful appearance, as she languidly walked along the flower-covered pathway.

The Princesses of the Royal family followed after her, in splendid costumes, and adorned with jewels almost as "rich and rare" as those of the Empress. Their trains were held by pages. Then came the ladies and gentlemen of the Court, in full dress. No foreign ministers or ambassadors took part in the pageant, as it was strictly a religious fête.

When the "host" appeared, borne beneath a glittering canopy, the long lines of soldiers all fell upon their knees, until it passed; then rising up again, formed two walls of gleaming bayonets, through which the procession moved. It required two hours to traverse all the principal streets of the city. Then it returned to the cathedral, where the "host" was replaced in the sanctuary. When this ceremony was ended, the state carriages were driven up to the door of St. Stephen. The Emperor's coach was a perfect mass of gilding and costly adornments of flashing gems. It was drawn by eight prancing black horses, whose harness we were assured was worth fifty thousand dollars. The Empress, seemingly exhausted with the fatigue of her long walk, leaned back wearily in the gorgeous equipage as it drove away, followed by many others of equal splendor. The carriage of Prince Esterhazy was magnificent, while its noble occupant was absolutely blazing with diamonds. They were like a coat-of-mail over his breast, entirely concealing the material of which his dress was made. Prince Liechtenstien had also a carriage of remarkable and superb elegance. Numerous servants, in rich liveries, with cocked hats, ran by the side of the horses of their lordly masters.

This procession of great pomp and parade, passing slowly up the street, disappeared at last. The soldiers marched away; the vast throngs moved off into by-streets, and we, bidding adieu to our genial host and hostess, returned to the hotel.

In the afternoon Col. Jackson accompanied us to the *Prater*, the fashionable drive of Vienna. It is almost as beautiful as the Cascine of Florence, and a most enjoyable place. It is upon an island formed by the streams flowing into the Danube. Delightful carriage-roads pierce through forests of oak and ash trees, and wind around verdant lawns and shaded dells, where there are herds of tame deer. As it was a holiday, vast multitudes of persons were walking along the paths, or sitting beneath the spreading branches of immense trees, while hundreds of equipages were dashing through the main avenues.

The Prater covers a space of many miles: thus we were often in perfect solitude, as quiet and lone as one of our own deep forests. Just by the entrance-gate, there was a scene resembling the Champs Elysées on a fête-day. There were punchinellos, swings, theatres, rope-dancing, jugglers, and an enormous quantity of eating, drinking, waltzing, and singing.

We ended our charming day at the opera house, where we saw a fine ballet, in which many of the "Viennoise Children," who made such a *furore* in the States some years ago, (now handsome women,) appeared in graceful dances.

Vienna, called by the Austrians "The Emperor's City," is truly magnificent, grand, and unique. It is bright, cheerful, and noisy. The inhabitants are good-looking, animated, and energetic. Although so gay and fond of pleasure, they are a commercial and business people. In truth, Vienna may be called the connecting link between the civilization of Europe and the barbaric splendors of the Oriental world. The inhabitants of both meet here as in a grand exchange. Persians and Turks, Numidians and Greeks, Hungarians and Bohemians, mingle in social mirth at operas, cafés, and gardens, with the English and French, the Italians and Americans.

The *Altstadt*, (old city,) contains a population of eighty thousand persons. It is upon the banks of a small stream, the Wien, from which it takes its name. Massive walls of great width surround it; upon them there is a delightful promenade, and a most charming panoramic view of the distant mountains. Around these walls there is a wide belt of land, called the *glacis*, once occupied by the fortifications of the city, and now converted into lovely gardens, and planted with groves of trees, so fresh and verdant, they seemed like an emerald setting to enclose the ancient city, built on the spot where the Emperor Marcus Aurelius died, and long the favorite home of Leopold the Glorious. Beyond this glacis there is a large city, with wide streets, and many fine houses. Contrary to the usual routine of worldly matters, the old city, and not the new, is the heart and centre of elegance and fashion. The royal palace is there, and private palaces of grand proportions, public buildings, time-honored churches, and numerous theatres.

The cathedral of St. Stephen is a noble old structure, erected during the fourteenth century. Its architecture is strictly Gothic, with a majestic tower, or spire, rising from its roof to near four hundred feet. It is elaborately carved, is light and graceful in outline, and met our eyes long ere we reached Vienna. Near the cathedral is the famous *Stock am Eisen*, (iron stick,) the trunk of a tree bound with iron hoops, the last relic of the *Wienerwald*, a dense forest which once covered the ground where the city now stands. For many centuries it has been the custom for all wandering apprentices, when leaving their homes to go out into the world seeking their fortunes, to come to this old tree, and drive a nail into it for "good luck." Hence it has become quite a mass of iron. There is a legend that the devil aided a workman to build a large castle in the midst of the forest; and for this reason, (in remembrance of the service,) all of the craft, ere departing from their native city, feel themselves bound to visit the old trunk, and to drive in a nail as an evidence of their faith in the oft-repeated story.

Vienna has many interesting monuments, among them the tomb of the Grand Duchess Maria Christina, in the church of St. Augustine. It is a lofty pyramid of grayish marble, with emblematic figures grouped around it, and is a noble work of Canova. In the palaces of Belvidere, divided from each other by an exquisite garden, there are more than thirty or forty rooms filled with pictures by artists of the ancient as well as modern schools. There are also splendid galleries of paintings in several private palaces.

In the Imperial Library we saw the noble statue of Charles the Fifth, and many precious and valuable books and manuscripts. There was a volume of the Psalms, printed by Faust in 1457, and a copy of "Jerusalem Delivered," with corrections in the hand-writing of Tasso. In the basement under the Library were the state carriages of the Emperor. They were splendid indeed—one with panels painted by Rubens. They were of all forms and sizes, from the heavy coach of a hundred and fifty years ago, to the light and graceful carriage of the present day. There were also many sleds of curious shape, with richly-adorned harness.

The National Armory was vastly interesting. We saw there the helmet of Attila the Hun, and the steel breast-plate of John Sobieski, which he wore when he defended Venice against the Turks. There were hundreds of tattered banners, captured from the enemy at various times. None awakened in my heart so enthusiastic an emotion as the standards taken from the walls of Jerusalem by the Crusaders, those heroic men who, following the dauntless Richard of the "Lion Heart," pressed on through all the blood and storm of battle, content to die if their eyes could take in with their last glance the Holy Sepulchre of our blessed Saviour. We saw also the helmet and sword of Godfrey de Bouillon, the crusader-king of Jerusalem, and many, many other relics of ancient days.

When the Emperor and the Court leave Vienna, the gay season is considered over. Their Majesties are occupying at present one of the surburban palaces, and only returned to the city to assist in the fête of Corpus Christi. Therefore, as etiquette ordains it, all balls and parties among the fashionables had ceased, though the opera and ballet still continued the delight of thousands.

Our kind friend Mr. G. gave us letters to Mme. Sophie Tedesco, and to Mme. Von Wertheimstien, two charming sisters, who reside here. They came directly to call upon us, and have been truly polite and attentive, placing their fine opera box at our disposal during all the period of our visit. Mme. Tedesco, a highly accomplished woman, was, unhappily for us, detained in the country most of the time by the illness of her child. Mme. Von Wertheimstien we saw frequently in her elegant house. She is sparkling and *spirituelle,* handsome and graceful, speaking French and Italian uncommonly well.

Col. Jackson kindly presented me to many of his German friends, with whom we were much pleased. They greeted us with such an honest, unaffected, and cordial manner, we did not feel as strangers among them. To him I was also indebted for the happiness of knowing Lady Westmorland, wife of the British Minister. It was indeed, Mamma, a happiness to know her, for rarely have I met a more fascinating and gifted lady; and the hours of our visit to her were an enchantment to the heart as well as to the mind. She is learned as a linguist, and accomplished as a painter; and yet, with all these varied charms, she is simple, frank, and unpretending—a high-bred woman of the English nobility, who are the noblest and best types of female character I have met in Europe. Lady Westmorland is the niece of the Duke of Wellington, daughter of Lord Mornington, (his brother.) The walls of their large and spacious palace (belonging to the British Government) were hung with many splendid pictures, the work of her own hands, and several the conception of her own genius. In the sweetest manner she described to me the peculiar inspiration which had produced them. One possessed such a charming interest, I must tell you of it. The picture was the likeness of her grandmother, Countess of Mornington. She is represented as a very aged woman, still retaining her beautiful features, in spite of years and many crushing sorrows. She is seated in a small boudoir, with three marble busts of her sons before her—the Duke of Wellington, the Marquis of Wellesley, and Lord Mornington. By her side, on a small table, is an open letter, signed by the Duke of Wellington, and dated the very night after the victory of Waterloo. The old mother has seemingly just read the few hurried lines from her son, and her hands are clasped as though in grateful prayer that he is safe. There was a pathos, an eloquence, (if I may thus apply the word,) about the picture truly touching. Lady Westmorland then told us, the letter in the painting was really written by the Duke. As she was painting it, her uncle came in, and said, "Let me copy the letter myself upon the canvas." Thus his autograph is there preserved.

Her daughter, Lady Rose, was like her ladyship, a delightful, well-educated person. When I called again, they were in great distress about Lord Raglan, (who is brother-in-law to Lady Westmorland.) Tidings had just reached them from her son, who was aide-de-camp to Lord Raglan, that the physicians had said he must die, if he did not leave the Crimea at once. This Lord Raglan resolutely refused to do, saying, "My Queen and her Ministers shall never say I deserted my post. I will die in the discharge of my duty."

We went one afternoon to the *Volksgarten*, to hear Strauss' famous band, to drink coffee, and to see the noble statue of "Theseus destroying the Minotaur." It is by Canova, and was designed by Napoléon to crown the summit of the Simplon mountain, at the loftiest peak, where the road turns to descend into Italy. What a grand position that would have been for it! and how impressive the effect! But here, it is cramped up in a kind of temple. At sunset the gardens were filled with well-dressed, robust people. They appeared very merry and happy, and many were seated by little tables, with wine and coffee upon them as refreshments, while others strolled along the deeply-shaded avenues, or lingered near the orchestra to listen to the enchanting music of Strauss. Dancing and music may be termed the *specialities* of the Viennese. In various parts of the city we looked in upon the *Tanzsäle*, (the dancing halls,) where the inhabitants assemble to dance very often, particularly on the Sunday nights. There is only a small sum paid at the entrance, and a man, his wife, and children, can thus amuse themselves the entire night, if they please. A fine band of musicians plays the whole time, and near by are supper-rooms, much frequented also; for the Austrians, like the Americans, deem "supper a part of the ball."

In the environs are many splendid *Casinos* for the higher classes of society, which are very charming resorts. For miles around Vienna there are chateaux and villas, and the hills which encircle the plain are sprinkled here and there with ruined castles of the feudal times.

One lovely afternoon we drove to the palace of *Schönbrunn*, where the Emperor lives during the summer. Maria Theresa often resided there in her day, and Napoléon made it his abode in 1809, while he remained in Austria. It is a fine palace, decorated, like all others, with paintings, gilding, and statuary. It was there the King of Rome (so named by his noble father, but called by his grandfather the Duke of Reichstadt) died in 1832, in the very room and upon the same bed his father occupied. We heard many anecdotes of the amiable young king, or duke, who was greatly loved by all his attendants, and is said (I know not if with truth) to have been adored by the Emperor his grandfather. The constant watchfulness over him was induced by a fear that some daring and enthusiastic Frenchman might steal or abduct him, for the purpose of restoring him to the throne of Napoléon, and thereby endanger his life. His portrait represents him as a handsome, noble-looking youth. He was only twenty-one when he died, and several persons who knew him well, told me he had a bold and resolute spirit, which not all the power of his grandparent could subdue, and which would one day have revealed itself as strong and firm as the "indomitable will" of his father; but God willed that he should early pass away.

The gardens of Schönbrunn are trim and artificial, resembling those of the French chateaux. The *Palm House* is a large conservatory filled with palm trees and other tropical plants. Near this is the *Menagerie*, where the beasts are most luxuriously lodged. We were looking upon an enormous lion, when we perceived a confusion in the crowd, and a speedy removal of hats and caps. Soon the cause was apparent: it was the Emperor Franz Joseph, with the Empress leaning on his arm. They had just come from the palace, and were sauntering about to enjoy the delightful scene. During their walk they also came up to the enclosure, and stood looking upon the deposed "monarch of the forest." As when we saw her in the pageant of Corpus Christi, her young face wore the same innocent and sweet expression. She was very simply dressed, in a colored muslin, plain bonnet, and black silk mantle. The Emperor seemed very tender of her, and his stern, cold eyes lighted up with a beaming brightness as they talked together. Their union was not like usual royal marriages, (matters of policy,) but one of ardent affection. He had always loved her, but another princess was intended for him by his ministers. Without informing them, he went off, and "wooed and won" his fair young cousin, telling them upon his return that he could make love for himself, and did not require their aid. So runs the story.

Upon a high hill in the grounds there stands a graceful temple with a colonnade called the *Gloriette*. Thence there is an admirable view of the city. Springing up in the centre of a thickly wooded vale, was the *Schöne Brunnen* (beautiful fountain), from which the palace takes its name. Almost every day we drove to some of the picturesque heights, or to the Prater, or to the gardens. It would seem as though more than half the population spent the long hours of sunlight in the open air. Every place we visited was full of people; families grouped under the thick branches of the the trees; lovers (I suppose) walking apart from the throng along the shaded pathway; and children romping over the grass. What an enjoyment these places give to the "sons of toil" and the "daughters of the needle," as some writer styles the poor workwomen. How often we regret we do not have parks with us! But there they would be useless. In the hurry, the rush of our existence, we have no time to stop to admire and be amused on the way upwards and onwards to the captivating "Paradise of Money." Therein we hope, like the Mahomedans, to revel in joy forever. Alas! alas! when attained, the power to be happy has departed, and we find ourselves crushed, like the Roman maiden, by the weight of our own treasure. I fancy I see you laughing at this little bit of moralizing, especially when I said "we." That was only to render my expressions more forcible. Thank Heaven for the capacity which has been given me to enjoy the simple flowers of earth as well as the costly plants of the conservatory; and the desire for great wealth never rippled the current of my life.

M. D. has made many charming acquaintances among the professional and scientific men. Dr. *Yocobovisc*, a most intelligent and pleasant man, has conducted him to several hospitals of the government, and to medical colleges, where there are vast numbers of students.

I was very glad, the other day, to meet Mr. and Mrs. Locke, of Savannah, whom you will remember we knew long years ago. They have been some years in Europe.

I must finish my letter. Col. Jackson will send it with dispatches home to America. He is now waiting for it. Were we not compelled to be in Paris for the Exposition, we would stay here a month. Oh ! such happy, happy days we have spent in the " Emperor's City." At twilight we leave for Dresden ; so now, farewell.

CHAPTER LX.

DRESDEN, SAXONY, *June 15th.*

WE travelled all night, and at morning came to the old city of Prague, built on both shores of the Moldau, over which is thrown a great bridge ornamented with the statues of numerous saints. Afar off we perceived the high cliff upon which was once the Castle of Libussa, the Amazonian priestess, who, when she was tired of her lovers, cast them down the precipice into the river. The legend says she found her *master* at last, for a young peasant so entirely won her affections, and had such power over her, that she yielded up her fortune, even her life, to him. On the mountain opposite to the Castle of Libussa stood the Palace of Wlaska, also an Amazon queen, who reigned seven years over half of Bohemia.

Prague has been a famous battle-field for centuries. There the fiery words of Huss stirred up the people to wild frenzy, and the armies of Wallenstien, in the "Thirty Years' War," poured over these hills like rushing torrents of destruction. On a lone peak the blind Ziska and his Hussite followers fought and conquered the combined soldiers of the German empire. As we neared the city, we passed the field where the memorable "Battle of Prague" was fought by Frederick the Great. How well I remembered that unfortunate piece of music which bears its name, so often murdered by beginners on the piano-forte.

Very brief was our sojourn in Prague, and then on through a fertile country, with great fields of hops, (used for making beer,) and vineyards from which the rich Bohemian wines are made. Then we passed extensive orchards of fruit trees, and miles of land planted with corn. Dresden we reached ere night. It is the residence of the King of Saxony, and lies in a valley divided by the Elbe. A noble bridge spans the river, said to be the finest in Germany. I am extremely weary, and must to sleep; good night, dear Mamma.

Wednesday night.—We have passed a most charming day. Quite early in the morning we went to the picture-gallery, which, after those of Madrid and Florence, is decidedly the finest in Europe. There are multitudes of rooms, all hung with rare and exquisite creations of celebrated painters. " La Notte " (the night) by Correggio is a wonderful picture. It portrays the scene in the manger, with the Virgin-Mother bending over the child Jesus. All the light which illumines the darkness comes from the body of the infant, and falls upon the enraptured faces of the shepherds, and touches, as with a halo of glory, the divine features of Mary, as her gentle eyes are resting with tender love upon the little being she holds within her arms. Another precious gem is the " Madonna di San Sisto," by Raphael, purchased from a convent of Piacenza, in Italy, for an enormous sum. The figure of the Virgin is represented as soaring upwards to the heavens, clasping to her bosom the infant Saviour. Her face is beautiful, and its angelic expression truly enchanting. The pious and saintly Pope Sixtus, (from whom the painting takes its name,) Santa Barbara, and two children, fill the lower portion of the picture, and are gazing with adoration upon the lovely vision before them. There are many Titians, Paolo Veroneses, and Domenichinos, besides Rubenses and Rembrandts, of great value. In truth, dear Mamma, I could spend one month in the gallery, finding some new treasure each day. This you can readily believe when you hear there are more than two thousand pictures, all by the great masters of the Dutch, Flemish, German, and Italian schools. So many, many hours have I given to the study of pictures, that I can immediately distinguish the artist from the peculiarities of the painting, as we do the hand-writing of a friend by a single glance.

Leaving the gallery, we went to the *Grune Gewölbe*, (green vault.) Is not the name suggestive of something dismal and gloomy? Vastly different is the reality, however. Upon entering, we were dazzled by a blaze of shining gems. It was like the cave of the geni, the famous slave of Aladdin's lamp. The Saxon kings in ancient days were exceedingly rich. This was long before America was discovered, when the silver mines of Freiberg were a boundless source of wealth. It was their custom to collect great treasures, in jewels, carvings, and objects of *vertú* in the precious metals, and place them in vaults under their palace. As the walls were painted green, it thence derived its name. There are immense quantities of precious stones carved and polished exquisitely; vases of rock-crystals; the largest onyx in the world, and a pearl of fabulous size; several tables of mosaic, with wreaths of flowers all composed of costly gems, inlaid upon the marble; then wine-coolers of gold, quite large enough for a bath-tub for Netta, and an *egg of gold*, containing a jewelled-covered chicken, which, upon touching a spring, opened and revealed a diamond crown just fit for a fairy. Well, here are millions and millions in royal toys and *bijouterie*, locked up for ever. How many sad hearts, worn to despair by unceasing toil, might be made happy by a slight portion of these treasures, skilfully invested! You see my American ideas of utility will always be starting up, when I look on such unemployed wealth.

We have had great pleasure in meeting Mr. and Mrs. Westfelt, and the cordial welcome they gave us was really delightful, and increased, if possible, the high appreciation we have always experienced for these charming and refined people. They are living in a large chateau near the city. It is a lovely spot, embowered in trees and radiant-hued flower parterres, sparklingly bright with pretty little fountains. We spent several hours with them, and saw their family of handsome, blooming children. It is for their education Mr. and Mrs. Westfelt reside here, as the schools are admirable.

Give my kind love to dear Mrs. E., and tell her I have seen her son. He is a fine-looking, intelligent youth. I am sure his parents will be much gratified at his improvement.

Dresden is called by the Saxons "The German Florence," since it is so rich in works of art, and is the home of many literary people. It is indeed a pleasant, quiet city. There is no bustle of business in the streets, or the confusion and rush of traffic we note in other places. There are quite a number of museums, containing antiquities, cabinets of engravings, and curiosities of the mineral, vegetable, and animal kingdoms. Among them were the teeth of the *zyglodon*, brought from Alabama by Dr. Koch. The *Gallery of the Tournament* is filled with the arms and armor used in the days of chivalry. Many suits of armor are of rare workmanship, and form most interesting relics of the past.

The drives around Dresden are very numerous. We went to the *Grosse Garten*, on the banks of the Elbe, and passed over the battle-field where Moreau was killed by a cannon-ball. There is a monument on the spot. You remember Moreau lived several years in the United States, after his banishment from France by Napoléon; and when the invasion of Russia took place, he returned and joined the Allies. It is said Moreau was standing by the Emperor Alexander, when Napoléon brought his wonderful spy-glass to bear upon him, and directed the cannon to be fired, which shattered his body in a manner so frightful, he died very soon.

The gardens of the *Japanese Palace* are extremely pretty, but the *Terrace of Brühl* pleased us most. It is upon the banks of the river, raised high above surrounding objects. Groves of immense trees give a dim and pleasant shade, almost like the twilight, while here and there are concert-rooms and coffee pavillions. The view over the country is extensive, and afar off were the heights of Saxon-Switzerland.

The peasants of Saxony are a contented, well-fed people; but a painful feeling always oppressed me when I saw women ploughing and reaping in the fields, and drawing small carts, assisted often by dogs and cows, but *never by men.* Old women, with snow-white hair, we frequently saw wheeling along a kind of hand-car, loaded with a burden almost too heavy for a horse. What a contrast is the lot of these aged females, to that of your old negroes at home, where every care and kind attention cheers the last feeble emotions of life.

"By-the-bye," as our friend Tom used to say, Mrs. Westfelt still has her two colored servants, William and Louisa, who accompanied her from the South. They were glad to hear about " home " (as they yet call Mobile). William is quite a pet with the Saxon *frauleins*, their favorite partner in the dancing saloons, when they meet on Sundays; but Louisa does not like the place so well. She said, " Ah! it is very hard to live without speaking to, or even seeing, black persons; now William, he takes to the white folks just like they were his own color; but I despise these poor hard-working people, and won't associate with them." Is there not a touch of aristocracy in this?

Berlin, June 17*th.*—A travel of eight hours over a level country brought us to Berlin, the capital of Prussia, on the Spree. The city is in a vast sandy plain, and, until the time of Frederick the Great, was a miserable village. This obstinate and eccentric monarch resolved that he would have a splendid city as his royal residence; so he enclosed a great space of ground with high walls, and said to his subjects, " Build up houses immediately." They, compelled to obey his mandate, began forthwith; and, the sooner to accomplish his orders, they gave immense length to their houses, instead of height. Thus there are often twenty windows on one floor, and rarely more than two stories to any building; and the streets are unusually wide.

We are staying at the *Hotel du Nord*, a superb hotel, on the street *par excellence*, called " Unter den Linden," (under the lindens,) from the broad avenue of these trees stretching along its centre. We have an elegant parlor, with half a dozen windows opening upon this beautiful street; and so charming is the view, I almost regret to be compelled to leave it, and go down to dinner at the table d'hôte. In all the cities of northern Europe, there are these tables d'hôte at different hours of the day, thereby saving one the trouble of ordering dinner.

We have now been several days in Berlin, and constantly

and agreeably occupied in visiting its palaces, museums, public gardens, galleries, and monuments. Upon a broad pedestal of red granite is the bronze equestrian statue of Frederick the Great. It is truly magnificent, and of colossal proportions, with *bas reliefs* and figures of many of the soldier-king's generals grouped around him, in dignified attitudes. This monument is by Rauch, a Prussian sculptor, and is considered the largest in the world.

The *Egyptian Museum* is remarkable for its variety of strange and hideous objects, brought from the ancient cities of the Nile by Lepsius. There is a temple from Philoe, set up in one of the rooms, with the frightful figure of the god within it, and mummies by hundreds; besides every imaginable article of adornment, and even of dress, worn by people of Egypt about three or four thousand years ago.

Then we went to the gallery of sculpture, to the royal library; where we saw the Bible carried by Charles the First in his own hands to the scaffold, and given by him to the bishop who accompanied him. The Museum of Natural History, the University, and even the *Anatomical Museum*, we saw. The picture-gallery is somewhat inferior to that of Dresden, although there were some splendid pictures of Rubens.

The *Schloss* (royal palace) is of prodigious dimensions. The state apartments are gorgeously furnished. In the *Ritter Säle* there is some massive plate, and the White Hall is said to be the largest ball-room in the world. A legend says this Schloss is haunted by the *Dame Blanche*, (the white lady,) who always appears, to foretell the death of one of the royal family.

Driving through the streets, we were incessantly attracted by fine squares, with statues among the trees, and graceful bridges over the sluggish Spree. The Car of Victory surmounts the lofty structure, styled the *Brandenburg Gate*, and amid the rich foliage of the "Unter den Linden" is seen the statue of *Blücher*, who turned the tide of battle at Waterloo from France to the Allies.

Mr. Vroom, our Minister, a kind and amiable man, with his agreeable family, have been several times to visit us. He came one morning with his carriage, and invited us to accompany him to Charlottenburg, the summer Schloss of the royal family. We had a pleasant drive, and were delighted with our ramble through the gardens, where we saw multitudes of orange trees, (they are replaced in hot-houses when winter comes,) and the little lake filled with carp. They all came to the surface when the old custode rang a bell. Thus he summons them to be fed. In a retired portion of the grounds is a pavillion, containing the monument of Queen Louisa, of Prussia. She was a beautiful woman, and dearly loved by her subjects. Her statue is a recumbent one, lying naturally and gracefully, as though she were sleeping. She was only thirty-six when she died. Twenty-one years after her death, Frederick William the Third passed away from life, and was buried by her side, and a marble statue of him, also sculptured by Rauch, was placed by that of his lovely queen.

We saw the house of the present Crown Prince of Prussia, whom I met with the Princess and his son, Frederick William, at Buckingham Palace last year.

Oh! dear Mamma, I must not neglect to tell you, I went to look upon the mansion in which poor Sontag lived, while she was Ambassadress of Sardinia. So many incidents have been related to me of her goodness, her unostentatious charity, her kind sympathy for the poor and the suffering, her ceaseless efforts to relieve the sorrow-stricken, not only by money, but by pleasant words of comfort,—you will not wonder when you hear I wept as they told me of all these lovely traits of character, and as I walked through the great drawing-room where her entrancing voice had so often burst forth in joyous melody. I remembered so well the words in which she described to us the "beautiful home in Berlin where every body was so kind to me." The very tone of her voice came back to memory as I lingered in that room. Dear, charming Sontag! Her end was a sad one indeed!

Without the gates of the city is the *Thier garten* (park), where the people resort at evening. It is laid out in groves and flower-gardens. Within the walls are the *Lust gartens.* There are large conservatories, with tropical plants, where people assemble to drink coffee—and such coffee! The very best in the world is made throughout Germany.

Berlin is remarkable for its numerous theatres. We went one night to see *Emil Devrient*, an admirable artist. He has a noble classic head (like that of our handsome young Edwin Booth), and in passages of deep emotion, his face was startlingly expressive of fiery passion, although generally his acting was characterized by a calm dignity and a high-bred air. His voice seemed always in harmony with the sentiment he expressed; now swelling into strains of heroic eloquence, or sinking to the soft and soul-subduing cadence of the loving heart. The theatre was superb, and the audience genteel and well dressed. Here, as in Vienna, the gay season was over. The Germans are famous lovers of watering-places. They usually spend three months of the summer at the baths, and hence it is called *Kurzeit*, (the curing season.) The poorest people contrive to save a little money to go for a brief period. In truth, all descriptions of people visit the watering-places, and all throw off etiquette and form, and amuse themselves by dancing, bathing, walking, riding, drinking, and (above every other amusement) by gambling. When the *Kurziet* is over, every body returns to their palaces, their houses, or their shops, brightened in spirits and renovated in health. But the Germans do not fancy country houses; thus, save villas and chateaux near the large towns, we never saw any.

I regret to tell you, dear Mamma, we cannot go to Stockholm, as was our earnest intention. We had proposed going from Stetin over the Baltic in a steamer to Stockholm. But a letter from dear Miss Bremer, which has been pursuing me from city to city, has this moment reached me. She is in great sorrow: her mother is dead, and she has gone to the island of Gothland to pass all the summer months, but will return in September, when she implores me to make her a visit. I shall certainly do so, if it be within the circle of possibilities; that is, if I can get away from Paris. I love dear Miss Bremer so fondly, I do not believe that even the enchantments of all the European cities combined can keep me from her.

We are truly sorry to be compelled to leave Berlin without the satisfaction of seeing and knowing Baron Von Humboldt. A charming little note has just been sent to me from him, (through the kindness of Mr. Vroom,) in which he expresses the great pleasure it will give him to receive us next week, when he returns to the city; but unfortunately, we must be in Paris as quickly as possible, and cannot wait until then. As an author, naturalist, and geologist, Baron Von Humboldt is truly among the greatest men of the age. Although more than eighty years old, he is still engaged writing his "Cosmos."

We depart to-morrow, and I must send off this letter by the post to-night; therefore, darling Mamma, good-bye.

Coblenz on the Rhine, June 20th.—Yesterday morning we left Berlin about daylight, and travelled *four hundred and three* miles, to Cologne, in *sixteen hours*, stopping to breakfast and to dine. Was not that a rapid transit—a "speedy annihilation of space?" It was a delightful journey, through a rich, prosperous, and flourishing country. We came first to *Magdeburg*, whose fortifications are deemed among the strongest in Europe. Upon an island in the Elbe is the citadel where Lafayette was confined, and where the famous Baron Trenck was for so many long years imprisoned. *Brunswick*, capital of the Duchy of that name, was the next city we reached. The remains of the persecuted Caroline of Brunswick, wife of the cruel George the Fourth, are entombed in the vault of the *Döm* (cathedral) of St. Blaize. Then we stopped at *Hanover*, chief town in the possessions of the blind King of Hanover. It is said to contain many fine buildings and treasures of art. *Minden*, in Westphalia, was the next place of importance: it is upon the Weser. Besides these cities, we were frequently passing pretty, flourishing villages; and to my great delight, Mamma, we saw the *Hartz mountains*, so often, when I was a little child, Papa used to read me stories of the spectre of the Brocken, and the fierce, bold robbers there. The remembrance of all these wild legends came vividly to my mind, as we rushed along by the chain of *hills*. In truth, they are so low, and insignificant, they scarcely merit the title of mountains. From Berlin to the shores of the Baltic the country is a perfect level; and as these hills spring up in the midst of it, and form such a contrast to the surroundings, they appear in the eyes of its inhabitants gigantic mountains; and all their authors and poets have written of them as such, and invested them with a grandeur they really do not merit.

It was quite dark when we reached Düsseldorf, and we

had not even a glimpse of the town, so celebrated for its school of painting. In the railway carriage there had been all day a most charming and well-informed Russian, journeying on to Antwerp. He told us many interesting incidents of the Emperor Nicholas, and of the grief experienced by his people when he died. He seemed to think Sebastopol a second Gibraltar, and that not all the combined forces of Europe could take it. Well, *faith* is a great blessing, but the engines of war are too terrible now to be long withstood. At Cologne we parted, he going forward and we staying all night; and then this morning visiting the old cathedral again, and looking with delight upon the superbly painted windows.

At twelve we embarked upon a small steamer, and were soon amid the noble, grand, and picturesque scenery of the legendary Rhine. You may fancy, dear Mamma, by this time, I must be weary of beautiful scenery; but no, the glory and freshness of nature is to me as a fountain of unceasing joy. When we ascended the Rhine before, I had been entranced by its wondrous beauties, (of which I then sent long descriptions,) but to-day they appeared even more majestic; and stealing away from M. D. and Octavia, I ingratiated myself with the helmsman, by giving him a little piece of money; so he permitted me to sit in a corner of the elevated platform upon which he stood. There, free from interruption, I yielded up my soul to the influence of the wild and romantic scenery, and upon a tide of pleasurable emotions was borne far back to the dim and shadowy past. As mountain, castle, and ruined-crowned height seemed to sweep by me, as lovely visions seen in dreams, I almost held out my hands to implore them to stay, that I might stamp their beauty on memory for ever. Ah! that bright afternoon was to me as one long breath of enjoyment.

Just as we were landing at Coblenz, a slight shower veiled the landscape for a few moments; then the sun came out, and a rainbow, springing as it were from the Rhine, formed a glowing arch over the rushing river, one end resting on the lofty battlements of Ehrenbreitstein.

Coblenz is a strongly fortified town, belonging to Prussia. It is here Sontag was born, also the famous Austrian minister, Prince Metternich. We took a long walk through the city, and went out upon the bridge connecting it with the castle, where we stood until it was perfectly dark, looking upon the stern fortress, and wondering how the soldiers climbed up to take it.

Now we must to sleep. Good night.

Frankfürt-on-the-Maine, June 21st.—Leaving Coblenz early in the morning we reached Mayence ere mid-day, where we parted with the Rhine. The peasants in these regions call it "King Rhine;" and in fact it should reign supreme, as the most wildly picturesque of earthly streams. It is not a more noble river than our Hudson, neither are the lofty battlements of its rocky banks absolutely more beautiful; but the "romance of the past" invests it with charms beyond the power of words to describe. Each castellated height has been the scene of fierce warfare, or of impassioned love. Islands, rocks, valleys, dells, and mountains, have all their legends, some of despairing maidens, and others of "fairies bright and goblins grim;" some of dark oppression, and others of peaceful joy. All these memories, around which thought and fancy cluster, make the Rhine a peerless river. But we must part from it now, with a deep regret in our hearts.

Opposite to Mayence is the railway station. We crossed he river on a bridge of boats, and entering the cars, were swiftly carried to *Frankfürt-on-the-Maine*, thus called to distinguish it from *Frankfürt-on-the-Oder*. As the rain is falling, and we cannot go out " sight-seeing," I will finish my long letter, commenced last night upon the banks of the rushing Rhine, and send it off at once from here.

Wednesday night.—Among the most pleasant incidents of our busy day, has been a visit made by me to the father and mother of our friend Mme. Lienur. When I was leaving home, she gave me a letter to them, and I accompanied it to the house, waiting in the carriage until the parents had read it, and then going up to their parlor. Oh ! Mamma, it was so touching to see the aged mother ! Again and again she would say, " Kind lady, tell me more of my child, and of *her* child,—she has been so long away, and my heart is so weary, always hoping she will come." Then the good old father, with his snow-white hair, would exclaim, " You must excuse her ; she grieves sadly at separation from her children; but in time we shall all meet, never to be parted again." The father is a Lutheran minister, a highly cultivated and learned man. They told me all their children had left them for other homes, and the old couple lived alone. In the afternoon they came to see me, and we had a long and interesting conversation. There seemed such a beautiful sympathy between these aged people, such a calm contentment with life, and a love so tenderly expressed towards their absent children, that I was quite charmed with them. Family affection is very strong among the Germans, and the ties binding them together are rarely severed by time.

During the morning we drove to the garden of Bethmann, and saw the statue of *Ariadne* by Danneker. It represents a beautiful female riding upon a tiger. The light falls upon it through a rose-colored curtain, thus imparting a glow to the exquisitely rounded limbs, like life itself.

Then we drove to the house where Goëthe was born, and thence to the square adorned by his monument. The figure is grand and noble, and the face strikingly intellectual. There was a grandeur and a presence of majestic thought about that statue I have seldom seen in any other. It may be the admiration I have for the mighty mind of Goëthe, which tinges every object connected with his name with an especial interest.

Next we went to the house where Luther lived, and then to the Jews' Quarter, where multitudes of heads were poked out of the windows to look at us. It was there, in the *Judengasse*, that Rothschild was born, and lived until long after his prime, as a vendor of "old clothes." Then by a lucky chance he was selected by some duke (of Nassau, I believe) to secrete for him vast treasures of money he dared not keep about his palace or person, for fear the revolutionists would seize it. In a little time the duke was obliged to fly from his country. Years passed on, and he returned again. Then Rothschild came to him, and paid him back all the sums confided to his care. While the money was in his hands he had employed it in trade, and thus laid the foundation of that colossal fortune which has since almost controlled Europe at various periods. The wife of the first Rothschild, and the mother of the present "Money-Kings," refused for a long time to leave the Jews' Quarter, her dear old home.

We visited several galleries of pictures, and museums, and drove out into the gardens on the banks of the Maine. In one of the galleries there is a grand picture by Lessing —"Huss before the Council of Constance." It is wonderful for the expression of the faces and the grouping of the figures. Huss stands before the cardinals, pale and wasted by his long confinement in prison, but his eye is resolute, and stern energy pervades the whole figure.

It was our purpose to drive this evening in the environs of the city, but a violent rain-storm has prevented us. At dawn to-morrow we leave *Frankfürt* for Paris, going by the way of Strasbourg. I will not close this letter until we reach Paris, so I máy tell you of our safe arrival there.

And now, good night, dear Mamma.

Hotel de Castile, 7 *o'clock.*—We have just reached Paris, after travelling all night; and ere I take off my bonnet, I write these few words to tell my precious Mamma we are all well and safe. When our courier takes this letter to the banker's, he will bring me your dear letters, and I shall spend such happy moments in reading them. Good-bye.

CHAPTER LXI.

[We reached Paris in June, and remained there three months. During that period numerous letters were written by me, describing scenes and incidents of personal, political, and historic interest; for surely, upon a bright page in the history of both England and France, will be recorded the visit of the British Queen to the Emperor and Empress of the French. Selecting from this perfect volume of letters, carefully preserved by dear Mamma, the most spirited and graphic, I give them as "word-pictures" of several of the brilliant events which occurred during the summer of the Great Exposition.]

July 3d.—Paris is wondrously beautiful now, and far more charming than we found it when first we came here. It appears a continued gala-time, for the Exposition has summoned people of all climes and nations. To welcome and enchant them, the city is superbly embellished; and by way of rendering the fascination more secure, cordial words and smiling glances greet the strangers at every turn.

The splendid *Rue de Rivoli* is completed. The unsightly houses which before destroyed its fine effect, have all been removed, and spacious dwellings erected in their places. Every building has been freshly painted, and the shop-windows are absolutely glowing with gorgeous silks and rainbow-hued *moire antiques.* Even the little tables of the poor street-merchants, along the sidewalks, are covered with an unusual quantity of shining *bijouterie* and pretty trifles. Now and then, from the uppermost story of a house, we see the placard "*à louer*" (to rent) hanging out. This indicates clearly that all the best apartments have been already taken. Men by hundreds are sweeping the streets, both night and day, and not a leaf is permitted to remain a moment on the ground in the Gardens of the Tuileries.

A promenade along the Boulevards and the Champs Elysées is really enchanting, not only from the rich variety of curious and picturesque costumes, but from the life and animation presented there. It would seem as though thousands and thousands were assembled for a grand fancy ball *al fresco*—Turks and ruddy-faced Englishmen, fair Norwegians and dark Arabs from the Desert, brown Egyptians and pale Americans, Persians from Ispahan, and stalwart Germans, Italians, Spaniards, bronze-colored Moors, and negroes, blacker than the little ebony busts of "Uncle Tom and Topsy" we frequently see in the shops.

All these inhabitants of various countries have met here, a few for business, but many more for pleasure, to which they yield themselves with an epicurean enjoyment of the "absolute present," thinking neither of the past nor the future. The people of Paris, too, are in famous good humor, for they look upon this summer as their "golden time," and expect to make huge fortunes by the overflowing throngs who fill the hotels and lodging-houses, the theatres, cafés, shops, restaurants, and gardens.

We hear all languages spoken in the streets, and polyglot placards adorn the windows, such as,

"Hier mann sprecht Deutch!"

"Aqui se habla Español!"

"English spoken!"

"Se parla Italiano!"

In a merry mood, we sometimes go in, and address the shopkeeper in one of the advertised tongues; and it is rare fun to hear the strange answers, and to see the despairing grimaces and hieroglyphic signs of the puzzled traders. We saw a capital piece last night at the "Varieties," called "English Spoken Here," which convulses one with laughter, as it shows up the speculation these shop-people hope to make of the strangers.

We spent a pleasant social evening, (the one before the last,) at the American Minister's; and I am glad to tell you, Mr. Mason is rapidly recovering from his recent illness. Both Mrs. Mason and himself send you many cordial remembrances. At their house we met Mr. Squiers, author of that delightful book about Nicaragua, which I read to you last summer. He gave me many descriptions of the beautiful tropic land, which I wish I could send you.

We have seen our good friend Mr. M'Crea, and his lovely young wife, and Gen. Mercer, who, you recollect, served forty years in the Congress of the United States. He is indeed a wonderful man. Although *seventy-eight* years old, he is as bright in spirit and fresh in feeling as a man of thirty; and in spite of sad reverses of fortune, and numerous sorrows, he retains all his youthful belief in the goodness of human nature. The sunshine of his kind heart lights up every object upon which it falls.

We have often perfect *levées* of persons we have met in our wanderings; and Dr. Parker (the friend who went up Vesuvius with us) declared yesterday morning our parlor was the "Tower of Babel" on a small scale.

Since our arrival we have been at an agreeable party given by Mrs. Smythe, (sister of our dearly-loved Mrs. Ritchie.) She lives in elegant style in the finest quarter of Paris, and with her resides another sister, also a lovely woman. It seems that beauty is an especial inheritance of this family, for the two sisters here are almost as handsome as Mrs Ritchie.

We drove out near Neuilly a few days ago, to see Mr. and Mrs. Goodrich. They have a pretty villa in the midst of a sweet garden. Mr. Goodrich (the "Peter Parley" of our children's adoration) had gone to America, where Mrs. Goodrich and her family follow him in the autumn. They have lived in France for seven years; and being admirable people, have made vast numbers of warm friends, who most sincerely seem to regret their coming departure.

The beautiful Mme. Pilie, of New Orleans, and her charming sister, have just called to take us to drive in the *Bois de Bologne*; therefore I must end my letter to go by the Havre steamer. Good-bye.

CHAPTER LXII.

July 11th.—Fearing you may reproach me for my long delay in telling you of the Exposition, I commence this letter by a description of our first visit. We went at ten, and tarried there until six in the evening. The " Palace of Industry " is still in a most unfinished state; therefore we can scarcely decide upon its merits or attractions. It is a vast building of light-colored stone, roofed over with glass, and presenting a noble façade. Its length and breadth are prodigious, and its dimensions numbering so many feet, I dare not write them down here, for fear it may appear a fabulous amount. It rises in the midst of a grove along the Champs Elysées, while its long galleries, or wings, styled " Annex," stretch down to the bank of the Seine.

The grand nave is finished, and in its centre there is a fountain, encircled by flowers in full bloom. There are giant mirrors (one, twenty feet high), enormous glass candelabra, and lanterns for light-houses, quite as large as an ordinary room. The silver-ware and jewelry are splendid; the embroidery upon muslin exquisite, and the Brussels lace, shawls, dresses, and flounces, so delicate, so spider-web-like, they might have been woven in a loom by the fairies. Passing through many long corridors, where hundreds of men were at work, the clang of their hammers mingling in the confusion of tongues, we came to an immense oval room, lighted from a great dome above. The walls were covered with various specimens of gorgeous carpets, tapestries, pictures, and stained glass. In the centre was a kind of pyramid, and on its summit a small glass pavillion, in which were placed the "Jewels of the Crown," resting very nicely upon beds of velvet, and dazzling the eyes of beholders by their flashing splendor. There was the Regent diamond, bought for Louis the Fifteenth, weighing one hundred and thirty-six carats, and valued at five millions of francs (one million of dollars). Then a crown of diamonds and sapphires (worth nearly three millions of dollars of our money). Next we looked upon necklaces, bracelets, diadems, girdles for the waist, brooches for the bosom, clasps for cloaks, swords, and buttons for coats, all of diamonds, rubies, emeralds, and opals; all recently reset in the most tasteful manner, and surpassing any jewels we have ever yet seen, in size and profusion.

Quite a number of *gens d'armes* stood around the glass envelope of these precious treasures, evidently guarding them with watchful care. A constant stream of persons was pouring around it, who, however, were not allowed a very long time to gaze upon them, for the impatient cry was, constantly, "Passez, Mesdames! passez, Messieurs!" (Pass on, ladies and gentlemen.)

The portions I have described were actually the only ones completed. The rest of the building was precisely like the "moving-day" of a large family, when every thing, from a mousetrap to an enormous bedstead, is brought in and thrown down *pêle-mêle* upon the floor.

Our own flag floats over a great space, devoted to Goodyear's India Rubber articles, from big boots to small combs. Then comes Paine's Vermifuge, and Swaim's Panacea, similar medicines, and a few Daguerreotypes. We are so sorry we did not bring Mark's last picture of Octavia; it is immeasurably superior to any specimens of the kind here, and would certainly have taken the first prize if it had been placed in our department.

It is a source of regret to us that our Government has not dispatched a vessel freighted with some of the fine American fabrics. One of our countrymen told us they had, however, some machinery in the *Annex* "which would astonish the world!" Many people are disposed to call the Exposition a *fiasco* (the Italian for failure); but I doubt not in a week or so it will be worthy of Paris, and the pride of *La belle France.*

Another day, since my last letter to you, we spent in a large building not far from the "Palace of Industry," called *Les beaux Arts.* It is filled with four thousand pictures of living artists, and quantities of statuary. Mr. Powers, our excellent artist from New Orleans, accompanied us, and by his direction we only looked at the finest works of art. There is a most fascinating painting, by Winterhalter, of the Empress, and all her ladies of honor, seated on the green turf in the shady groves of Fontainebleau. Then a full-length picture of the Emperor, and another of the Empress, in their robes of ceremony. Horace Vernet's paintings of Battles were very grand, and in one of the saloons we saw the very same pictures which so charmed us at Sevilla in the *Casa de Pilatos.* The artist was then painting them for this occasion. The English gallery was exquisite. Several pictures of Rossiter were admirable, also some of Healy, and the noble head of an old man by Powers. The walls of several rooms were glowing with Italian paintings of scenery, of

Italian life, and the classic and beautiful faces of the inhabitants of that oft-remembered land. One picture, by a Swedish artist, was exceedingly unique. It was the "Midnight Sun," shining over the dreary wastes, the stern, gray mountains, and enormous rocks of the far-away Northern region. Dear Miss Bremer's painting, in exquisite language, had before made me acquainted with the wild grandeur of that scene, and we almost now seemed to look upon the reality. Then there is another picture,—but I must stop for fear of wearying you. When writing upon my favorite themes of painting and statuary, I quite forget the advice of the French authoress, "Never write more than four pages in one letter." Still, ere I complete this, I must tell of a wonderful scrap-book, or album, we saw at the American office in the "Palace of Industry." It belonged to Mons. Vattemare, (the international copyright advocate,) and contained many original sketches by great artists, and multitudes of autographs of famous people. We thought of your old "seventy-six," and wished we could bring you treasures like these to place within its ancient pages.

The servant waits to take my letter to the banker's; so farewell, dear Mamma.

CHAPTER LXIII.

July 20th.—A few nights ago we attended a magnificent ball at the palace of the Count and Countess de Walewski, on the banks of the Seine, near the Chamber of Deputies. The Count (now Minister of Foreign Affairs) was ambassador at the Court of St. James for several years, where both himself and his lovely wife were exceedingly admired. At Queen Victoria's state ball in Buckingham Palace, (during our first visit to England,) I had been presented to them, and was earnestly pleased to meet them again.

Twelve rooms were opened, quite as splendid as those of the Tuileries or the Hotel de Ville. They were each hung with a different-colored damask, and so highly gilded, they shone like the palace of the "Gold-King." The chandeliers were singularly pretty, formed of large bouquets of flowers, whence the light issued. Just beneath a large one, fashioned like white lilies, was an elegant crimson divan, the centre of which was a perfect bank of bright-hued verbenas, geraniums, and heliotropes. Around this spot the ladies were clustered, much more at home and as radiant as the flowers themselves. As it was the reception room, the graceful Countess stood near this group, greeting her guests as they entered with sweet words and gracious smiles. She kindly welcomed us to France, and gave us a seat near her, where we remarked the *entrée* of many distinguished and elegant people. All the "dignitaries of the state" were there, the ministers, and a number of the English nobility; among them the Duke and Duchess of Hamilton; then Prince Napoléon, President of the Exposition, and his two cousins, Charles and Lucien Bonaparte. The Turkish Ambassador has a very interesting face, with eyes of wonderful size and brightness. He was dressed in the modern costume, except the crimson *fez* upon his head; and then he wore no cravat, but a wide black ribbon around his neck, to which was attached a medallion of diamonds of dazzling light. He was accompanied by numerous young *attachés*, uncommonly handsome men, who were really the most caressed beaux of the ball. Their soft and beautiful eyes seemed to possess a magnetic power over the hearts of the fair ones around them. There were two Egyptians of noble presence, (quite as dark-skinned as our Betsey,) and a Haytien prince, entirely black. His manner was grave and dignified.

A few officers in glittering uniforms were present. Several had recently returned from the Crimea, and were still pale and weak from the wounds received there.

The ladies' dresses were very brilliant, and precious jewels sparkled on their bosoms, and bracelets of rare value clasped their arms. But to the vast circumference of the *petticoats* our eyes have not yet become accustomed. They are formed of crinoline (a fabric made of horse-hair), with a quilling of it around the bottom to keep the huge circle distended. They resemble half-inflated balloons, just rising from the ground, and the wearers appear compelled to push the skirts along as they walk. The *courtesy*, or *curtsey*, now in vogue, is most extraordinary. The ladies can no longer move back a step or two, and incline forward, (as was their custom formerly,) without knocking over some small man by the weight of their petticoats; therefore, instead of bending forward, they give a sudden " duck down," very much after the style of little Chloe when old Aunt Charlotte directs her in their Sunday visits to say, " How do 'ee do, Missis !" Yet how omnipotent is fashion ! How it reconciles us to utter monstrosities, and after a time makes us deem them undoubted beauties ! Hence you must not wonder to find us, on our return, pushing along our heavy skirts, and rolling to and fro like half-collapsed balloons !

Serving-men in gorgeous liveries were constantly handing around ices, although there was a sumptuous *buffet*, where every variety of refreshment was politely served to the guests.

We made the acquaintance of many agreeable people, among them the Princess Ghika, daughter of the reigning Prince of Wallachia. She is married to a French gentleman, who occupied some diplomatic position in her country. We found her a charming woman, and accompanied her and the Turkish Ambassador to supper, where we had a famously merry time. Not far from us was the Count de Morney, whom Talleyrand prophesied (when he was only a child) would be a Prime Minister of France. His devotion to the Emperor, at the time of the *coup d'état* of December, is known to the whole world. Count de Morney, although not more than forty-three or four, is quite bald ; he has a quiet, dignified air, and the self-possession of a man of profound intellect.

After leaving the supper-rooms, we went out into the gardens, which were lighted by colored lamps hanging from trees and shrubs. The scene was most inviting, and the fresh perfume of the flowers delicious. Music from the palace floated upon the air, and mingled with the sound of the falling waters of the fountains, while lovely forms flitted to and fro amid the green foliage. How delightful it was!

July 25th.—We went last night to the reception of Prince Napoléon, at the *Palais Royal*, accompanied by Colonel Coxe, a very agreeable gentleman, who once lived in Alabama.

Prince Napoléon is cousin to the Emperor, and son of Prince Jerome, (the offspring of his second marriage.) He is a fine-looking man, about thirty years old, and bears a most wonderful resemblance to the portraits of the First Napoléon. His sister, Princess Matilde Demidoff, aided him in receiving the guests. She is a superb woman, of commanding figure, with an exquisitely formed neck and bust. Her toilette was beautiful, of some light material, trimmed with multitudes of delicate flowers.

There was a splendid band of music, but no dancing. It is decreed by the " world's goddess " that the weather is too warm for such really severe exercise, and yet the temperature was only like our spring weather. Fashion, however, repudiates dancing in summer, and banishes such winter pastime to watering places and country quarters.

Conversation, and promenades through the long suite of rooms, delightfully filled the hours of the evening. We were told the élite of Parisian society were there assembled, and we observed many distinguished literary, political, and artistic people.

During the evening we were seated by the side of a lady attired in elegant taste, and wearing many diamonds of a dazzling radiance. We soon began a conversation, she addressing me in Spanish, supposing we came from Spain, as Octavia so much resembled an Andalucian. When I said we did not, she still insisted we must be compatriots, from my pronunciation of some particular word. As she was guessing my native country, Prince Napoléon approached, and made me acquainted with her, as the Countess de Montijo, the mother of the Empress. I was truly glad to know her, for I was anxious to have tidings of her lovely daughter, who is now at a watering place for the benefit of her health. While in Madrid, we had often met warm friends of the Countess and of the Empress, who had spoken of them with admiring friendship and appreciative regard; among them several ladies, who had been the youthful companions of the beautiful Eugenie. In describing her to me, they always ended by saying, " She deserves her high position, for she is as good and kind as she is enchanting and gifted." It was delightful to hear the Countess Montijo speak of her daughter. Her heart seemed overflowing with joy as she mentioned her. The Empress's health is vastly improved, but she will not return to the Palace of St. Cloud, (where the Emperor and herself are passing the summer,) until just before the arrival of Queen Victoria. Prince Napoléon said this would certainly be the 18th of August; and then he remarked, the Exposition would be entirely finished, and magnificently adorned.

Apropos to the Exposition, I have never yet informed you that I am the only " lady-commissioner " duly accredited to the World's Fair. Our Governor comes in for a large amount of compliment for his selection, and for his gallantry. But what think you? Alabama has not a single article in the " Palace of Industry!" If there were only a few cotton-seed, it would " serve to swear by." When I meet the commissioners of other nations, and they inquire, " Pray, Madame, what products of Alabama have you in your department? " I am obliged to point to *Octavia* as the only one we have. Whereupon many flattering words are uttered, and Alabama is not so much in the shade as might be supposed.

Excuse this little digression, and let me tell you how proud we are to hear of the brave conduct of young Jerome Bonaparte in the Crimea. He has greatly distinguished himself, and is aid to one of the generals, and often the medium of communication between the two armies, as he speaks English and French equally well. He is always in the midst of the battle, and the soldiers call him the "brave American Bonaparte." An old French count was speaking to me of young Jerome at the party last night, and said, "How quickly the blood of the great Napoléon showed itself in this young man! When he found himself in the thickest of the fight, he had all the coolness and daring of an old veteran." Earnest pride of country flushed my cheek with excitement as I answered, "Ah, Count, you forget his training in our admirable school for soldiers, *West Point.* There he acquired those military tactics you so much admire, and on our frontier, the practice of bold warfare." Marshal Pelissier has written excellent accounts of our Bonaparte, and the Emperor will give him the Legion of Honor, there is no doubt. Please tell Melancthon of this, and say I have forwarded the letter to the Crimea, to his young fellow-soldier.

We had the pleasure of becoming acquainted with the Duke and Duchess of Alba. The Duchess is sister to the Empress, and, though she has dark eyes and hair, is extremely like her. She is a lovely creature, with most unaffected and sweet manners.

From my description you will know how charmingly we spent the evening; and now, dearest Mamma, adieu for a few days.

July 28th.—We were wishing this morning, by some *spiritual clairvoyance* you could see your children, dear Mamma, and behold how enchantingly they are situated. We have apartments on the *Boulevard des Italiens*, just over the *Passage de l'Opéra*. This Boulevard is the great centre of vitality and animation in Paris, like Broadway to New York, the favorite street where all the gay pageants pass, and the highway for elegant equipages, heavy omnibuses, and common carts. It is of great width, and the sidewalks are about the breadth of an ordinary street. Rows of trees (called " trees of heaven ") are planted along the pavement, and spacious houses, hotels, cafés, restaurants, and shops, are built on either side. (Shops signify in this country large stores.) The Boulevards, having been once the walls of the city, have many curves. In one of these turns is the house where we are lodged; and thus we have an extensive view, at least three miles in length, of the most superb and brilliant street in the world. We sit upon our balcony at evening and at night, and look down upon the moving panorama below us. It is truly amusing and delightful. Our only grief is that you and my precious Cara Netta cannot enjoy the scene with us. Therefore I so minutely describe it to you, that, through my eyes, it may also charm you.

This is the first day we have passed at home since our arrival in Paris. Then your dear letters were to arrive, and no pleasure was half so welcome. With the afternoon came a furious rain-storm, which entirely flooded the streets. When it ceased, and the lamps were lighted, from our charming balcony-seats we beheld the Boulevards in a new phase. The sidewalks are extremely wide, and of smooth asphaltum, which, when wet, shines like a mirror; thus, when illuminated by the street-lamps and those within the shops and houses, reflecting every object so clearly that it seemed as if there were another Paris beneath the pavement. It was a curious sight, and we remained gazing upon it long after midnight.

During this morning we had a visit from Mrs. May, of Washington city, (the sister of Mrs. Gales.) She was accompanied by her young daughter, Juliana Gales May, who, I have been assured by excellent judges, possesses a most superb voice. Mrs. May has been several years in Italy, where Juliana has studied with the finest masters of music; and at Verona (the city of Romeo and Juliet) she made a successful *début*, and then played several triumphant engagements in that "land of song," beautiful Italy! Juliana has an exceedingly fine *physique* for the stage. She is tall and graceful, with an admirably developed form, large, expressive eyes, and a perfectly self-possessed manner. There is not a shadow of doubt but she will make a *furore* when she appears as an opera-singer in Paris or America.

To-day the Emperor has set all sight-loving Paris in consternation by announcing the "Fête of 15th of August" will not be celebrated. The money spent upon it will be appropriated to the widows and orphans of the soldiers who were killed in the Crimea, fighting bravely for the "glory of France."

Among the most stylish equipages we have remarked along the Boulevards, during the fashionable hours of the afternoon drive, is that of two negro Princes from Hayti, some of the black Emperor Soulouque's nobility. Their carriage is gorgeous, and glittering with adornments. They have a white coachman, *chasseur*, in a cocked hat, riding alongside, and two dashingly liveried footmen. These dark aristocrats lean back in their luxurious barouche, and give orders to their white servants in a loud tone of assumed importance, and a violent attempt at regal dignity.

We were occupied all of yesterday in making visits. One,

to the Countess Walewski, was very charming; and the palace was even more splendid by daylight, than when we saw it the other night so radiantly illuminated. The Countess's boudoir, in which she received us, is a darling gem of a room, hung around with many sweet pictures. Those of Queen Victoria, Prince Albert, and all the royal children, were beautiful in execution, and admirable resemblances. The Countess, in her simple morning dress, was really lovely. As she has just returned from England, (only a few weeks ago,) she could give me late tidings of my English friends, many of whom, I was deeply pained to hear, were mourning the loss of loved ones in the frightful war of the Crimea. The Countess said that the kind heart of the Queen was often agonized by the horrible details of battles and the terrible sufferings of her soldiers.

Oh! Mamma, fearful is this war! What noble men have perished there! Lord Raglan is dead. He was not killed in battle, but died from anxiety of mind, from the climate, and the unceasing attacks of his enemies at home. How much sorrow his death will give dear Lady Westmorland! When we parted, she was so grieved about him, and dreading the sad result.

We visited our cousin Jane Dixey, too, yesterday. She is pleasantly situated in the Champs Elysées, where the family will remain all the summer. Little Anna has quite forgotten her English, and only speaks French now.

When we came home to dinner, Octavia was made very happy by finding her sweet young friend, Annie Cox, waiting for her. She is a bright, spirited, gifted little girl, extremely accomplished, and well mannered. We all went to drive at evening in the *Bois de Bologne.*

Two nights ago we went to *Le Français*, accompanied by Dr. Gage, formerly of our city, (who resides permanently here now.) He is a very clever man, and has been most kindly polite to us. Rachel was playing her last engagement in Paris, ere she departs for America. The play was *Phedre*, and her acting most impressive and grand. She looks much thinner than when I saw her in London last year, and at times her voice was faint and weak, as though she were suffering from some severe illness.

Octavia, awakening from her sleep, summons me by a loud call from my nice little boudoir, where I write, to tell me it is past one o'clock. I must conclude my letter with blessings upon my dear Mamma.

CHAPTER LXIV.

August 1*st.*—You remember, dear Mamma, my deep regret at not meeting De Lamartine when we were in Paris before. Inquiring for him this time, we heard he was again in the country, and I was sadly disappointed. Speaking to a friend of the poet the other evening, at Prince Napoléon's reception, of my earnest wish to know him, I received the pleasant intelligence that De Lamartine was just now in the city for a few days. The next morning we drove to his apartments. As he was not at home, we left our cards and a kind letter to him from Hon. Dudley Mann, introducing us. Then came an invitation to spend the evening with himself and Mme. Lamartine. There were only a few literary persons present in addition, and I passed some of the most enchanting hours I have known for many years, with the historian, his wife, and friends.

Monsieur De Lamartine resembles much more an American or an Englishman in manner, than a Frenchman. He is tall and thin, has white hair, and an expression of face indicative of constant and intense thought. There is a dreamy, poetical look about the eyes; and he speaks slowly and with marked emphasis. He is calm and self-possessed, but full of cordiality, and his words are both genial and kind. He is captivating in conversation, earnest and eloquent; with so much feeling in his language, as impresses one constantly with his sincerity. He received me with the utmost warmth and charming *empressement*, and seated me by his side, so that I had all his attentions to myself. The thread of conversation was unravelled by the usual topics, until it flowed freely from the ball; and then it soon wove itself into a thousand pleasant themes.

A sparkling little episode, "like the flight of a shining arrow," flashed over the evening's pleasure, so gratifying to me, I must tell you of it. We were speaking of the adoration bestowed upon relics in Rome, when one of the company remarked that all nations possessed objects insignificant in themselves, but dear from associations of the past. De Lamartine turned to me, and said, "Your country, Madame, has the most precious manuscript in the world—the *signed Declaration of Independence!* Do not your people make pilgrimages to look upon it?" Think how my heart swelled with joy as I answered him, "Yes, it is sacred to all our citizens, but most precious to me, since my grandfather's name, which I proudly yet retain, is thereon inscribed, as one who gave his blood and his fortune to perpetuate our free institutions." De Lamartine rose up and bowed to me profoundly, exclaiming, "Madame, in that name you have a noble heritage. It is the true patent of nobility, and you rightly cherish your descent from such a brave and heroic patriot with honest pride!"

Not all the concentrated compliments of the titled, the wealthy, and witty of France, could have touched my soul with the same thrilling delight, as those heart-warm words from De Lamartine; and truly the evening spent with the historian, poet, and orator, has given me more happiness than all the splendid fêtes I have seen in Europe.

Mme. De Lamartine is a most charming person, highly accomplished and intellectual. She seems tenderly loved by her husband, and admired and honored by her friends. She is an Englishwoman, and the circumstances attending their union were exceedingly romantic, she having become passionately interested in the author from reading his beautiful thoughts expressed in his "Meditations." When they did meet, the warm sympathy between them changed into love, which has cheered and brightened the poet's life, and sustained him under its terrible trials. Over her pale face there often stole a deep sadness, as of long past sorrows, whose shadow still lingered. When she told me she was childless, I no longer wondered at the cloud. She had been the mother of four lovely children; all had been gathered, as spring flowers, by relentless death. In the East, at the Holy City of Jerusalem, the last, a precious blooming girl, had been taken from them, and the stricken father and mother were left alone with their great anguish. How sincerely we can feel for these fond parents, thus bereft—we, whose hearts have "travelled the same dark track."

De Lamartine is no longer occupied with politics. He devotes eight or nine hours of the twenty-four to literary pursuits. Indeed, his wife said, but for her entreaties he would give much more time to them. They live in a quiet, comfortable style, and go early in the spring to their grape-farms near Macon. The illness of Mme. De Lamartine had compelled them to return for a brief period to Paris, to consult physicians; and while they were here, I fortunately saw them. In parting, they told me it was quite probable they might visit the United States in a few years.

I have written to dear Papa a long description of my visit to De Lamartine. It will give him great satisfaction, I am sure. The post closes in an hour; so, farewell.

CHAPTER LXV.

August 5th.—We have just returned from a concert at the Imperial Conservatory of Music, where we went with Mr. and Mrs. Smith, of Alabama. They are most agreeable and delightful young people, and have been very kind to us. What will you say when I tell you the concert was at *nine o'clock* in the morning! It was in the theatre of the Conservatory, and was a trial-scene of the candidates for musical fame. These were scholars who had been studying for several years. In a large box, in front of the stage, were seated Auber, (the composer of "Massaniello" and "Fra Diavolo,") Halevy, (composer of "La Juive,") besides other distinguished musicians. They were the jury to bring in a verdict upon the trembling *débutantes.* Scenes from operas were given, in full costume, and solos. There were several splendid voices, which will ere long charm the musical world; but the effect of the whole spectacle by daylight was not pleasant, and our sympathies were so much excited for the poor creatures who failed, we could not enjoy the success of the fortunate ones.

Last night we saw Mme. Doche, in the famous play, written by Alexandre Dumas, (son of the author of "Monte Christo,") called "La Dame aux Camelias," translated into

English with the name of "Camille." For nearly two years it has been played every night, and its attraction is still undiminished. It is the sad history of a young life given up to the wild abandonment of passion, reclaimed by the power and purity of a true love. Deep affection, with its endearing and fond caresses—dark despair, with its fierce and stormy struggles—and death, by the slow wasting away of terrible consumption, were all so touchingly portrayed by Mme. Doche, the entire audience were in tears, and for several hours afterwards a painful feeling oppressed us. This drama, or tragedy, is founded upon truth; and only a few days since, in the cemetery, we saw the tomb of the wretched being whose tumultuous life had furnished the incidents for it.

Alexandre Dumas, the most prolific writer of the age, sat near us. He is quite as dark as our Quadroons, and his features bear the strong type of the negro race, in the thick lips and crispy hair, now very gray.

We have been several times at the Grand Opera, where Cruvelli, Alboni, and Roger are singing. In "Le Prophète," the music of Fides fell to Alboni; and it is peculiarly adapted to her fine contralto voice, and requires, happily for her, but very little action; for she is now so very large, any display of energy would appear ridiculous. Her deep tones were entrancing as she poured forth, with thrilling pathos, "Ah! mon fils."

Cruvelli's voice resembles Sontag's in its quality, but her *tours de force* (if I may use the phrase) were far beyond even those of Jenny Lind. She utters prodigies of sound, and sustains the upper notes with most amazing clearness and precision; but she does not possess that electric power to touch the heart, which was one of the great gifts of the lovely Sontag.

We have a charming young acquaintance here, Dr. Atkinson, of Virginia, who often comes for us to go to the different theatres where spectacles are exhibited. A few evenings since he invited us to go to the *Porte St. Martin* theatre, where "Paris" was represented. You will deem this a very peculiar drama when I tell you it occupies a period of twenty-five hundred years, and only four or five centuries elapse between the acts. It begins with the history of "Paris," from the time of Merlin the Conjuror, renowned in nursery rhyme-books, and continues on with the most remarkable events, either of war, glory, or love, which have in those long ages gilded with brightness or stained with blood and shame its records. The distribution of the eagles is the last scene. In one act occurs a singularly pathetic interview between Louis the Fourteenth and La Vallière. There is a grand ballet, danced by the beauties of the court, and led by Mme. Montespan, her rival in the king's affection. When it is time for *Louise* to appear, the royal lover calls for her, and she comes forward in the dress of the religious order she has embraced, and folding the crucifix to her bosom, exclaims, "Louise La Vallière exists no more; she is now Louise the Carmelite!"

At the *Opéra Comique* we have seen "L'Etoile du Nord," with Caroline Duprez as prima donna.

A letter has just been placed in my hands from Mrs. Kinney, my kind friend in Florence, Italy. Oh! she gives me such sad tidings of that city. The cholera is raging with most frightful power, sweeping away whole families on its tide of death. Only one week after we left the beautiful city, the cholera appeared in the *Casa del Bello*, where Mrs. Kinney lives, and both the wife and child of Buchanan Read died in a few hours, and were buried side by side. Many others of my friends have suffered severely, but life has been spared to them. In Bologna, Ferrara, Padua, and Venice, the pestilence has come forth in all its horrors. It appeared in those places a few days after we had been in them, and we often say how grateful we should be for our escape from danger and illness. Oh! Mamma, how good has God been to us! and you must not think, in the gay whirl of Paris life, we forget the many blessings bestowed upon us. We never fail each night to send up a prayer of thanksgiving from our heart of hearts. And now, farewell.

[Letter to a friend, describing Ristori.]

August 8th.—We have seen the Italian tragédienne several times. She is certainly one of the greatest actresses of the world. She has wonderful talent, perfect grace, and a voice of thrilling power. Her features are not absolutely beautiful, but their expression is charming, for her impassioned soul lights them up, like a lamp in an alabaster vase. The enthusiasm of her acting takes all hearts captive, and her graceful gestures, aiding the touching intonations of her voice, create the wildest *furore* I ever beheld. For, remember, there are very few among the audience who understand Italian; hence you may judge somewhat of Ristori's power —of the magic of her action—when, without this advantage, she thus enchants.

The tragedy of "Maria Stuarda," in which we first saw her, was written by Schiller, then translated into Italian by the poet Maffei; and it gives a new phase to the characters of Elizabeth and Mary Stuart. Contrary to history, a meeting takes place between them, wherein the scorn and hatred of Mary burst forth like the lava-flood of a volcano, and calling down such fearful curses upon the cowering queen, that she quails and retreats from her fierce anger, while Mary, rushing towards her, exclaims, "Oh! this one moment of triumph repays me for years of anguish!" The effect of these frenzied words seemed perfectly magical, and many, many moments passed ere she could again proceed.

Schiller gives a key to the terrible act of revenge which has stamped eternal cruelty upon the character of Elizabeth, in the fact that Leicester loved Mary passionately in early life, and this was never to be forgiven by the stern Tudor.

It is said, when Rachel witnessed this scene, she rushed from her box in wild excitement, and declared she must again appear on the French stage, or the Parisians would forget all she had once been to them. Hence we had the pleasure of seeing her again. She is indeed also an admirable *artiste*, as you will say when she visits the South. But it is in the fierce and bitter passions of woman's heart she triumphs most; not in the gentler emotions of the soul. On the contrary, Ristori is full of love. The little god lurks in her soft eyes, and plays about her beautiful mouth. Think what a miracle she must be, when, in an almost unknown tongue, she awakens such enthusiasm, and above all, among the people of Paris, who often proudly and unhesitatingly declare, "None but the French are good," either as actors, singers, or dancers. To win admiration in this city, is therefore much more difficult than elsewhere.

The second time we witnessed her performance, a box was placed at our command by Mons. Delamarre, one of the editors of *La Patrie*, a most elegant, refined, and highly intellectual gentleman, to whom we were often indebted for polite courtesies. During the representation of the tragedy of "Mirra," (written by the poet Alfieri,) Mons. Delamarre related to us the incidents of her first night before this critical audience. During two acts there was manifest coldness, and even profound silence. But in the third, so remarkable was the power and electric radiance of her genius, the enchanting grace of her attitudes, that, like the universal languages of music and of love, they were perfectly understood by the vast throng, and received with loud acclamations of delight, and a constant flight of bouquets, until they carpeted the whole stage.

Mme. Ristori is a native of Venetian Lombardy. She was educated in Rome, and there made her first appearance. After playing a few years, she married the Marquis of Capranica, and retired from the stage. In the retirement of a happy home, she devoted herself to intense study, and to the perfection of every womanly grâce and accomplishment. The memory of her triumphs, and the incense of applause, still clung around her; and to renew them, to increase them, she again came forward, matured in personal charms, her mind richly cultivated, her talent more dazzling than ever; and now she has received the seal and the stamp of celebrity from a Parisian audience.

And now, I trust this letter, (interesting as I am sure it will prove to you,) will make my peace for the long silence which has hung between us.

August 16*th*.—You can readily imagine, dear Mamma, how happy we have been to meet Mr. Fillmore again. He has recently arrived here from a pleasant tour in Scotland and Ireland. In London (as you have no doubt seen already) his reception by Queen Victoria, Prince Albert, and the Court, was extremely courteous and flattering.

Mr. Fillmore looks uncommonly well, but the sadness of the great grief he experienced in the loss of his gifted daughter, still presses upon his heart. We have had the pleasure of accompanying him, and playing the part of *cicerone* during his visits to the majestic *Louvre*, along the tomb-environed avenues of *Père la Chaise*, amid the rare wonders of the museums, to the "Garden of Plants," to the monuments and triumphal arches. We have also been with him several times at operas, parties, and theatres. His noble and distinguished appearance, his quiet, unostentatious manner, so perfectly elegant in its republican simplicity, has charmed every one; and our American pride was constantly gratified by the high respect and admiration he awakened whenever he appeared in public. He has had a private audience with the Emperor, who welcomed him to France with warm cordiality, and many agreeable words of appreciation.

A few evenings since we drove with Mr. Fillmore to Neuilly, to visit Mme. Calderon de la Barca, whom we knew in America. She is a charming woman, whose high literary fame is well merited. Her husband, Chevalier de la Barca, was Minister of State at Madrid, and during the last revolution was compelled to fly from Spain. They are living here very quietly, "biding their time," as a few months may bring another change, and again their party come into power.

As it was Mme. Calderon's day of reception, we met a number of persons of distinction; of course, a number of Spaniards, (as there are now ten thousand residing here,) and Mexicans, and South Americans. Among the many people presented to me, I was especially pleased with Mr. George Sumner, (brother of the Senator of that name.) He is a most gifted, learned, and agreeable man.

Leaving the pretty villa of Mme. Calderon, we proceeded to the *Bois de Bologne*, and reached it just about twilight—the fashionable hour when the gay *élégantés*, in their fresh and voluminous toilettes, leaning back in splendid barouches, were driving around the lake. Wonderfully has the wood been improved since our first visit to Paris. It has been greatly enlarged, and beautified beyond belief. There are broad roads for carriages, deeply-shaded avenues for *equestriennes* and their attendant beaux, and winding pathways for lovers, (I suppose they are such,) as *flirtations* are not among the institutions of society here. Within the lake are several islands, adorned with Swiss *chalets*. Numerous boats were skimming over the waters, filled with merry parties. When it was entirely night, the scene was truly picturesque. Hundreds and hundreds of carriages were driving around the lake, and their lamps, reflected upon its clear surface, gave us a perfect illumination.

We attended the wedding of Mrs. Meike (sister of Mrs. Ritchie), and Dr. Borroughs, this morning, at the house of the American Minister. The ceremony was performed by a *Swedenborgian*, and was quite long; but impressive and touching, very unlike the Protestant service, although a ring was given as " a sign and token of a union, that was to last on earth, and be eternal in the heavens."

In a foreign country, the marriages of all Americans must take place in the residence of the Minister. Thus, immediately after the greetings of the newly-wedded pair and their friends were over, we all went to the *Rue du Cirque*, to the mansion of Mr. and Mrs. Smythe, where a magnificent banquet (a *déjeûner à la fourchette*) awaited the guests; and we spent several charming hours in a large circle of American acquaintances and friends. Our agreeable friend, Mr. Bloodgood, and his sweet and interesting daughter, (who is so like her lovely mother), were there; they have just returned from Egypt, where they passed many months most delightfully. Mr. Thompson (the pleasant gentleman I have mentioned to you before) accompanied them in their voyage up the Nile. We also met many acquaintances we had made in Naples, Rome, and Florence. They had all gathered here for the Exposition, and for the coming fêtes for Queen Victoria.

Returning home, we had barely time to make our toilettes for a dinner party at Mr. Armstrong's, our near neighbor on the *Boulevard des Italiens.* During all our visits to Paris, we have been much indebted to him for many polite and graceful courtesies. He is an American gentleman of fortune, who has made Paris his home, and lives in elegant style. His sister and two pretty young nieces received the guests with charming cordiality. There were two very handsome girls present from the West, the Misses Fellows, who, with their father, a frank, warm-hearted man, have been some time upon the Continent. The dinner was admirable, and we passed the hours most pleasantly until eleven, when we returned home, and I seated myself to tell my dear Mamma all the events of the last ten days. But it is quite impossible for me to write half the kind words of remembrance with which I am charged by friends who knew us in other days. I am sure you have a vivid recollection of Mrs. Stewart, whom we so often saw in Washington city, with her beautiful daughter Delia, (who is now married, and lives in England.) I have had great pleasure in renewing my acquaintance with Mrs. Stewart. She is an accomplished and intellectual lady, and still retains her fine form and elegant manner.

We have spent two or three evenings with Mr. and Mrs. Rossiter. We met them in England during our first visit there, and were truly glad to see them again. Oh! Mamma, they are certainly the happiest and most charming couple I ever saw. Their home is so beautiful, with its walls adorned with exquisite pictures painted by themselves, (for both are fine artists). Mrs. Rossiter has twins, lively little creatures, one year old. Paintings of them, and marble busts, are seen in all directions, their parents are so proud of them. Rossiter is now painting a large picture of Anna (his wife) and the twins. The mother is seated in a neat little boudoir, while the two French nurses, in the picturesque costume of Normandy, have just brought the children to her, and she is stretching out her arms to take them, while her noble face is glowing with delight.

Vast numbers of Americans live here constantly, while others are only visitors like ourselves. I have been with Gen. Mercer to see two very agreeable families from Boston, the Brooks and Thorndykes. We had a visit a few nights since from a delightful young friend of ours, Dr. Kennedy, of Mississippi. He has been residing in Paris several years, and is going in a few weeks to the Holy Land, to Egypt, and up the Nile. He proposed that we should join his party; and believe me, we are extremely tempted to do so. This journey and voyage would, however, occupy us six months at least, and we have already been near one year away from you; and we do not think we could endure an absence so much prolonged. Still, it would be an enchanting visit to that sacred land, the first touched by the footsteps of our blessed Saviour. Another time when we cross the ocean I shall go there, but not now.

Our Boulevard is never silent, either night or day. Until three o'clock in the morning, there is an incessant stream of carriages and peeple passing. When that ceases, the street-sweepers come. They consist of large parties of men and women, with brooms and rakes. Being often up writing to you at that hour, I go out on the balcony to look at them and absolutely tremble, when they turn their fierce and savage eyes upon me. What frightful creatures they are. Almost the semblance of woman has been crushed out from the wretched forms, by their hard and disgusting life. With them there were always the "rag-pickers," huge baskets on their backs, and a long staff with an iron hook in their hands. They fished in the gutters, and turned over every scrap of paper.

The street-sweepers usually completed their work about daylight, when they crept away to their dark holes and garrets, like so many evil birds of night. With the sunlight came again the bright, gay, joyous life of Paris.

Through the heavy curtains of my window a ray of the morning's dawn is just stealing, warning me to end this letter. So good-bye, dear Mamma.

CHAPTER LXVI.

August 18th, morning.—All the long night these Boulevards have been thronged with excited people, either as spectators, or busied in the countless preparations for this day's spectacle. Workmen by hundreds are engaged in adorning the arches of triumph, or of welcome, or raising on lofty poles the flags of France, England, Sardinia, and Turkey, by thousands. It is impossible to picture to you even a tithe of the excitement of Paris—of all France, indeed, at the coming of the British Queen. The world seems absolutely wild, (all Paris certainly is.) Vast multitudes from the Provinces, who never saw the great city before, have come up to catch one glimpse of a real, live English sovereign, as the guest and friend of France. To gratify this earnest wish, no fear of expense stops them. Think of the sum of two thousand francs being paid for the use of a balcony for one day on the Boulevards, and three or five hundred francs for a single window!

We have a long balcony belonging to our apartments, and five windows; and we have surely had over a hundred applicants for them. But what could we do? To make all "free and equal," as good Americans should, was impossible; so we were obliged to select a certain number, and then decline the other applications. Our company is compelled to assemble at two, although the *cortége* is not due until six; but after the hour appointed the *Boulevard des Italiens* will be impassable. Our courier, Luigi, has had the floors waxed until they shine like Venetian mirrors, and all the covers are removed from gay furniture, in due arrangement for a grand day. Even now the street is perfectly radiant. From every window flags are floating, and all the balconies are draped in velvet, fringed with gold. Nearly opposite to us is the Triumphal Arch of the Grand Opera; it is of immense height, crowned with two giant eagles, and hung with crimson draperies studded thickly with gold bees. Garlands of flowers likewise adorn it, while the flags of the four nations are waving gracefully over it.

It is a glorious day, and a delicious breeze renders the air as cool as our spring weather. All Paris is abroad, all smiling, all in good humor, and joyous expectation of seeing the English Queen. It is now four hundred and fifty years since a British sovereign has visited France; so there is no fear that any one can compare this pageant with one on a similar occasion. For nine miles, from the Strasbourg station to the Arch of Friendship, the streets are lined on each side with soldiery, four deep. It is said there are a hundred and fifty thousand under arms; and all along the line, banners float out, with sweet words of welcome. The sidewalks are one dense mass of human beings, but the centre of the Boulevard is kept clear by numerous *gens d'armes.* The very housetops are crowded, and the chimneys, peeping over their nine or ten stories, are covered with people, as treetops sometimes are with birds. At a window *vis-à-vis* to us, in the tenth story, even now there is a large placard, "*à louer*" (for rent), displayed. As it is nearly two o'clock, we must prepare to receive our friends.

Night.--Before proceeding with the day's festivities, I must relate an episode, which will please you vastly. The first glance this morning at the myriads of flags brought vividly to mind our own loved " stars and stripes," and I at once resolved they should float as proudly as others, at least from my own domicil. We wrote to the American Minister to obtain one; but those belonging to the Embassy were already engaged. M. D. was too patriotic to permit me to be disappointed, so he started out, searching highway and byway, until he found, bought, and brought home, a standard flag, and a number of hand colors. We raised the proud emblem of our country in the centre of our balcony, and flanked it on either hand with the flags of England and France. Crowds soon gathered to look up at it, as many people from the interior had never before seen an American flag; while a party of our countrymen, catching the unusual sight in such a place, after profoundly saluting the banner, rushed up stairs to compliment my patriotism. Several laughingly declared they expected we should be forced to take it down, as there was a whisper stealing through Paris that the United States fraternized with Russia; and they were curious to know what answer we would make to such a command. Just as we were asserting, " We will never strike our flag," the Chief of Police came in to thank us for the attention shown to the " Guest of Paris," by unfurling in her honor our national flag. Our friend Mr. Fillmore, too, who saw the banner at a distance as we were loosening the tangled folds from the staff, and casting them out upon the free air, raised his hat involuntarily, and bowed to the banner with deep reverence; then, when he came in, said such sweet words of approbation, as quite gladdened our hearts, telling Octavia, as he looked upon her half enveloped in the banner, she seemed the Genius of America, protecting and protected by the " stars and stripes."

At six o'clock in the evening we all took our stations on the balcony. Music was constantly floating on the air, and gay sights filling the eyes, so we felt no weariness in waiting so long. At length the cannon from the " Invalides " boomed forth the announcement of the arrival at the Strasbourg station of the royal visitors. A murmur of relief, multiplied by the watching thousands, rose like the sound of an avalanche. In half an hour more the *cortége* was in sight. Wearied by the long delay, the multitude had lost much of their enthusiasm, and darkness was fast coming on. Thus the absolute reception seemed but tame, when judged by its expectation. Millions and millions of francs were thus uselessly expended by poor persons, who had almost starved themselves for weeks that they might have money enough to hire a place whence they could have a good look at Queen Victoria.

As her Majesty passed our balcony, instead of waving handkerchiefs as many of the ladies did, we waved the guide colors from our national flag. The Emperor called her Majesty's attention to this compliment, and she most graciously bowed to us in acknowledgment of it.

By the time the Imperial party reached St. Cloud, a brilliant illumination was glowing throughout the city. All the public buildings, the Tuileries, and the great Exposition edifice, shone out like palaces of light, glittering until long after the midnight.

My eyes are weary with the sights and scenes of the day; therefore I must say good night, dear Mamma.

CHAPTER LXVII.

August 23*d*.—We spent a very pleasant morning on Monday last, at the Exposition of the *Beaux Arts* (the picture-gallery), during the visit of Queen Victoria to it. Our handsome and agreeable friend, Col. Starke, accompanied us, and we saw a vast throng of royal personages and distinguished people. The Emperor was devoted in his attention to the sovereign of England, walking constantly by her side, and pointing out the most attractive pictures. She seemed delighted, and expressed her pleasure in charming words, with the enthusiasm of a young girl. Prince Napoléon was in attendance upon the Princess Royal, who is a sweet, modest-looking little creature, apparently not more than twelve, (she is, however, fourteen.) Both herself and the Queen were very simply dressed. The Prince of Wales is a bright, intellectual boy; his remarks concerning the pictures were intelligent and appropriate. Prince Albert was (as he always must be) elegant and dignified, with the same kind, benign expression of face, and cordial manner, which so charmed me when I first met him in England. The Queen stood with the Emperor for quite a long time before the beautiful picture of the Empress and her ladies in waiting, painted by Winterhalter, (I described it to you in a previous letter,) and expressed loudly her admiration of it. Then the royal party proceeded through all the different rooms, and after spending two or three hours viewing the splendid pictures and statuary, they drove away to the Tuileries, where a lunch was prepared for them, and afterwards returned to St. Cloud, which is their home during their sojourn in France.

We had rare amusement watching the anxiety of the people to see the Queen. Several times, when she passed groups of English people, they appeared so enchanted, they could not repress their exclamations of "God bless our Queen!" When she heard these words, she would invariably turn, and bow to her loyal subjects. The love they feel for her is so honest and real, it always pleased us that we were near to hear this earnest expression of it.

Tuesday morning the Queen visited the Exposition, where a much greater crowd awaited her than at the *Beaux Arts*, and the eagerness to see her was so great, it was almost impossible to keep back the vast throng. She does not dread fatigue much, for she walked through all the galleries, great saloons, and even went down into the *Annex* to see the machinery. But the most brilliant event of the week thus far has been the royal visit to the Opera, and I must devote a whole letter to it; so, good-bye.

The Queen at the Grand Opera.—All the windows in the vicinity of the Opera House were illuminated with colored lamps, and the front of the theatre adorned with flowers, hangings, and shields, bearing the arms of England and France. A line of fire ran along the frieze of the building, with the initials of Queen Victoria and the Emperor in jets of gas.

Passing through the *passage de l'Opéra*, we soon entered the Opera House, and seated ourselves in an excellent box, whence we had an admirable view of the royal party during all the evening.

I must tell you, now, who composed the party in our box. There was Mr. Fillmore, our noble-looking and distinguished Ex-President; Mr. Corcoran, the rich banker from Washington city, and his lovely little daughter; Mrs. Ewing, an agreeable lady from Tennessee; and your two Octavias. M. D. and Judge Davies preferred seats in the parquette.

Several of the boxes fronting the stage had been removed, and the space converted into quite a room, which was richly carpeted, and furnished with enormous crimson satin chairs. The draperies around the box were of red velvet, embroidered with gold, and suspended from the talons of an immense imperial eagle with outstretched wings. There were two of the *cent-garde* in their glittering uniform, standing like statues at each side.

The other boxes were all filled with the rank, wealth, and fashion of Paris. Every lady had a new toilette of amazing elegance, and jewels of dazzling splendor. Every gentleman was in ball dress, or in uniform. In the Emperor's box, where he usually sits, was the Prince Adalbert of Bavaria, (our former *compagnon du voyage*,) and not far off, the Countess Montijo, and the Duke and Duchess of Alba. These ladies were superbly attired with a profusion of diamonds, while the Duke was in a suit of black.

About eight o'clock we heard loud shouts from the street. Then the orchestra played "God save the Queen," and the Emperor entered the state-box, leading in the sovereign of Great Britain. A burst of joyous acclamation resounded through the edifice, and "Vive la Reine!" was heard on every side. Queen Victoria bowed and curtsied many times ere she could take her seat; then the Empress and Prince Albert came in, and they were saluted in the same manner; next Princess Matilde and Prince Napoléon joined them. When they were all seated, the Queen of England

and the Empress of France side by side, the Emperor by Victoria, and Prince Albert by the fair Eugenie, the curtain arose, and the performance began. There was a trio from "William Tell," and Hummel's variations exquisitely given by Alboni, and the "Bolero" of the "Vêpres Siciliennes" by Cruvelli. There was no applause of the singers until the note of approval came from some one of the royal party. In truth, we did not listen much to the music; we were absorbed in looking around us upon the magnificent scene.

Both Queen Victoria and the Empress were dressed in white, with blazing diadems around their brows, and necklaces and bracelets of great splendor. The Empress wore the crown jewels, and their weight appeared almost overpowering. Across her bosom was the cordon of the order of Isabella the Catholic, while her Majesty of England displayed the Ribbon of the Garter. The Emperor wore the uniform of a general officer, while Prince Albert was in a Field-Marshal's dress. Both had gleaming stars and orders upon the breast.

The Empress is a lovely creature, with a radiant, *spirituelle* expression of countenance. Her manner is gentle, graceful, and winning, and a soft and tender charm pervades her every movement; she was very pale, and is evidently in delicate health. She conversed frequently with Prince Albert and the Queen. They all seemed in cheerful spirits, and greatly to enjoy the spectacle before them.

Queen Victoria looked uncommonly well, and gratified by the enthusiasm of her reception. A sweet smile was constantly playing around her full red lips, and lighting up her clear blue eyes. She appeared really happy and delighted.

When the ballet of *La Fonti*, danced by Rosati, Plunket, Petitpas, was ended, the curtain rose upon the last *tableau*, which was a representation of Windsor Castle; the French and English flags forming clouds around it, amid which were the prettiest and youngest girls of the *corps de ballet*, and little children to represent angels, suspended in such an artistic manner, they absolutely seemed floating in the air. The Castle was illuminated by electric light, which produced a very wonderful effect. Then Roger, Alboni, and Cruvelli, stepped forward in front of the theatrical company, who were all upon the stage, and sang the English national anthem. When its first note was uttered, the whole audience rose up, and the house, from the parquette to the ceiling, presented the most magnificent appearance imagination can picture. "Vive la Reine Victoria!" burst from a thousand lips, while handkerchiefs were waved, and hands were clapped. Her Majesty curtsied and bowed; then curtsied and bowed, again and again; still the same wild delight continued. Three different times she left the box, and was led back by the Emperor, when she gracefully acknowledged the tumultuous enthusiasm of the audience. At last, the imperial party were permitted to leave, and every where along the Boulevards, as they passed, the houses were illuminated.

Thus ended the brilliant pageant of the opera; and now, dear Mamma, good night.

CHAPTER LXVIII.

August 24th.—Well, the grand ball is over! Before the spectacle has lost one tint of its radiance, let me daguerreotype it by its own brightness. Yet, how can I picture the scene of enchantment? That I may give you, at least, a good sketch of it, I let no intermediate objects or time interfere between it and you, for it was near daylight when we reached home.

After having slept a few hours, I will now to my pleasant task. Where shall I begin? Ah! with the rush, the crush, and eagerness of ticket-hunting, the triumph of success and the regret of disappointment; for although twelve thousand tickets were issued, there were at least five hundred thousand strangers in Paris, all equally anxious to attend the ball. Of course, therefore, many could not accomplish their earnest wish. Mr. Piott, Secretary of the American Embassy, called, and kindly brought us invitations, while a distinguished French gentleman sent them also. Thus we fortunately had two sets of tickets, and were enabled to make our pretty friend from South Carolina, and Mrs. S., of New York, most happy by sending them these cards of admission. M. D. gave his invitations to D. and Mr. S., who accompanied us. Col. Pryor, of Richmond, *en route* as Minister to Greece, was also with us. Thus we had three of the handsomest and most elegant beaux of the ball.

We left our apartments at half past eight, and on reaching the *Rue de Rivoli*, we fell into a train of fifteen hundred carriages. "Faites la queue!" shouted the soldiers on guard, but this said "long tail" was equal to a sentence of midnight arrival. Still we stopped, for bayonets are peremptory things. But our courier is a man of the moment. What was to be done, though? A dashing young officer came riding by; he said to him, "Monsieur, the ladies in the barouche are of high rank—a glance will prove it—they wish a speedy arrival at the ball!" The gallant soldier gave us a *look*, the sentinel a *sign;* and thereon we dashed triumphantly towards the *Hotel de Ville.*

Every street leading thither was illuminated, but the square on which it stands was a miracle of light. Pyramids of variegated lamps! Giant initials of the four sovereigns in jets of gas! with Drummond lights on the summit of the Hotel, and upon the old Tower of St. Jacques! Flags and garlands fluttered in the air; martial music pealed up from the square; while thousands of soldiers, and multitudes of *gens d'armes*, made the ground one glittering surface. High over all shone the bright, pure moon. Oh! how contrasted was the light of the scene above and below.

The front of the vast Hotel was decorated with huge bouquets, from whose flowers and leaves brilliant streams of gaslight seemed to issue, and every cornice and frieze was glowing with long lines of flame. All was so bright, it appeared impossible the interior could exceed this external view. Truly were we mistaken; for soon we entered a scene of fairy-like enchantment. The grand staircase was tapestried with living flowers; from their fragrant clusters peeped out little nymphs with vases, whence gushed streams of water, sparkling a moment, and then darting away amid the green leaves and clinging vines.

The spacious *Gallerie des Fêtes* was the ball-room of the night; and there we witnessed a quadrille danced by Queen Victoria, the Emperor, Prince Albert, Princess Matilde, and other royal personages to complete the set. The lovely Empress was too much indisposed to appear. The Queen wore a dress of white silk, covered with costly flounces of Brussels lace, and a splendid diadem of diamonds, with necklace, brooch, and bracelets of the same precious gems. Her face was bright with animation and pleasure. As the heat was excessive, the imperial party danced but once, and after walking through the principal saloons, they withdrew about twelve o'clock.

Strauss's band "discoursed most eloquent music" all the evening, but the throng was too dense to think of dancing; so we wandered from room to room, thirty-five in number, and each seemed more beautiful than the other. The walls of the "Gallery of Mirrors" is all of glass and burnished gold, while in the "Hall of Flora" the walls as well as the ceiling were covered with morning glories, whose bell-shaped flowers and shining green leaves were so natural, we often put forth our hands to pluck them. In several of the apartments there was a light, soft and tender as the moon's rays; and on the sides or in the centre, were fountains reflecting the pale beams, and giving forth a music in their gushing waters that was heard above the voices of the crowd.

But the most wonderful was the "Court of Louis the Fourteenth," roofed over with glass, and formed into a hall. In each arcade was a magnificent chandelier, and between the columns, fountains encircled with flowers; while far above were numerous Cupids, bearing clusters of lights intermin gling with immense candelabra. In the centre was a staircase built for the occasion, light, graceful, elegant. Fresh flowers were twining around its golden balustrades, while directly where it sprung from the floor were the statues of England and France, with links of the olive-branch between them; and quite near these were grottoes occupied by naiads, emblematic of the Seine and the Thames. From vases they held flowed two sparkling streams, which soon mingled into one, and then rushed over ledges of rock, chafed into white foam, like a mountain cascade; and thence dashed over myriads of lamps, protected from extinction as though by magic. After a noisy and brief career the waters fell into great basins, whence they glided calmly away. The lotus and other water plants floated upon the surface of these fountains, while around them banks of rare flowers exhaled a gentle and delicious perfume, that pervaded one's entire system. It was a scene more beautiful than the visions of "Vathek."

There mere multitudes of exquisitely dressed women, graceful and stylish, but not so lovely as the women of our own country. There were people of all nations, and every variety of the "types of the human race." The wife and sister of the Haytien Prince, black as Africans, were attired in silk of their own color, while a negro from Abyssinia wore the Turkish costume, and flirted with the freshest and fairest in the ball. The four Arab chiefs, too, were present; and at the termination of the quadrille, the Emperor commanded the superior one of the party to salute the Queen! The Arab knelt with native grace before her, and pressed the Queen's knees between his two hands. (This is the Arab token of submission.) So greatly were we all diverted, that a laugh would have been a safety-valve; but the presence of royalty forbade such a relief. However, even her Majesty looked as though she would gladly have laughed if etiquette had permitted. When the second Arab approached she shook her head, declining another such presentation of homage.

The refreshments were tea, iced coffee, sherbets, creams, and punch; but no "champaigne" or "boned turkeys," the important luxuries of an American supper. Until long after twelve o'clock the guests were arriving, and even at three, as we were descending the great stairway, we met several just going up, the occupants of the last of the fifteen hundred carriages.

The glorious ball exists but in memory now. If my description has given you one ray of the pleasure we experienced, I am truly content. Ever your fond child.

August 30th.—The week of royal fêtes and festivities ended on Monday last, by the departure of the Queen. Grandly and nobly has she been received and entertained by the Emperor and Empress of France. Every variety of amusement awaited her. There were superb pageants, gorgeous balls, brilliant operas, visits to the monuments and neighboring palaces, and military reviews of thousands and thousands of soldiers upon the *Champs de Mars*. Never has there been a more splendid spectacle since the meeting of the two Kings upon the "Field of the Cloth of Gold," long years ago.

Queen Victoria was certainly enchanted with the warmth and the magnificence of her reception. We often remarked the bright look of pleasure and satisfaction expressed in her face. Louis Napoléon is a wonderful man, and has shown himself, in these times of war, a skilful ruler of the destinies of France. He seems to bear a "charmed life," for the bullet of the assassin Piornora struck him fully upon the breast, but rebounded. Only a few years ago he was a wanderer, almost without money, in London; now, he is the sovereign of a great people, and welcomes the proud Queen whose dominions are from the "rising to the setting sun," as his guest.

The anxiety to see Queen Victoria was beyond credibility. We have known many persons to stand twelve hours calmly waiting for her to pass, that they might catch one glimpse of her. Even a poor sewing woman, who brought us home some work the day of the Queen's arrival, told me she had given *forty francs* for one place at a window on the Boulevard, where she might see her as she went by. When we observed to her, "Is not that a vast amount for you to pay?" she gaily answered, "Oh! yes indeed; and to pay for it, I must sew all night for two weeks at least, scarcely sleeping a moment. But then, I shall have the delight of saying, I have seen the sovereign of England!" There were thousands of instances like this, I doubt not.

The departure of Queen Victoria was quite as magnificent as her *entrée* into Paris. By nine in the morning (last Monday) the soldiers were drawn up in long lines, with glittering bayonets, along the sidewalks, and all the flags thrown out to the breeze. About eleven the *cortége* came up the Boulevards, and moved slowly on to the Strasbourg station. In the imperial carriage were the Queen, Emperor, Princess Royal, and Prince Albert. This equipage was superb in all its appointments; it was drawn by eight black horses, each with a groom leading him by a gilded bridle. In another carriage was the Prince Napoléon and the Prince of Wales. Marshal Magnan and General Loewenstein rode near it. Then came an escort of "Guides," and the carriages containing the suite of her Majesty. After them marched the *cent-garde* (hundred guards) in their gorgeous uniform, with gleaming breastplates, and the foot-soldiers in "serried ranks." It was indeed a stately and imposing procession, as it moved grandly onward, glowing in the dazzling sunlight; drums beating, and trumpets sounding, while the soldiers presented arms as it passed, and the vast throngs on the pavements, at windows, upon galleries and housetops, shouted loudly, "Vive la Reine! Vive la Reine!"

CHAPTER LXIX.

September 2d.—We passed yesterday at the *Chateau de Croissy*, with the charming family of Mr. and Mrs. Henderson, of New York. Miss Henderson, a fine, noble-looking woman, had been several times to visit us, and had invited us to spend some days with them in the Chateau, which they have rented for the summer; but our numerous engagements had prevented us from accepting, although an excellent friend, Dr. Elliot, had called once or twice to accompany us there. When Queen Victoria departed, and there was a lull in the wild rush of gaiety, young Henderson came for us, and we went down by railway within a few miles of Croissy; at the village station a carriage met us, and we drove through a pretty country, just by the banks of the Seine, up a grand avenue of trees, to the Chateau, built in the time of Louis the Fourteenth, in the Italian style of villa, with immense rooms, and marble terraces, whence we descended into the gardens, radiant with flowers, and walked through long aisles of green; entered grottoes, overshadowed by cedars of Lebanon; and went up to the summit of the observatory, where we commanded an extensive view over the whole country.

But the greatest charm of the Chateau consisted in its having been the residence of Josephine. In the principal saloon the conqueror of many lands, the victorious General Bonaparte, had been married to the fascinating Mme Beauharnais. (This Chateau was the property of her first husband.) As I sat in that room, where the lovely Josephine had given herself to Napoléon, a flood of remembrances rushed over my mind, recalling the hours of my first recollection, when, a little child, I used to place myself at your feet, and beg you to tell me stories of the good Josephine. How often my heart had then been touched with indignation at the thought of her cruel abandonment.

Miss Henderson, perceiving how much feeling I manifested in the memory of the good queen, drove me to *Mal Maison*, (now belonging to Queen Christina of Spain.) It was there Josephine retired after her separation from Napoléon, and lived in solitude and sorrow, seeking out the poor and afflicted, whose sufferings she soothed, until death released her pure spirit from its earthly tenement, and upon angel-wings it soared to heaven. We saw the long gloomy avenues where she wandered in desolate grief, when parted forever from Napoléon, finding her only consolation in the exercises of her holy religion. In the small town of *Rueil*, near to *Mal Maison*, she is buried in the village church, beneath a monument "erected to her memory by her children, Hortense and Eugene."

After many weary trials, and sad, dark days, Hortense died, and her body was brought to France, and laid by the side of Josephine. I hope the Emperor will build a grand mausoleum to his mother and grandmother. During the lifetime of his mother (Hortense) he was remarkable for his fond and devoted affection towards her, and the unceasing tenderness with which he watched over her.

Returning from *Mal Maison*, we passed *Saint Germain* and *Les Maisons*, built by Louis the Fourteenth for Mme.

Du Barri. On the summit of a hill we saw the ruins of a Roman aqueduct, in a wonderful state of preservation. At eight we dined, and by eleven were at the station, and soon after in Paris, quite charmed with our agreeable day. Mrs. Henderson is the niece of Miss Hannah F. Gould, the sweet poetess, who so captivated my heart when we met many years since in New York.

We are going to-night to the opera to hear Cruvelli in *Les Vêpres Siciliennes*, the last production of Verdi; and must now cease writing, to make our toilettes. Farewell, dear Mamma.

September 6th.—The " Palace of Industry," as the Parisians call the Exposition, is now completed, and overflowing with splendid varieties of rich fabrics, costly furniture, precious jewels, and wonderful machinery. It is open constantly from daylight until dark night; but there are two especial days when it is seen to peculiar advantage,—the *aristocratic* day, when the nobility, rank, and fashion, resort to it, (then the admittance is five francs;) only superbly dressed women and elegant men are there during those hours: Sunday is the *people's* day, when all the hard-working inhabitants of Paris and its environs are permitted to enter by paying *four cents;* thus a poor man is enabled to bring all his family with him. We went there last Sunday purposely to see the vast multitude. It numbered more than *one hundred and twenty thousand persons*, and yet the immense building was not crowded. A most pleasant sight it was to watch these " children of toil," they appeared so perfectly happy and contented, looking at the diamonds, and commenting upon the beauty of the laces and embroideries. There were family groups of especial interest: an aged grandmother, with snowy hair, neatly curled, accompanied by her daughter, and grandchildren and great-grandchildren; then an old man, supported on the arms of a bright-eyed young girl, his grandson's daughter, tottering around, and exclaiming in feeble voice, "Ah! we had none of these beautiful things when I was young, but we were happier then." Many of the throng remained all day, and when they were wearied, they seated themselves upon the crimson sofas and divans around the great fountain, and the children played on the floor. It was a scene of merry enjoyment, and often did we admire the wisdom of the Emperor, who commanded or suggested this cheap day for the laboring classes.

There was never a crowd during the *aristocratic* day. The last time we were there, we remarked a large woman, exquisitely dressed, with a profusion of light hair clustering around her face in delicate curls. She was neither young nor handsome; yet there was an indescribable charm about her which compelled me to follow with admiring eyes her every movement. I felt I had seen her before, and that some singular interest connected with this person captivated and riveted my attention. Several inquiries brought me no information, until we met the Marquis de Molins, from Madrid, walking with the lovely Marquesa; so, running up to them, I explained the strange spell this woman had woven around me, when they both laughingly said, "Is it possible you do not know who she is?" Assuring them I did not, they told me she was the renowned *Countess Giuccioli*, beloved by Byron, and almost immortalized in his poems; and that I had seen her portrait in a certain palace at Venice, although her name was not attached to it. I well remember the fresh and delicious beauty of that picture, with the long fair curls, "bright as sunbeams," floating over the plump round shoulders, and nestling in the full white bosom. And this was the original of that fascinating painting, and hence I had been drawn so irresistibly towards her. The Marquis informed us then that the enchanting portrait we had seen, represented the *Countess Giuccioli* about the time Byron loved her. She is now the wife of a French Count, and resides in Paris.

We are just going to drive, so good-bye.

September 10*th*.—We have made several charming visits to the Countess de Montijo. She lives in the Champs Elysées, in a beautiful house the Emperor has purchased for her, and adorned with exquisite taste. Sunday is her reception day, and we often met there very distinguished and celebrated people, among them many of the grandees of Spain, who are surely the most noble, dignified, and elegant men we have seen in Europe. These morning *réunions* were exceedingly delightful. The Countess is remarkable for her tact in conversation, and the charm she throws around the social circle, rendering all her guests happy by presenting congenial persons to each other, and not allowing any to feel themselves a stranger in her splendid saloons. The Duchess d'Albe is only now twenty, has been married three years, and has several children. She is passing the summer with her mother, the Countess Montijo. During our pleasant visits to their hotel, we often heard them speak of the sweet Empress. Although still in delicate health, there is a hope she will ere many months be perfectly well. The physicians have ordered she shall remain quietly upon her sofa, and not encounter the slightest fatigue. They told us what delight Queen Victoria had expressed at seeing Paris, and in the magnificent festivities prepared to welcome her. The Emperor so entirely won the heart of the Prince of

Wales, that the little fellow implored his mamma to leave him for a time with the Emperor, when she returned to England.

I think, in some of my letters, I have mentioned Matilda, a *protégée* of dear Miss Bremer, whom she has sent here to learn engraving upon silver and gold—a *métier* or trade particularly adapted to young women. As she was exceedingly occupied learning this art, (from seven in the morning till seven at night,) she could only come to see me when there were holidays, and the shop shut up. She was a fresh, innocent-looking, artless girl. Though ignorant of society, she possessed a highly-cultivated and well-stored mind, a beautiful character, and great refinement of feeling. Her gratitude to Miss Bremer was profound and touching; often with gushing tears she told me how good and kind she had been to her, when, a desolate, homeless, friendless little creature, she had been cast out upon the world. Then the warm philanthropy of Miss Bremer's noble heart manifested itself by rescuing this girl from a life of degradation, and making her a useful, industrious, and thoughtful woman. It was a true pleasure for me to talk with her.

Last Sunday, just as I was entering the carriage to drive to the Countess Montijo's, a letter came from Miss Bremer, saying to me, " In September my magnolia flower from the sweet South must come to me, and she shall be truly welcome to my heart, my home, my friends, and all that is best in Stockholm." Then followed kind words to Matilda, whom she begged I would see, and cheer a little in her loneliness, for she was a total stranger in Paris.

After the Countess's reception was over, in driving home, my thoughts dwelt frequently upon Miss Bremer, and the disappointment I must inflict when she received my letter, informing her I could not go to Stockholm, in consequence of the lateness of the season, and our fears of the autumn storms of the rude Baltic. I had never been to see Matilda where she lodged, and having her address in my card-case, I told the coachman to drive there. He looked astonished when he heard the direction. However, he proceeded to a gloomy, narrow street, where the houses were about eight or nine stories high. When he stopped, the *concierge* (the woman who attends the door) came out, and I inquired for Matilda. "Yes, Madame, there is such a person here, a fair, rosy girl, from the North of Europe. She has been here a long time, but no one ever came to see her before; and surely, Madame with her elegant toilette would not go up to the seventh story?"

Being resolved to see her, I told the coachman to wait, and I began the ascent. You may judge by the time I reached the seventh story I was quite breathless. Knocking at a door, it was opened by a wretched-looking woman, who started back at seeing such an applicant for admission. "Does Matilda live here?" "What! Matilda, the Swedish girl? *Ciel!* Madame cannot wish to see her! no one ever asked for her since she has lived in that room," replied the pale shadow, pointing to a door near by.

I tapped upon it, and a soft voice cried "Entrez." Opening it, I went in, and there, at a little table, Matilda was seated, with an open Bible before her, and the picture of Miss Bremer just above it, like the image of a holy saint within this humble shrine. For a moment Matilda could not speak for astonishment, and then she sprang up, and with warm and enthusiastic words poured out her gratitude to me for my kindness in coming, and imploring me to pardon her for calling out so abruptly, "Come in." "I thought it was the *concierge*, for no one save herself ever knocked at my door since I came here."

Poor Matilda! She was indeed lonely, in a strange land; but she seemed quite happy, and told me, just as I saw her upon entering she spent all her Sabbath days, reading her Bible, and looking upon the picture of her only friend. She begged me to be seated, but turning her eyes from my gay dress to the rude bench (her only seat), she cried out in distress, " What shall I do ? " Relieving her anxiety, I seated myself upon her neat little bed, and she drew the bench near me, and then we had such a long and pleasant *tête-à-tête*. The room was no larger than one of our closets at home. There was only one window, whence the view extended over a great world of housetops. It was a wretched, miserable garret-room, and yet it had for me a pure and touching interest. The gentle and sweet young creature who made it her home, appeared to sanctify the spot with her lovely piety, and heart-warm affection for her benefactress.

Was not that a morning of contrasts ?—from the gilded and magnificent saloons of the highest fashion, to the humble garret of the workwoman !

In your last letter you inquire about Prince Jerome. One morning when we went to call upon the Princess Matilde, we met Prince Jerome (her father) just driving from the door. He is a stout old gentleman, resembling slightly the portraits of Napoleon (his illustrious brother) ; but Mr. Bonaparte (his son, and the son of his American wife) is the most striking likeness of his uncle I ever beheld. We have had the pleasure of seeing him several times. He has the simple, cordial, pleasant manner of a Baltimorean. For some time past he has been living in Paris, and has many appreciative friends here.

Our friend Portz comes frequently to see us, and we agree perfectly in our admiration of Paris. He has recently returned from a long visit to Symrna, Constantinople, and the Crimea. Although he is so happy here, we sometimes tell him his heart is yet lingering about Mobile, and he will go back to seek it.

When you see Dr. Terrell, tell him we have made many visits to his charming niece, Mrs. Rice. Her sister, the Countess de Sartiges, has come lately from America. The Count has been decorated with the Legion of Honor since his arrival here.

The courier has just tapped at the door, to tell me the post will leave without my letter, unless I send it quickly. Therefore I must say, good-bye.

September 13th.—A few nights since we went to the *Italiens*, a large and splendid theatre thus called, where the Italian Opera was formerly presented. Ristori plays there now, and the performance was "by command," which signifies for the especial pleasure of the Emperor, who had informed the *impressario* (the manager) he would be there. Of course this announcement of "by command" never fails to make the evening a gala one. The ladies were in beautifull ball-dresses, glowing with trimmings of flowers, and sparkling with jewels, while the gentlemen were all in evening costume. We were accompanied by Lieut. Churchill, of our army, a gallant, handsome young officer. We had a fine box, and an admirable view of the brilliant scene. Soon after we were seated, we heard a hoarse murmur of thousands of voices, which seemed to surround the house and rush through the corridors. Ere we could inquire the cause, the Emperor entered his box, (not far from us,) and the entire audience started up and screamed, "Vive l'Empereur!" with a frantic enthusiasm. Several times before we had seen him at theatres and operas, and no manifestation like this awaited his entrance. The Emperor came forward to the front of the box, and bowed repeatedly, while the cries continued. He was excessively pale, and we fancied had just received bad news from the Crimea. But in a few moments after we discovered an attempt had been made to kill him as he entered the theatre. A young Frenchman, (always rather a bad subject,) resolved to take the Emperor's life; and arming himself with a pistol, he climbed a lamp-post in front of the theatre; and when the royal carriage drove up, and the crowd called out " Vive l'Empereur ! " he fired into it. Happily the Emperor was not in it, but in the next one. The aim of the assassin, however, was not very sure ; for, although there were four ladies of the Court in the carriage, they all escaped untouched.

Ristori even surpassed her usual admirable acting. The eloquence of her gestures was a language in itself, and the pathos and power of her voice were perfectly magnetic, holding the listener captive to their bewitching spell. She was recalled to the stage *ten different times*, ere the excited audience would permit her to withdraw, and bouquets and garlands were cast at her feet by hundreds. She is indeed a great actress. When the tragedy was over, Ristori appeared in a little comic after-piece, styled the " Jealous Lovers," in which she enchanted every one by her vivacity and sprightly grace. She looked wonderfully like our friend in Mobile; she has the same manner and stylish air.

On Monday evening we were visiting Mrs. Rossiter, and did not leave her parlor until after night. Coming down into the *Place Vendôme*, we found all the public buildings illuminated, and soon after we discovered the occasion of this brilliant display, by the loud cannon of *Des Invalides* speaking the nation's joy in the capture of Sebastopol. Our coachman drove madly down the Boulevards, crying out constantly to approaching carriages, " More glory for France

Sebastopol is taken!" In all directions we heard words of exultation, always ending with "Sebastopol has fallen! The French army are victorious!" This wild delight brought to mind my grandmother's story of the night the news came to Philadelphia that Cornwallis was taken. When the watchman calling out the hour, said, "Past twelve o'clock, and all's well, and Cornwallis is taken!" then windows burst open, and heads were thrust out, and in one hour the whole population were dressed and in the streets, rejoicing with a right good will.

Think how frantic with gratified pride, how wild with joy, these excitable people of Paris must have been! There was no sleep that night. Immense crowds thronged the streets until day dawned, and it still continues, for the Te Deum is to be celebrated this morning at *Notre Dame.* It is a day of fête. All the theatres are open gratis—all the various places of amusement too. Every one is abroad—every one triumphant. The poorest workman in the streets had as proud an air, as though he had accomplished the taking of the Malakoff tower himself.

But the dead of Sebastopol appeared quite forgotten. Yet the victory was only won by fearful sacrifice of human life! As we gazed upon the joyous scene, how often came to me the thought of the desolate mothers, the fatherless children, and sorrowing wives of the brave and daring soldiers who gave their lives that day for the glory of France. These sad attributes of war were not remembered. In the silence and solitude of blighted homes, crushed hearts were mourning; but joy delights in the sunlight, and universal was the rapture of the entire French nation when the tidings flashed along the electric wires, "Sebastopol is taken!"

Now good-bye. A friend has called to take me to see the pageant of the procession on its way to *Notre Dame de Paris.* I shall not write again for several days.

CHAPTER LXX.

September 17*th*.—The Te Deum at *Notre Dame* was a grand spectacle, and the procession through the streets really magnificent. The Emperor was in his carriage of state, which is a superb equipage, lined with white satin, and adorned with heavy gold fringe. Then followed all the dignitaries of the empire, all the distinguished generals, foreign ambassadors, and soldiers by thousands and tens of thousands. Flags were thrown out, balconies decked with garlands of flowers, and martial music filled the air with strains of inspiring melody. When night came, the illumination was brilliant and dazzling beyond all others ever before seen in Paris. Every street was radiant with myriads of lamps, of varied colors and descriptions. All the palaces and governmental buildings were like vast structures of fire, glowing and blazing, yet unconsumed. The great edifice of the Industrial Exposition was revealed in flame, while the fountains of the gardens in front shone in the light like spectres rising from the ground, or like Undines holding out their shadowy arms to us. Over the façade of the entrance to the palace is an enormous figure representing France, and in the gleam of the many-colored fires a smile of triumph seemed to linger about the colossal lips of the statue. Along the banks of the Seine, and upon the bridges, were thousands of lamps, and the very waters of the river were turned to a hue like burning lava. Except the illumination of St. Peter's on Easter-Sunday, we have never looked upon a more gorgeously bright and glorious spectacle. Such was the happiness of the people, their mirth and joy, it absolutely appeared as though Paris had but one heart, throbbing with delight and exultation.

I have several times mentioned to you, dear Mamma, my anxiety concerning the unusual silence of our beloved Lady Emmeline. A letter has just reached me from Lord John Manners, informing me of a sad accident which has befallen this cherished friend in the Holy Land. Her only son, Captain Stuart Wortley, of the Rifles, was in the Crimea, where he has been several times in fierce battles, and constantly distinguished for his brave conduct in these engagements with the enemy. His mother, wearied at his long absence, went to Sebastopol to see him; and thence returning to Constantinople, she proceeded to Syria. While in Jerusalem, she was riding with her daughter upon the Mount of Olives, and had stopped to gaze on the sacred environs of the Holy City, when Victoria's horse rushed suddenly against Lady Emmeline, breaking her leg in the most frightful manner. The dragoman lifted her from the horse, and laid her upon the ground; which was soon crimson with blood; for the flesh had been torn away by the furious blow, and mingled with the broken bone. Death seemed inevitable. Springing upon a fleet horse, the dragoman rode furiously to Jerusalem; as he entered it, he met a gentleman just arriving, to whom he told the sad story. It was Mr. Edgar Drummond, who had been many months in Egypt, and had that moment reached Jerusalem. He dashed up the mountain, and on reaching the spot, knelt by the almost lifeless sufferer, to staunch the swiftly-flowing blood. Imagine his horror to find it was his honored aunt, Lady Emmeline Stuart Wortley! With the aid of his Arabs he formed a litter, and she was borne to the city and placed under the care of a physician. Since that time the bone has united, and Victoria writes she is doing well, although excessively weak. Of course, all her family are in deep distress, and the Duke of Rutland (her father), himself in feeble health, has been quite overpowered by this sad intelligence. You well know what pain it has given me, and not meeting her in England will greatly destroy the happiness of my visit there.

Every one tells us it is too cold to go to Sweden, and we have therefore abandoned entirely the thought of making that much-desired visit to dear Miss Bremer. The regret this occasions me is the only cloud which has passed over the sunlight of my visit to Europe. Truly have we floated on the crest of pleasure's waves.

In one week we shall leave Paris, and go to England, Scotland, and Ireland, ere we return westward. Our long valued and pleasant friend, Dr. Smith, of Texas, accompanies us. Thaddeus Smith, of Mobile, a fine, noble youth, goes over to America with us in the "Arago;" Dr. Henry, also, who has just come back from the Crimea, from one year of hard service before Sebastopol.

One day of last week we devoted to visiting, making our parting calls upon the many kind and affectionate people who have welcomed us so cordially. During the first days of my sojourn here, I had met an old Countess, the widow of one of Napoléon's generals, and had made her a visit then. Since, she had been absent, but we concluded to leave a farewell card. Driving to her hotel, I sent up for the maid-servant, to give a message for her mistress. Finding, however, she had returned a few days ago, I begged the servant to tell her we were about departing and wished to see her ere we left. She replied to me, "I will give your message, Madame, but this is the Countess's *day of memories*, and she never sees any one when that comes round." Then away she ran up the stairway, while I sat wondering what could be the meaning of those words, "day of memories." Soon she came down, saying, "As Madame leaves so soon, the Countess will break through her usual custom, and receive Madame."

So I went up, passing through many handsomely-furnished rooms, until I came to a pretty boudoir, where the aged Countess was seated, in deep mourning, with a sad expression upon her face, always before so animated and cheerful. The evident grief in her countenance touched my heart with warm sympathy, and seizing her hands, I exclaimed, "Dear Countess, what great sorrow has befallen you?" She looked intently upon me for a few moments, then replied, "I was sure (though I had only seen you in gay scenes) that your feelings were tender, true, and warm; therefore I have permitted you to see me this sacred day, when I always shut myself up, remaining in perfect solitude and silence until after midnight; for you already know this is my day of memories!" Her hands dropped listlessly in her lap, and she seemed lost in a profound revery. I dared not break upon the silence, so I remained motionless, gazing upon the sorrow-worn face, while to my mind came the many days of terrible memories enshrined within my own soul, and dark clouds from that fearful past, never to be forgotten, were rapidly surrounding me, and bringing burning tears to my eyes; when the Countess aroused herself, and said, "Would you not like to hear why I call this day, the of memories? Seat yourself near me, and you shall hear." I drew my chair near her, and she began a little history of herself.

"I was once young, lively, loving, and beloved; the wife of a gallant and noble husband, a general of the great Napoléon, who was our dearest friend, and that picture was painted for me (pointing to a fine portrait of the first Napoléon). I was the mother of two sons, glorious boys, who, like their father, would be soldiers. They went with the Emperor to battle, to fight for the glory of France, and in one engagement father and sons were all killed, and I was left utterly desolate and perfectly alone, for both my husband and self were orphans, and in the veins of no human being save our two beautiful children flowed one drop of our blood. When the news came they were all dead, and that I was alone in the world, I ceased to remember events for many long years; then reason returned, and I found I must live my allotted time upon earth, so I resolved to gather all the flowers thrown in my pathway, and be gay and cheerful. For near half a century (for I am very old now) I have given this day, the anniversary of their death in fighting the battles of France, to the memory of the past. Here I sit, with my eyes upon their portraits, and recall, one by one, the joys of my life when they were with me; and I recall, too, every word spoken to me, every visit made me, by our dear Emperor. Thus passes *my day of memories*, and when midnight comes I leave the room, and the next day occupy my thoughts with busy Paris life; with visits, parties, operas, and dinners. I strive to forget the 'long-gone days' in present amusements. But oh! it is terrible, desolate, and mournful, to be all alone! all alone! all alone!"

Thanking her for the touching narrative, I endeavored to draw her into conversation, but her thoughts seemed wandering along the "corridors of time," and I bade her farewell and left her, my heart saddened by the remembrance of the interview, and very often shall I think of the "day of memories."

CHAPTER LXXI.

September 21st.—Our enchanting visit is over, and in the bouquet of pleasant memories I have placed the last sweet flower, the happiness of having seen the kind and beautiful Empress and the noble Emperor, that wondrously gifted man, who has made France the glory of European nations.

Leaving Paris is like another separation from home. We have found such charming and excellent friends here, that my heart is overflowing with good feeling towards the whole world.

During the morning we wandered through the Gardens of the Tuileries, and along the Champs Elysées, paid some parting visits to persons who have lavished many delightful tokens of friendship upon us, as though to deepen the regret we feel in saying farewell.

It is now after midnight, and the last cordial adieu is still wringing in my ears. In the little boudoir where I have passed so many happy hours in writing to you, I end this letter, after taking one more look upon the gay and joyous Boulevard.

Good-bye! good-bye!

My "Souvenirs of Travel" must now end. The enrapturing days of wandering amid the classic and historic scenes of the Old World are over. Again we return to "our own green forest land," the land of freedom and of love. 'Tis true, we passed several weeks in the "happy homes" of England and of Scotland, ere we embarked upon the Atlantic; but the record of those hours cannot now be made.

> "My task is done; my song hath ceased; my theme
> Has died into an echo; it is fit
> The spell should break of this protracted dream."

God bless the Old World! God bless the New!
Dear friends and kind readers, *farewell!*

THE END.

www.ingramcontent.com/pod-product-compliance
Lightning Source LLC
LaVergne TN
LVHW010155110826
845151LV00002B/522